I0119327

Gender and Psychoanalysis.
Clinical Contributions

Gender and Psychoanalysis.
Clinical Contributions

Edited by
Teresa Lartigue and
Olga Varela

Guadalajara Psychoanalytic Association (Provisional Society)
Mexican Psychoanalytic Association

XV Anniversary of COWAP (1998-2013)

First edition 2013

All rights reserved. This book, or parts thereof, may not be reproduced or transmitted in any form or by any means, electronic or mechanical, including recording, photocopying, offset, or by any information storage and retrieval system without permission in writing from Architecthum Plus S.C.

©ARCHITECTHUM PLUS S.C.
Díaz de León 122-2
Aguascalientes, Aguascalientes
México CP 20000
libros@architecthum.edu.mx

Cover Design:
Based on a poster by Verónica Segovia González
Composition and design: Lola Sosa Valdés

ISBN 978-607-9137-13-7

Alcira Mariam Alizade, our dear friend, companion and colleague,
died on March 6, 2013, forever depriving us of her
affection, intelligence and libidic presence.
As we all know, Mariam was always a point of reference,
a 'driving force' behind the COWAP Committee.
Her super efficient enthusiasm, and her constant creative optimism,
in combination with her personal warmth,
all contributed to a special atmosphere in our manner of collaboration.
She invested her intelligence, passion, and vitality in
the theoretical and clinical studies on femininity.
As psychoanalysts, we should all be particularly capable
of dealing with and working through death.
However –precisely because we are psychoanalysts–
we can't easily make use of our defenses,
and therefore the pain of loss can be even more acute.
Our only consolation is the continuity of Mariam's emotional
and psychoanalytical legacy that we all share.
We miss her immensely.
We –all of us– dedicate this book to her memory.

Contents

PART 1
CLINICAL PERSPECTIVES

About the Authors

Luz María Abatangelo de Sturzenbaum Professor of Literature. Graduate in Psychology. Affiliate Member of the Argentine Psychoanalytic Association. Collaborator of COWAP-APA. Member of the Children and Adolescent Department of the Argentine Psychoanalytic Association. Supervisor of the Pediatric Consultation Team and Coordinator of the Ballint Group in Pediatrics at the Hospital de Clínicas "Gral. José de San Martín" affiliated to the School of Medicine of the University of Buenos Aires.

A. Mariam Alizade Psychiatrist and training analyst of the Argentine Psychoanalytic Association. Overall Chair of the IPA Committe on Women and Psychoanalysis (2001-2005). Former COWAP Latinamerican Co-Chair (1998-2001). Author: Feminine Sensuality; Near death: Clinical psychoanalytical studies; Time for women; The lone woman and Psychoanalysis and Positivity. Editor of some IPA- COWAP- Karnac Series and of the collected papers of COWAP Latinamerican Intergenerational Dialogues. Scientific Secretary (1996-2008) of FEPAL (Latinamerican Psychoanalytical Federation).

Giovanna Ambrosio Training Analyst of the Italian Psychoanalytical Association and the International Psychoanalytical Association. Past Secretary of the Italian Psychoanalytical Association. Chief Editor of the Journal Psicoanalisi. Consultant of the IPA Committee on Women and Psychoanalysis; former (2005-2009) overall Chair of the IPA Committee on Women and Psychoanalysis (COWAP) and past European Co-Chair of the Committee on Women and Psychoanalysis (2001-2005). She is author of several essays and Editor of several books.

Doris Berlín Clinical psychologist (M.A) from Bar- Ilan University (Israel). Full member psychoanalyst of the Caracas Psychoanalytic Society. Teacher and Supervisor at the Clinical Psychology Department at the Universidad Central de Venezuela. Currently Co-Chair for the Latin-America for COWAP (Women and Psychoanalysis Committee, 2009-) at the International Psychoanalytical Association. Her contributions are mostly in the area of Psychoanalysis and Gender.

Alicia Briseño Mendoza Psychoanalyst, President, Full Member and Training Analyst of the Psychoanalytic Society of Mexico. Holder of an MA and PhD in Psychoanalysis. Lecturer at the Training Institute of the Psychoanalytic Society of Mexico, Spokesperson for the Raise Your Voice Against Violence Campaign in Mexico (AVON). She coordinates FEPAL's Myths Committee. Her research areas include Gender Studies and Myths.

Matthew Brown DO. Resident in Psychiatry at the University of Missouri Kansas City Department of Psychiatry. Doctor of Osteophathy from the Kansas City University of Medicine and Biosciences, Kansas City, Missouri,USA.

Ángela Camacho-Durán MD. Psychiatrist, Director of the Consultation Liaison Service, Truman Medical Centers. Assistant professor, University of Missouri Kansas City. Graduated in Psychiatry from University of Massachussets Medical Center, Boston, USA.

Delia de la Cerda PhD. Doctor in Psychology, analyst and child-adolescent psychoanalyst from the Mexican Psychoanalytic Association (APM) and full member of the IPA. Graduated of the 1st Class "Serge Levobici" of de International Association of Parenthood. Coordinator of the Diplomate or Master Program in Psychoanalytic Psychotherapy for Children and Adolescents of the APM (2002-2011).

José Cuenca is Research Assistant at the Division of Psychiatry in the Institute of Mental Health of the University of Nottingham. He received his bachelor's degree from Ibero-American University and his MSc degree from the University of Nottingham. He recently completed his PhD studies at the University of Nottingham, and is currently conducting research on young people's experiences of medical and psychological treatments for neurodevelopmental disorders.

Patricia Dávila Zárate PhD. Doctor and Master degree in General Psychotherapy, Mexican Psychoanalytic Association (APM) and Family Therapy (Family Institute, IFAC). CONACyT Grant on the investigation project for master degree "STD/HIV-AIDS and Personality Disorders in Pregnant Women and their Couples". Private practice with adolescents, adults and family. Current residence in Brazil.

Constanza Duhalde PhD. Doctor in Psychology Buenos Aires University DEA (Master) in Clinical Psychology, Paris V. Diplomat in Infant Psychopathology, Paris XIII, Professor and Researcher University of Buenos Aires. Candidate in the Argentine Society of Psychoanalysis (SAP). FEPAL Award 2008 for Psychoanalysis and Society "Concebir la posición analítica en un grupo de pacientes con problemas en la procreación. Encuentro en la comunidad" (Conceptualizing the analytic stance in a group of patients who have fertility problems. A meeting with the community). 2001-2012 Psychological advisor of Concebir (Support group of infertile patients). Member of CAPSIR (Argentine Center for Psychology and Reproduction). Author Así fue como llegaste (This is how you come to the world), a three children's books on medically assisted reproduction.

María Teresa Flores Psychiatrist and psychoanalyst. Full Member and Training Analyst of the Portuguese Nucleus of Psychoanalysis - IPA Study Group; Member of the SEPEA (Société Européene pour la Psychanalyse de l'Enfant et de l'Adolescent). Private practice with children and adults. Former COWAP European Co-Chair (2005-2009).

Kenia Gómez PhD. Assistant professor at UMKC Psychiatry Department and clinical psychologist at Truman Medical Center. She obtained her PhD. at Loyola University Chicago, where she researched the relationship between subjective well-being, ethnic identity, and family satisfaction among pre-adolescents. Her interest are in areas of child development, mother-infant attachment, mind-mindedness, early childhood trauma, resiliency, family therapy, and psychological assessment.

Itzel González Psychologist, holding a Postgraduate specialization in psychoanalytic psychotherapy in child and adolescents and a Master of psychoanalytic psychotherapy, as well as PhD studies in Psychoanalytic Psychotherapy. Graduated of the 1st Class "Serge Levobici" of de International Association of Parenthood. As researcher at the National Perinatology Institute of Mexico (1999–2009) she produced number of scientific articles regarding maternal depression. With years of experience in Psychotherapy, she currently works in private practice with children, adolescents and adults.

Elizabeth Haworth Clinical psychologist, with Bachelor's and Licentiate in Psychology from Pontificia Universidad Católica of Peru (PUCP). Diploma in Gender & Development at the International Development Research Center (IDRC) and St. Mary's University, Halifax, Canada. Training as a Candidate Member of the Peruvian Institute of Psychoanalysis (ongoing). Extensive training and experience in clinical and social psychology with specialization in problems of domestic violence against women and children, human rights abuses and women's leadership.

Silvia Jadur Member of the Argentine Psychoanalytic Association(APA); FEPAL Award 2008 for Psychoanalysis and Society "Concebir la posición analítica en un grupo de pacientes con problemas en la procreación. Encuentro en la comunidad" (Conceptualizing the analytic stance in a group of patients who have fertility problems. A meeting with the community). Board member of COWAP- Latin America (2009-2012). Psychology chapter coordinator of the Argentina Society of Reproductive Medicine. Director of CAPSIR (Argentine Center for Psychology and Reproduction). Master in Public Mental Health. Buenos Aires University. 1995-2012 Member of the advisory board and coordinator for psychology of Concebir (Support group of infertile patients). 1976-2000, Psychologist of Dr.Gutierrez Children's Hospital. Author Así fue como llegaste (This is how you come to the world), a three children's books on medically assisted reproduction. Member of Concebir.

Teresa Lartigue PhD. Doctorate in research psychology Iberoamericana University and Chair of the Psychology Deparment (1977-1981). Training analyst and analyst of children and adolescents for the Mexican Psychoanalytic Association (APM), and Full Member of the IPA. Past president of APM (2002-2004). Chief of the Department, Department, Reproductive Epidemiology National Institute of Perinatology (2000-2007); Former Director of the Mexican Institute of Psychoanalysis APM (2004-2006). Former COWAP Latinamerican Co-Chair (2005-2009). Member of the Sub-Committee on Evaluation of Research Proposals Results of the IPA Research Committee (2005-) and of the Sub-Committee on Training in Research Methodology, Reviewer for Latin America of The International Journal of Psychoanalysis (2010-).

Ahmed Maher MD. Resident in Psychiatry, University of Missouri Kansas City Department of Psychiatry. Medical degree from the University of Alexandria, Egypt.

J. Martín Maldonado Durán MD. Associate professor of Child Psychiatry, and Gynaecology and Obstetrics, University of Missouri, Kansas City, Department of Psychiatry.Associate Clinical Professor, University of Kansas. Perinatal, infant and child/adolescent psychiatrist and family therapist. Faculty, Greater Kansas City Psychoanalytic Institute.

Johanna Mendoza Talledo Clinical Psychologist at the Pontifical Catholic University of Peru (PUCP). Candidate in training of the Peruvian Society of Psychoanalysis (SPP). Magister in Theoretical Psychoanalytic Studies (PUCP). Obtained PhD in Philosophy (PUCP). Scientific Secretary of the Peruvian Association of Psychoanalytic Psychotherapy for child and adolescents (APPPNA). FLAPPSIPP member. Editor and author of The Motherhood and its vicissitudes, today (2006) and author of articles related to the areas of intersubjectivity, body and gender.

Dolores Montilla Bravo Psychoanalyst graduated at the Mexican Psychoanalytic Association (APM) and full member of IPA. Clinical work with adolescents, adults and seniors, specialized in eating disorders. Member of the COWAP (APM) team in studies related to gender. Clinical work in public hospitals as well as in private consultation. She has a Master degree in Clinical Psychology (UNAM), is engaged in her PhD in Psychoanalytical Psychotherapy. Member of the APM board of directors and has written several papers and book chapters. Also engaged in training in Child and Adolescent Psychoanalysis.

Manuel E. Morales Monsalve. Psychiatrist, child/adolescent psychiatrist, Karl Menninger School of Psychiatry.Psychoanalyst. Faculty of the Greater Kansas City Psychoanalytic Association. Member of the American Psychoanalytic Association and the International Psychoanalytic Association. Assistant professor of Child Psychiatry, University of Missouri Kansas City School of Medicine.

Edoarda Paron Radvany Psychologist and psychoanalyst. Associated Member of the Brazilian Society of Psychoanalysis of Sao Paulo, SBPSP and of the International Psychoanalytical Association, IPA; Coordinator of the Section of Community and Culture of the SBPSP (2001-2003); Coordinator of the study group "Psychoanalysis and Gender". Member of the Scientific Board of Directors (2009-2010), Member of the committee of Community Affairs (2006-2009). Her papers on Feminility, Paternity and Culture have been published in books and specialized journals on Psychoanalysis.

Martha Pérez Calderón B.S. in Psychology Iberoamericana University; M.Sc. in Theoretical Psychoanalytic Studies University College London; M.A. in Psychology, City College of New York; M.Phil. in Clinical Psychology and PhD Candidate in Clinical Psychology, City University of New York. Research interests: trauma and its comorbidity with substance abuse/dependence and with personality disorders, migration processes, and gender studies.

Joséphine Quallenberg Psychiatrist and psychoanalyst (IPA, Canadian Psychoanalytic Association and Mexican Psychoanalytic Association) in full private practice and lecturer for three decades. She has published articles on psychoanalysis in various countries; Training in Psychoanalysis in Montreal, Québec, Canada at the Canadian Institute of Psychoanalysis, CPS (IPA); Master's in Art Therapy in Montreal at Concordia University; Fellowship in Child Psychiatry at the University of Montreal; Professor Developmental Psychology.

Cândida Sé Holovko Psychologist and psychoanalyst. Full Member of the Brazilian Psychoanalytical Society of Sao Paulo (SBPSP) and the IPA; Editor of the Psychoanalytical Journal of the Sao Paulo Institute of Psychoanalysis (biennium 2009-2010); Member of the Committee of the Community Care Board for SBPSP (2009-2010), Member of the COWAP Committee for Latin America (2005-2007); COWAP Liason member for SBPSP (2005-2008). Published works in psychoanalytical journals and books on themes such as: Femininity, Masculinity, Mind-Body Relations and Perversions. Regional Editor Revista Latino Americana Calibán (FEPAL) and in training in the Instituto de Psicosomática de Paris.

Débora Regina Unikoswki Psychoanalyst and Clinical Psychologist (Université de Paris V – René Descartes – Sorbonne). Full Member and Training Analyst, Rio de Janeiro Psychoanalytic Society - Rio1 (SPRJ).

COWAP representative of Rio 3 Psychoanalytic Society (2005-2010) and of Rio de Janeiro Psychoanalytic Society - Rio1(2012-2013). Treasurer of ABEBE (Brazilian Association of Infant Studies). Adult, Child and Adolescent Psychoanalyst; Private practice in Rio de Janeiro, Brazil.

Matilde Ureta de Caplansky Psychologist (UNMSM, Peru), Master in Mental Health and Social Sciences of Leon University Barcelona España. Teaching Full Member and former president of of the Peruvian Psychoanalytic Society (1998-1999). Former Director of the Peruvian Institute of Psychoanalysis (2005-2009). Former Director of the Graduate School of the Lima Center for Psychoanalytic Psychotherapy. Founding Director of the Psychosocial Counseling and Development Center (CEDAPP). Former Co-Chair and worldwide consultant of COWAP-IPA for Latin America (2001-2005).

Olga Varela Psychologist (ITESO, Guadalajara, Mexico), Master degree in Psychoanalytic Psychotherapy; Full member and training analyst of the Guadalajara Psychoanalytic Association (Provisional society) and the International Psychoanalytical Association (IPA), Past President of this association. Editor La mujer desde la antigüedad hasta nuestros días (Lumen Publishers), Nuevos paradigmas de la mujer (Lumen) y Locuras Privadas (Lumen). Director of Extension (communications) of the Latin American Institute of Psychoanalysis (ILAP).

Juan Vives MD. Psychiatrist and training psychoanalyst of the Mexican Psychoanalytic Association (APM) and full member of the IPA. Past president of APM (2000-2002). Member House of Delegates (2001-2003) International Psychoanalytical Association; Training analyst of the Asociación Mexicana de Psicoterapia Analítica de Grupo; Associated Director of the Latin American Institute of Psychoanalysis (ILAP, 2006-2009). Editor of the International Journal of Psychoanalysis and of the Revista Latinoamericana de Psicoanálisis and Cuadernos de Psicoanálisis.

Viviana Wainstein Master's degree in adult clinical psychology. FEPAL Award 2008 for Psychoanalysis and Society "Concebir la posición analítica en un grupo de pacientes con problemas en la procreación. Encuentro en la comunidad" (Conceptualizing the analytic stance in a group of patients who have fertility problems. A meeting with the community). Member of the Argentinian School in Psychoterapy for Graduates. Master's degree in Reproductive Medicine. Master's degree in Sexology.2006 -2012; Psychological advisor of Concebir (Support group for infertile patients). Member of CAPSIR (Argentine Center for Psychology and Reproduction). Assistant professor of Psychoanalysis at the Belgrano and Favaloro Universities.

Carmen Rosa Zelaya Pflucker Clinical Psychology and Master's Degree in Theoretical Studies in Psychoanalysis from Pontificia Universidad Catolica del Peru (PUCP). Candidate at the Instituto Peruano de Psicoanálisis. Past president of Asociacion Peruana de Psicoterapia de Niños y Adolescentes (APPPNA). Child and adult psychotherapist. Researcher and author of articles related to issues of maternity, early attachment, sexuality and gender.

Acknowledgements

First of all we would like to express our gratitude to our patients, as most of the ideas in this book have been inspired by our clinical work; through the work with them we have been able to integrate theoretical psychoanalytic concepts with the actual clinical practice. We tried to unify meta-psychology with the day to day work in the consulting room, be it on the couch or in a face to face psychoanalytically oriented psychotherapy. We also want to acknowledge the work of the colleagues of the Asociación Psicoanalítica de Guadalajara (Provisional association) in organizing the VII Latinamerican Intergenerational Dialogue, between men and women, which took place in the city of Guadalajara, México, and whose proceedings constitute the core of this book. The Spanish translation of the first fifteen chapters can be read in the book *Género y Psicoanálisis. Contribuciones Contemporáneas*, in the webpage of the Guadalajara Psychoanalytic Association. Our gratitude also to the authors of this volume who took care of its translation into English. Four of the remaining chapters were the results of investigations which were supported by the Research Committee of the International Psychoanalytical Association, to whom we want to express our deep appreciation, and in particular to Dr. Peter Fonagy. Without their generous support we could not have carried them out. We also want to thank the Consejo Nacional de Ciencia y Tecnología (México), and the Instituto Nacional de Perinatología. The last chapter is the result of investigations carried out by the team at the University of Missouri Kansas City, USA. With this volume we wish to contribute to the celebration of the 15 years of existence of the Committee on Women and Psychoanalysis (COWAP) of the International Psychoanalytical Association.

Introduction

This year[1] we celebrate the tenth anniversary of our Committee, so I should like to begin by saying a few words first about our history and then about our policy. COWAP was formed in 1998 as a Committee dedicated to the exploration of themes specifically concerning women. As of 2001 –when Mariam Alizade, from APA, was the overall chair and I was the European co-chair– COWAP has gradually become no longer a Committee concerned specifically with women, but a Committee governed by women and, of course open to all. Priority has been to focus on themes of high social impact, adhering closely to a psychoanalytical viewpoint and starting directly from our own clinical experience. Allow me a small gesture of immodesty, shared by my Committee: it is a source of pride to all of us that the President and the whole Board of the IPA put forward COWAP as an example to all the other Committees, both on account of the scientific quality that we always try to maintain in our meetings, as well as for its energy and vitality.

Our approach, not only continues to be significant from a socio-cultural perspective, but it has often contributed to up-dating and revising certain psychoanalytic concepts. During recent years, at the Conferences of Ravello, Buenos Aires, Lisbon, Rio and Catania to mention some of the most significant, we are very proud to have brought out of the shadows to which they had been relegated by the psychoanalytic literature, such important themes as incest and trans-sexuality.

Here, we have to walk the difficult tight-rope between clinical-theoretic psychoanalytic thinking and these crucial themes; it is also our tradition to work around a feminine and masculine image seen as a "whole", while we try to bring into the light the possible "grey zones". In fact, our meetings have always been characterized by the tendency to measure ourselves against the whole possible range of feminine -as well as masculine- psychopathologies in all their various shades of meaning. And I think that the works presented at this meeting follow in the same direction.

But especially -and always starting from our clinical experience- we have tried to rescue the feminine image from the Freudian triad of 'masochism, passivity, narcissism' (to which weakness of the superego has often been added), restoring it to its libido-aggressive instinctuality and its responsible

1 COWAP 10th Anniversary (1998-2008) "Gender and Psychoanalysis", Guadalajara, 30-31 May 2008.

subjectivity. We well know how the process of feminine psycho-sexual development has been, and continues to be, at the centre of speculation and debate.

The first paradox, in my view, was the disparity between the relentless criticism of Freud (in spite of his cautious and doubting style), and the absence of such intense criticism against his first women disciples (Helen Deutsch, Lou Andreas Salomé, Marie Bonaparte, Jeanne Lample-de Groot) who raged so ferociously against the "feminine", sometimes unfortunately 'acting out' this ferocity on themselves (Bonaparte). As we all know, it was not until the 'anticipatory' revolution of Melanie Klein and the thinking of Karen Horney and Ruth Mack Brunswick that psychoanalytic thought 'restored' to the woman a different image.

The pathways of psychoanalytic thought on the 'feminine' have been anything but linear and numerous revisions have been made according to the different theoretical-clinical models. Regarding sexuality in general and feminine sexuality in particular, today we have at our disposal a much wider range of studies that have re-examined the complex development processes of how women's gender and sexual identity are constituted, and have re-signified, within the relational dimension, all the classical parameters of the 'masculine'. A review of the relevant international literature would take too long, so I will only mention, among others, Chasseguet-Smirgel, McDougall, Pines, Argentieri, Alizade, Welldon. However, this often rich and creative archipelago has unfortunately seemed to be repetitive and confused. I agree with some of my colleagues who have described it as "a labyrinth, full of seductive pathways but with no way out". Today our meeting will try to discuss the theme of Gender and Psychoanalysis and I think that we, as psychoanalysts, have to guard against certain risks that we may meet:

1) First of all, putting excessive emphasis on a partial aspect, thus losing sight of the complex whole of the development process. During our international debate, we continually come across a succession of phases – almost of 'fashions' – in which, for example, maximum attention is turned towards very early levels of development, bypassing the importance of the oedipal cross-road; or, vice versa, attention is focused on the Oedipus as being the synthetic moment of the process. This is where we should perhaps continue to focus the 'lens' on the role of narcissism and on the crossroads between Narcissus and Oedipus; an area that is certainly more impervious and susceptible to great variations according to the different internal

development processes of the individual.

2) The second risk concerns the use of language: what do we mean when we use a certain term? As Sandler says, each of us has their own implicit theories but also their own clinical-theoretical models of reference. So we can use different words for saying things that are the same or similar. Perhaps it would be helpful if each of us were to mention their own model.

3) The third risk —in my opinion— derives from the reappearance of prejudice in disguise often closer to ideological inclinations. An example of this regards the so called 'politically correct' that pervades the realm of gender identity.

Obviously, during these first ten years COWAP's activities have varied in different ways according to the different 'regions' and to the single countries within them. To my way of thinking, the interesting aspect of this experience is its so-called 'multi-cultural' quality (common, of course, to all IPA Committees), in which different elements continually adapt themselves to the relationship with the Other by coming to terms, as far as actually 'doing' is concerned, with the reciprocal differences (the various histories and cultures to which we all belong). And what is more, always trying to use the differences as a source of enrichment and resource —something that is often not easy to do.

Today, being able to 'think' psychoanalytically without renouncing a rigorous stand from the meta-psychological point of view, means increasingly having to navigate between the Scylla of violent reactionary moralism -often backward- looking and repressive –and the equally dangerous Carybdis of ideological psycho-conformism that is unfortunately spreading, presenting us with something that, although at the visible level it may appear to be a hypocritical simplification, within the analyst's room and within the transference play of the couple at work, can assume the subtle form of Bleger's collusive ambiguity. On this point, Simona Argentieri rightly speaks of a "short circuit of the senses", the consequence of "two opposite ways of avoiding the effort of doubt and the responsibility of one's own ideas."

In conclusion, our way of celebrating is to be here today, in Guadalajara, and during the present year in many other places: London, Hamburg, Istanbul, Mexico city, Sao Paulo, Melbourne and so on. We are here not only to share our ideas and discuss them, but also to do so in the most pleasant way possible - as is our tradition. I'm pleased to share with you the satisfaction of our joint endeavours and I want to send my best wishes to what I believe will be another rich and stimulating Conference. Warmest regards to you all.

Giovanna Ambrosio
Overall Chair of the Committee of Women
and Psychoanalysis (2005-2009)
International Psychoanalytical Association

PART 1
CLINICAL PERSPECTIVES

1

Thinking Beyond the Pioneers: a Non-Traditional Psychoanalytical Approach in the Case of a Difficult Patient

Doris Berlín

Lorena's case is interesting for several reasons. Firstly, she is a difficult patient whose background shows a great deal of the cluster of events that come attached to women's suffering in a patriarchal society: mother-daughter intergenerational rejection, sexual abuse by the father which has repeated itself in the marriage relationship; work place abuse, rape; desired, ambivalent and finally truncated maternity. The approach to her treatment is permeated by my gender perspective and included interventions such as contact with other medical and legal professionals, and giving her access to information sources.

Secondly, because from a technical point of view, the shortcomings she experienced in her early childhood irradiated enormous difficulties, especially in the initial phase of treatment: the acting out, the session interruptions, the phone calls, all of which forced me to make concessions in the setting, to be able to build a bond that would allow me to attend the case. Particularly in the first phase of treatment, in which if I had not insisted that she return, she never would have accepted that possibility. At the same time I was interested in treating her when I realized her desire to live and her ability to overcome adversity.

In other words, it is a psychoanalytic work that articulates with a gender perspective, has changes in the setting, making it more permissive so that the patient could accept the treatment, while remaining true to our tradition of questioning discontent as well as to central concepts of the theoretical corpus of psychoanalysis: the unconscious, transference, repetition, etc. The four years of treatment can be divided into three parts: the first I call the resistance phase which culminated in the construction of a setting. The second is when, besides becoming aware of her problems, we were able to connect some early events with her identifications, and the third phase is the present one, in which important achievements in autonomy can be seen and the difficulties that still remain can be assessed.

Part One: Resistance phase and the construction of an analytic setting
Lorena first came because of her family's insistence, following the loss of
her first child, a boy. With cries of despair and anger, she expressed her
protest at coming to treatment. She would say: "If I had had my son I never
would have needed psychoanalysis, I would be in the playground with other
young mothers like myself and not with a psychoanalyst". Between screams
and protests, she gradually told me about the drama of her childhood and
adolescence. A borderline mother, who made her travel amongst the homes
of various relatives, she suffered from constant moving and economic
hardships. This daughter was foreseen as a prostitute by her mother however
she worked since her early adolescence and sheltered herself through going
to church, and the illusion of a marriage that would give a firmer base to
her life. It was clear, then, that with the loss of her first baby, her project of
having a home for the first time and of repairing her damaged childhood had
failed. Even more so when the relationship with her partner, their projects,
conversation topics, and games had been constructed around the shared
illusion of having a family.

The loss of her first pregnancy brought her a deep feeling of emptiness
and abandonment. In addition, with that death an important attempt to
satisfy her ideal of a "happy family" had failed. My intervention with her
at the time, that the lost child sealed off a series of things she had lacked,
and in that sense, had he been born, would have carried on his shoulders the
weight of filling her voids, was very difficult for her to accept at the time.
The symbolic intervention could not compensate her desire to fill her needs
in a concrete manner. Thus, there were frequent absences, after which I
always invited her to return. She also communicated with me and required
my attention on the phone, was absent after vacations, asked for appointment
changes. I understood these maneuvers to construct the framework in her
own way as a need to deal with the analyst by re-editing an enmeshed bond.

Parallel to this way of bonding with me, she kept insisting on staying
joined to the lost baby. Lorena spent many hours crying, thinking the child
was alive, in a secret communication in which, although she knew he was
dead, he reappeared through an intense connection with him. The inner void
was filled with a delusional idea that sealed off the lack. However, when it
seemed almost impossible, she overcame this loss after long and painful
months.

In that first year of treatment she began studying graphic design, which
she successfully completed. Designing, using her creativity and aesthetic

sense to meet her customers' demands, has provided her with a livelihood and with great job satisfaction. In addition to practicing her profession, she has shown management skills that allow her to plan for her different customers and for mass production orders. It should be noted that during that time, her husband supported her treatment. However, as she became more autonomous, important difficulties came up between them, his jealousy and physical violence.

Part two: The unfolding of the various identifications as a woman.
The married woman, the wanton, the "pretty girl", and the murderer
I identify a second phase of the process, at which time, beyond the chain of acting outs that have characterized this patient, it is possible to elaborate the identifications that organize her inner world. A relationship of extreme submission to her husband appeared, which is the only way she found to not upset him and be able to continue their marriage, but instead of lessening the husband's violence, it seemed to exacerbate it, as if he sensed that at the same time she was submissive, Lorena was pulling away from him. There is also an extreme submissive relationship with her mother, in which she is unable to deny any of her material demands. This is how she can hold a place for her mother, through gifts, and through staying married to a professional provider.

She told me about her sexual fantasies of being a conquered prostitute, rescued and transformed. With this theme, the patient expresses her masochistic pleasure in surrendering to someone who has her at their disposal, but she also expresses the desire for a new beginning, in which someone will give her a helping hand and be willing to build with her. Given the imminence of losing the fragile bond with her husband, pressure to have a second child arises. I insist that she think about it, but instead she does an acting out in which she leaves the treatment and gets pregnant for a second time, planning with a specialist to conceive a boy. In this manner she also ignores the information she possesses, which makes her a candidate for high-risk pregnancies.

She returned to treatment, asking me to help her preserve her couple relationship. When she found out she was expecting a girl, anguish and rejection followed at the thought of bringing an unprotected being into the world, prone to many aggressions and unable to defend herself. We worked on her murder fantasies with this pregnancy, which she came to desire. However, late in the pregnancy very strong contractions ensued that led to a caesarean. The baby was born with problems and died a few days later. She developed a very severe crisis with the persecutory idea of being a murderous mother. Just as after the first loss she stayed connected to the memory of the lost baby, in this second case, she stayed connected to her daughter through visual hallucinations in which the baby looks at her and cries. The daughter had become a murderous monster, by virtue of her mother's disaffection. Thus the trans-generational rejection she suffered was re-edited. Memories arose of her mother in her early childhood, in which she assaulted her by throwing any number of objects at her.

After a year she elaborated her pathological mourning. She would say: "I didn't want that pregnancy, my body rejected it, my body is wise. It's not that I had bad intentions toward my baby, it was just survival". Once she elaborated the loss of the child, Lorena decided to separate from her husband. Difficult events continue to happen, but she seems to have the strength to face them.

The husband showed an increase in his cruelty, with highly sophisticated tactics that I will not describe. Without going into the gruesome details of the harassment she was subjected to, Lorena gradually lost her fear and insisted on getting a divorce, which after extensive efforts she achieved. This happened contrary to what even I expected, as he was the only family that loved her and on whom she could count. It was decisive here to have worked over her ideal of being the perfect-married daughter for her mother, which allowed her to overcome the relationship of extreme dependency and violence with her partner. There is an analytical elaboration of her divorce. She states that it is who has given her the most support, was really her only family, but because of his violence she no longer desires him, she cannot be forced to make love.

Part three: Autonomy and Loneliness

Lorena has gradually managed to establish more worthy work contracts. She says she is supported by her job, the pleasure it gives her to see the satisfied look of her customers when she delivers an order. The pleasure of producing in order to enjoy the moment of pleasure she gives to others seems like a sublimated version of her enmeshed surrender. It is also a more refined way of nursing others that has not been thwarted.

Regarding the analytic relationship, from a demanding position that exerted an intense countertransferential pressure, it has become a relationship of a person who is committed to a twice-a-week setting. She envisions a world of social relations through her latest job. She feels she has progressed a lot, and marriage and a happy household no longer seem like the solution to her life. She has become a working woman, and feels it is not that bad to be one. She is one more among the crowd of divorcees, but not a whore because of it. One could say that her suffering has become more like common suffering, expressed as a secondary process, and is less a series of acting outs. However, her couple relationships are still an area of numerous difficulties. Although fortunately she enjoys sexual relationships, she has trouble establishing close bonds. From an indiscriminate submission that promotes domestic violence, she has gone to a distant, defensive self-sufficient and sarcastic position.

From a medical point of view a recommendation to not try to get pregnant again has been defined. The relationship with the analyst is still very particular. The analyst puts up with the patient determining just how deep she can think in each session, and how much of the day to day problems can be faced without thinking. Regarding this case I present the following thoughts.

The diagnosis

We can see her as a case of character pathology with narcissistic features, with the tendency to lose the subject-object differentiation around conflicting issues such as maternity. The suicidal thoughts, the flashbacks with her dead daughter, the reference ideas and other psychotic symptoms that arose after her daughter's death and have not repeated again, are all consistent with a posttraumatic syndrome after her baby's death. The strong ambivalence toward this female baby made her experience its death as induced by her, which led to a posttraumatic situation. Obviously, her husband's hidden and unacknowledged pathology also put pressure on her.

Most of the time, the use of defenses such as denial and isolation, together with her vitality, good humor, good looks and personal charm, allow her a competent and stable performance at work. Her childhood idea that she was more capable than her brothers, supported by her father and later on by her mother, pointed toward a narcissistic core around which she was able to organize herself. This idea of herself that she had to hold on to at any cost as a way to maintain her identity, of being a married woman to please her mother and to not feel like a wanton woman, she changes during her treatment and substitutes it for a self-concept based on projects and gratifications that are more her own. However, she is still a fragile person afraid of being used if she is dependent and establishes rather superficial ties.

Setting construction

In the first part of the treatment, despite coming three times a week, the patient needed to call me on the phone, she usually held back from interpretation, because she inevitably felt any interpretation as judgment. Also, the analyst's vacations generated absences and threats of interrupting treatment, at which time she was called and invited to return. Working in different sessions from those previously agreed on was accepted.

I think the way I found to work with this patient was tolerating her maneuvers in the hope that later she would try to understand. Only much later will she be able to understand her omnipotence, the imposition she attempts, in order to control the separations.

Maternal transference

Lorena displays a maternal transference in which she brings a very difficult relationship, demanding at times, rejecting at others, with primitive needs and ties. In the initial phase, where it is necessary to support the transference in this difficult case, the identification of the analyst with the maternal role enables a bridge that allows the progressive construction of a setting and the patient to be won over to the analysis task. To a large extent I think the improvement obtained in this case is because the analyst contains the transference of the maternal bond, from which Lorena can review some notions about her own identity without being judged.

Affirmative intervention

Given the difficulties of understanding symbolic interventions, in the cases of patients with deficits in the structuring of the self, interventions that provide recognition of resources and capabilities of the self are privileged over those that are directed to doubts, conflicts and unconscious aspects. These interventions have been called affirmative interventions, a technical concept developed by Killingmo and which I explain in a previous paper (Berlin , 2001). In this paper I explain how women who have been socialized to take care of the needs of others frequently present a deficit in the structuring of the self.

Group supervision amongst colleagues

I want to point out that I consider supervision amongst colleagues to be essential in this case, because it creates a space for benevolent reflection that decreases the conflict produced in us as analysts, when the demands of neutrality and abstinence that are foundational in our profession are difficult to maintain. For example, in this case there were times when legal problems were raised or when medical problems required recommendations. As well as sharing her medical problems or information, after her baby's death about where to go to be cared for until she overcame this predicament. Or simply by helping me endure some very difficult moments such as the crisis after the death of her second baby, when she threatened to commit suicide. And also to share the symbolic gifts that she left me much later on, without having to feel that by receiving them I was going against the Freudian requirements of abstinence.

Psychoanalysis and gender

The work with Lorena allows us to illustrate that a gender perspective is not in contradiction with the psychoanalytic approach to an individual case but rather complements and enriches it. Familiarity with the effects of incest, of domestic violence, gives the analyst tools to contain and think about a case which otherwise would have been considered borderline or psychotic. Likewise, understanding the denigration of femininity in its trans-subjective dimension as a historical legacy that is part of the mother-daughter relationship, as could be seen in two generations in this case, from the mother to the patient and from her to her daughter.

In Lorena's case, psychoanalytic treatment allowed her to question the paths she felt her parents forced her to follow. On her mother's side, to form the stable home she had not had herself, even at the cost of being abused. Lorena manages to think about and get out of that maternal imposition. As far as her father, the mark of incest seems indelible, leaves its print in serious intimacy difficulties, but at the same time that father-daughter bond, by giving her the feeling of being special, also organizes her and gives her the desire for self-improvement.

For analysts, it is necessary to establish a permanent dialogue with theoretical and clinical tradition, and to try to renew it. Several authors have been interested in studying why in scientific communities or communities of thought, theoretical postulates in disuse are maintained anyway within the community's background of knowledge, and are not questioned (Fleck, 1981 cited by Yonke & Barnet). The community of thought is constituted by a number of people who hold intellectual exchanges, share common postulates, thus rejecting new concepts that generate contradictions, and tending to repeat ideas. In this way the community tends to recognize and replicate the thinking of the founders, and ignores novel contributions. Besides the desire to maintain theoretical consistency, the preservation of the psychoanalytical institution has also been important, as it is an object of affection and belonging for the analysts, and a source of emotional and economical stability.

Torres (2007) has been concerned with the difficulties for psychoanalysis to get involved in openly discussing and changing concepts that belong more to the history of psychoanalysis and are not used by analysts, such as phallic logic, penis envy and female castration complex. She uses the cybernetic metaphor of the recycling bin to describe the effect of concepts that are not used, but are not discarded, irradiating effects on new conceptualizations, which often repeat the old concepts, with more modern versions. According to the author, along with a clinical practice in which analysts are indeed working with more innovative concepts, we are lacking statements that affect the theoretical, technical and clinical principles.

In this sense, for analysts interested in women's issues it may be very important to review and then to state which of the theoretical assumptions are confirmed or ruled out through clinical observation. In the case of Lorena, in a retrospective review of the theoretical concepts with which I approached this case, I find several that have been meaningful to me. The importance of the early relationship of the daughter with her mother in the shaping of her feminine identity, as stated by Klein and others who have theorized about gender construction (such as Chodorow, Stoller and others). The notion of motherhood as structural in woman, whether she has children or not, as stated by Chasseguet Smirguel. The idea of the rejection of femininity which is transmitted across generations, as worked on by Teresa Lartigue, and also the contribution of Leticia Glocer who examines the different meanings that the desire for a child may have. From our founder Freud, I have not seen the feminine castration complex or penis envy in this patient. However, I have received as a heritage, the love of research and the deep conviction that people change through the exploration of unconscious conflicts

To question the founders, then, involves thinking beyond them, not just repeating; understanding the theory according to the findings of a particular historical period, and reinventing the technique in those cases where it is necessary.

References

BERLIN, D (2001). Los vínculos en la mujer. Observaciones dentro y fuera del espacio clínico. *Trópicos.* Revista de la Sociedad Psicoanalítica de Caracas, III: 16-24.

TORRES, A. (2007). *Historias del continente oscuro. Ensayos sobre la condición femenina.* Caracas: Editorial Alfa.

YONKE, A. & BARNET, M. (2001). Persistence of Early Psychoanalytic Thought about Women. *Gender and Psychoanalysis*, 6: 53-73.

2

Body and Psychic Pain: Romina and Milena

Matilde Ureta de Caplansky

Every historical period and every society has its own subjectivity, which is a form of the *psyche* linked to predominant identificatory models, objects requiring sublimation and social imaginary significations. Thus, in the development of the *psyche*, society affects clinical formations. Just as the ego is a roving fragment of the institution of society, psychic suffering bears the marks of belonging to a particular social, historical context. We will see the consequences of all this in clinical praxis.

We can say then that psychic reality with fantasizing, for example, social reality from logging human links and the reality of the body, shape the complex structure which human beings must face. Its boundaries are unclear, except when conflicts or symptoms appear. The symptom produces a cut in the continuum and it is in the space of the split where the pathology appears. It is in this context that the body is present, not only as an anatomical reality but also as a fantasmatic reality where the representation and signs of illness and aging are present, from the experiential presence coming from the perception of the patient's erogenous and sensual capacity. Living in one's own body with its dimension of bereavement and death breaks with the omnipotent narcissistic illusion of exclusion from suffering. Suffering can be projected by the subject, via the split, onto the strange property that is the body.

In this work I present a reflection on the body-*psyche* relationship. When speaking of *psychosomatic*, we confront a difficult, complex field, because the first thing we find is that the illness becomes a mixed product: it is the set of symptoms itself and at the same time a defense protecting, so to speak, the subject of a major catastrophe. I turn to some authors who give theoretical support for the clinical vignettes.

Depending on different requirements that remain to be clarified, the mental representations of *soma* are renegades, treated as nonexistent, or if they are noted, are considered devoid of importance and lacking in significance. The relationship with other people runs the risk of falling into the same apparent "disaffection". This kind of dialogue of the deaf between the soma and the *psyche* characterizes the "psychosomatic" body. To understand better the psychological function of the psychosomatic body, it seems to me the question of the representation of pain, somatic and affective, is nodal. Thus, through the complex mediation of the mechanisms of splitting, projection and psychic repudiation, the human spirit is capable of avoiding, denying or even totally destroying any trace of perception of physical pain, thus revealing the dislocation of psychosomatic unity. All are manifestations of attempted self-healing in order to resolve conflict in the intolerable system of psychic "facts" that for each individual constitute his psychosomatic self.

Romina and Milena are two women who have made their respective bodies speak their problems and psychological traumas; in both cases we see how gender, emotions and corporal experiences are dramatically represented. It also confirms what Winnicott raises in terms of splitting, and how the traumatic experience has produced this change—passing to the body what belongs to the area of the mind. Romina is able for the first time to associate her pains with the experiences of several (seven) abortions, and Milena her pain of living through bodily ailments to unprocessed grief over the death of her sister in a plane accident.

Theoretical aspects: the split

"As Freud said many decades ago, the ego is based on a body ego ... The splitting of the *psyche* from the soma is a retrogressive phenomenon employing archaic residues in the setting up of a defence organization. By contrast, the tendency towards psychosomatic integration is part of forward movement in the developmental process. 'Splitting' is here the representative of 'repression' that is the appropriate term in a more sophisticated organization" (Winnicott 1989:112). We know that the split is as much in the self as in the object. Returning to the theoretical, we recall Winnicott who writes: "The illness in psycho-somatic disorder is not the clinical state expressed in terms of somatic pathology or pathological functioning (colitis, asthma, chronic eczema). It is the persistence of a split in the patient's ego organization, or of multiple dissociations, that constitute the true illness. ...This illness state in the patient is itself a defence organisation with very powerful determinants, and for this reason it is very common for well-meaning and well-informed and even exceptionally well-equipped doctors to fail in their efforts to cure patients with psycho-somatic disorder" (103). We see then that the psychosomatic issue becomes the object of several inquiries.

"Psycho-somatics is in many ways a curious subject, for if one ascends into the sphere of intellectualisation and loses contact with the actual patient, one soon finds that the term psycho-somatics loses its integrative function"(106). This in the general plan of Winnicottian theory on this point. But now let us deal with/take up central definitions.

Key definition: "Am I beginning to convey my meaning that *in practice* there does exist a real and insuperable difficulty, the dissociation in the patient which, as an organized defence, keeps separate the somatic dysfunction and the conflict in the *psyche*? Given time and favourable circumstances, the patient will tend to begin to recover from the dissociation. Integrative forces in the patient tend to make the patient abandon the defence" (106).

"Psycho-somatic illness is the negative of a positive; the positive being the tendency towards integration in several of its meanings and including what I have referred to ... as a personalisation. The positive is the inherited tendency of each individual to achieve a unity of the *psyche* and the soma, an experiential identity of the spirit or *psyche* and the totality of physical functioning" (111-112). "Our difficult job is to take a unified view of the patient and of the illness ... the real illness being the patient's personality split which is organised out of ego weakness and maintained as a defence against the treat of annihilation at the moment of integration" (114).

As far as Melanie Klein is concerned, she describes the way objects are separated by their good and bad aspects; according to her, it is the most primitive defense against anxiety.

The psychosomatic image plays such a fundamental role in the constitution of the identity of the self, that the way an individual experiences his body tells us much about the structure of his relationship with others. In neurotic relationships it is the repressed fantasies of the erogenous body that create the symptoms, and consequently the alteration in relationships with other people. It is the "neurotic" body. But when that same body no longer signifies what distinguishes it from others, the interior from the exterior, when the subject no longer believes he inhabits his body, relationships with others threaten to become confusing, even terrifying. The confusion may also take the form of mixing up one body part for another or an entanglement of zones in the representation of the body itself. This is the "psychotic" body.

This corporal experience is much like what is repressed neurotic fantasy, and is part of the material of everyone's dream life.

McDougall presents this as a paradox. The dilemma lies in that the body, outside its ability to be represented mentally, has no existence for the ego. Thus, the analyst is concerned with the "somatic self" of their analysands only to the extent the somatic self demands a mental representation. And when there is representation, it will still need to be communicable and that the other wishes to transmit it.

First vignette: Romina

Romina is a young woman of 37, chestnut-haired with light eyes and very pretty, of medium height, with a very sweet, feminine expression; she is successful in her profession. She has been married for 12 years, and has two children, a girl, 11, and boy, 7. Her marriage is a source of unhappiness and continual tension, because of her husband's infidelity and lack of money. She comes to consultation for severe "depression" that will not allow her to sleep or live with joy and tranquillity. Romina relates that for years she suffered urinary problems and that these led her to constant consultation with a specialist. The vignette I am presenting below took place in a special situation: Romina has just had a bladder operation for precancerous polyps and felt she was still convalescent, in addition to which we had been separated for a month's vacation, and suspension of sessions has always been a source of distrust and sadness for her.

Romina: *I feel a nail in my bladder ... It hurts horribly ... despite their having operated on me, the pain doesn't go away ... it's horrible.*

Analyst: Maybe the bladder is representing other pains you have, not just itself ... as though it were a spokesman ...

Romina: *That could be, couldn't it? ... I thought the bladder and the uterus are the same ... at least for me ... and I even saw illustrations of both but in my mind I united them ... (she starts crying).*

Analyst: How would that be? Are they the same thing?

Romina: *Yes ... I don't know how to say it ... it makes me remember my abortions... seven ... the first one when my mother made me ... I didn't want ... it was dreadful... (crying...) and then the others... until my marriage ... I wanted to have seven children... and look what happened to me... I ended up aborting them (crying heavily).*

That's why I don't know ... what's what ... more now after the bladder operation ... I hurt all over, I didn't ever want to get out of bed again or leave the hospital ... nothing made sense any more ... not much before either, the truth ... I felt my uterus and bladder were one single organ ... a bag ... that hurts ... a lot ... really a lot ...

Analyst: Perhaps it is important that both of us here, try to differentiate them not just as two organs but also their particularities and their functions ....

Romina continues to cry and in a labored way says she has never spoken about her abortions with anybody, not even with me in spite of the time she has been coming to therapy ... that they are experiences she prefers to forget forever ... because they are irreversible and painful.

Analyst: But I get the impression that your bladder pain and discomfort are responsible for reminding you all the time ... Maybe it would be better to throw some light on them, cry about them, understand them and so be able at some time ... to forgive yourself and move ahead under better conditions in your physical and psychic life ...

Romina: *It is possible... But that would suppose that I would have to recognize that my husband has been good and tender with me like my mother never was ... and that would change the panorama a lot ...*

Analyst: Do you mean the therapeutic panorama?

Romina: *... that, too ... no?*

Analyst: Possibly... but perhaps that would help to feel better and leave everything more clear and on more just terms for you, your husband, mother, family and between us.

Romina: (pausing, no longer crying)... *doctor... How strange ... the nail isn't still.... it has disappeared ... and it doesn't hurt.*

Some reflections

The psychoanalyst notes a sign in the organic incident, a prospective message, even healthy, that should serve as a wake up call, as if it were an alarm signal from the body faced with a way of living that ignores its claims; and also as the body's attempt to enroll itself in the psychic apparatus to restore the mind / body unit. Metapsychologically it is understood as a fusion and indifferentiation between one aspect of the ego—split from the corporal ego—the ideal of the ego and the "dominant cultural value".

When the stimuli from the body do not integrate into the psychic processing, the psychic processing is ill from a deficit resulting in the preeminence of exteriority over interiority. When such dissociation leaves psychism out of the body, the only recourse of the body is to express itself at the level of physiology or the neurovegetative system. The body is just

an "anatomical" body and the psychic interiority is erased. Its conflicts are always interpersonal. Let's see how this process would be:
• Mind-body split: the state in which the *psyche* is temporarily suspended and the soma responds biologically. Physical demands fail to send alarm signals.
• The somatic event is a defensive act of the mental structure, which appeals to evacuative actions.
•Serves as defense against corporality. The body is a symbolic psychic instance, a representational instance.

Second vignette: Milena

Milena, 42-year-old married woman with a college degree, and has a 10-year-old daughter. Consultation for severe depression and permanent anxiety.

Milena: *Everything hurts, first my head, then my stomach, spine, legs ... one thing after the other ... it is terrible and I can't do anything about it ... and it began when they told me that Juliet* [her daughter] was going on the school trip ...

Analyst: And all this fear?

Milena: *I don't know, ever since I was 10 years old, I have had the image that we were at the airport waiting for my sister... her plane never arrived, everyone cried and screamed desperately ... it was horrible ... since then I can't look at a plane much less board one, and to think of my daughter getting on a plane for that damn school now kills me...*

Analyst: Is the pain in your body killing you?

Milena: *Do you think so? Could the memory be that strong?* ... (she cries)
...

Analyst: It seems that it is, you say that it hurts part by part ... your head, your stomach, your spine, your legs ... as if you have identified with the fantasy of the body of your dead sister in the plane...

Milena: She cries intensely ... *how awful, how awful ... poor little thing ... poor little girl ... all in little pieces ... she was so little ... she was just 13 years old ... and I myself was on a vacation trip ... I have never been able to forget it, nor my parents either ... it was 35 years ago and it is as if it were today ...* (she continues to cry).

Theoretical reflections

Regarding the pathological bereavement Milena presented, it should be noted that mourning is a more or less prolonged process which needs the ego, essentially in order to come to accept the definitive loss of the object in reality. Desire must be taken away from every moment remembered, the ones that leave a trace. One can see the most important factor in overcoming grief would be reality testing, on which Klein agreed with Freud, along with the introjection of the good internal object. If for Freud the work of mourning consisted of a gradual letting go of the object, Klein considered that in achieving the work of mourning, the reinstallation of the lost object in the inner world is produced, keeping the libidinal link.

The "longing for the lost object" has been pointed out by Freud as well as by Klein, although the motives were libidinal in the one case (Freud) and restorative and reparatory in the other (Klein), and did not contemplate the urgency of the survivor to cry out to and look for the lost person. According to Bowlby such urgency has primitive roots. The *crying out to* and *searching* had survival value for human and animal babies. Hallucinations, illusions, dreams, identification, suicide attempts and even behavior such as wandering around and fleeing in a dissociative state, are found to be motivated by the unconscious search for the absent one.

Lutenberg describes how a seemingly banal separation or bereavement can often trigger *invisible emotional storms* that are inexplicable from the point of view of the emotional log, but which then become a psychosomatic threat which can even jeopardize the patient's life. Such is the patient's psychic primitivism that any frustration can set off a crisis affecting somatic physiology, such as occurs in babies during the perinatal period. These patients almost always fail when an elaborative bereavement, however small, is demanded. This contrasts with the extreme overadaptation to the "reality" they show outwardly, since they feign mental health resistant to any test. It is a question of *"mental orphans"* who have compensated their inner emptiness with a structural shell that *reverses their helplessness*; they are hypermature people who manage perfectly well on their own at all times, without anybody's help.

The psychoanalytic mobilization produced during analysis may give rise to the manifest appearance of unexplained somatic symptoms; their emotional reason remained frozen during the splitting. The patient's psychic apparatus regards these "contents" with total "pleasantness", particularly when it comes to emotions. For this reason, the psychic pain itself from the split and the anguish and longing, are not experiences processed by mental work; they automatically seek and find in the particular biological systems and in the physiology of the whole organism a compensatory cushioning for unthinkable emotions.

Epilogue

Everything is in order in that landscape, as happens in nature. Order which accommodates creator chaos and tranquil diversity, the dark and the luminous, the simple and the complex, that which changes and that which stays the same, in a harmonious whole that does not try to be anything but what it is. There, against the strong, kind and containing bay, the alert traveler may have a foretaste of what she has come to find in herself, which will surely help her find it.

... [W]hat if our body, with its guts and joints, with its flesh and bones, its liquids and neural networks, is a guide full of wisdom, whose messages also tell us how to transcend the self and connect with the whole?

Norma Osnajanski (*2004*)

The vignettes presented here recount—and tell how, even though the psychosomatic concept is debatable—there are patients to whom it happens that the leap from psychic to corporal is a dramatic event producing that paradoxical situation I call "double pain", pain of the soul and of the body. One notices with Romina as well as with Milena, this double pain; in one case, where the only expression of pain is at the physiological level, intense pain driven into the body, and in the other, pathological mourning, where the pain caused by memories kills the organism.

To conclude, I want to emphasize that it is in the context where the body appears not only as anatomical reality but also as psychic reality, where inhabiting one's own body with a painful, deadly feeling, produces a split with the omnipotent illusion of exclusion of suffering, a vain attempt, we should call it, so as not to say something radically impossible.

References

FISCHBEIN, J.E. (2000). La clínica psicoanalítica y las enfermedades somáticas *Psicoanálisis* (APdeBA), XXII(1). El cuerpo presencia o intromission, Buenos Aires.

JURI, L.J. (2006). Duelos intersubjetivos. El duelo segregado de Charles Darwin. *Aperturas psicoanalíticas* 23 (August). Available at http://www.aperturas.org/23juri.html

LUTEMBERG, J. (2007). *El vacío mental*. Lima: Siklos.

MCDOUGALL, J. 1993 [1978]. *Alegato por un acierta anormalidad.* Buenos Aires: Paidós.

OSNAJANSKI, N. (2004). Prologue to *La voz del síntoma* by Adriana Schnake S., Santiago de Chile: Editorial Cuatro Vientos.

VALLS, J.L. (1995). *Diccionario Freudiano.* Madrid: Ed. Julian Yebenes.

WINNICOTT, D.W. (1989). Psycho-Somatic Disorder. In *Psycho-Analytic Explorations,* ed. Winnicott, C., R. Shepherd, M. Davis, Cambridge, Mass.: Harvard University, 103-118.

3

The Development of the Maternal Feeling in Child Analysis: Ana and Diana

Débora Regina Unikowski

Motherhood is a part of every woman's life. In the interplay of fantasy and reality, becoming a mother can constitute either a desire or a non-desire; can be a project to be carried through or not. Or it can even cause fear or disgust. We are born from a woman that joined in marriage a man that is forbidden to us, and from their marriage we develop in our inner world a capacity of joining in marriage another man, to engender a child and become a mother. Independently of giving birth to a child, be it a fruit of our womb or adopted through a fairly successful process, we become a mother. This process includes the working through of the Oedipus complex, the identification to the feminine and masculine aspects of father and mother, the capacity of being alone, the capacity of thinking and of being able of revêrie. Furthermore, the perception of the flesh and blood child separated from our own body and the erasure of the idealization of the imaginary child provide the psychological birth of the child as well as that of the mother.

As a child analyst, I see mothers and fathers in search of help for their children, parents who need analysis but out of possibilities of investing in themselves. What I listen from them interest me, especially in order to grasp the family dynamics and to delineate the child's history, trying to preserve the place of the little patient. However, the changes brought about by the child's analysis reflect on the other family members. Transference and countertransference extend to parents that can take advantage of the cont function of the analyst. Thus, the family's space for thought and playfulness is broadened, enhancing the ongoing process of "becoming father and mother".

In this paper I would like to think about the development of the motherly feeling during the treatment of a child. I will present the cases of two mothers who couldn't bear their first child but in their forties, and brought to me a demand of help for their conflicts on motherhood. The first one, that I'll call Ana, adopted a baby girl when she was forty five, and the other, Diana, could bear her daughter at forty. During the analysis of their daughters, these mothers blossomed. They became more caring, improving their affective tuning, investing more harmonically in their lives and their families, and above all fostering the child's individuation.

Ana

Ana came to see me asking for an assessment of her four years old daughter, wishing I could also treat her or at least guide her as for the "hard role of being a mother". She described the girl as reserved, rough in her caresses and aggressive towards her little friends. Ana's relation to Marina was a constant "drop arm", a true war. Ana was worried about the girl's normality, fearing their mutual aggressiveness and harboring matricide and filicide fantasies. She wished she had a perfect daughter and so she quite rigidly programmed all her education.

Being married for many years, Ana postponed motherhood as far as she could, investing a lot in her profession. When she moved to another city, she believed it was time to have a child and decided to adopt one. She took upon herself the prenatal assistance of a young woman who was willing to give away her baby, and this way Ana got Marina since her first days of life. The adoption of the desired daughter coincided with the loss of a maternal figure, and a depressive moment followed. Unable to get back to her job, Ana felt worthless and it exacerbated her guilt feelings for not being able to beget a child. She felt herself a disaster and asked herself how such a disaster could be a mother. With her self-esteem down on her feet and being extremely demanding on herself, nothing she did could be well. She always remained attentive to the baby's education, setting limits and sternly requiring the keeping of all rules, but without the counterpart of sweetness which, for her, would mean neglecting the education. She felt as a "naughty mother" while the father was always the "nice" one. Her husband was more moderate and flexible, but was also very wavery, allowing the girl to do a lot of mischief, not imposing limits until he got tired and yelled at her and punished her.

Ana and Marina had a well built story about the "belly mother", that could not keep her, and the "heart mother Ana". Mother and child were linked in the abandonment anxiety and the feeling of helplessness. The girl seemed to dress up an omnipotence shield, similar to Ana's. Asserting that she didn't need anybody, she often took the mother's place, making decisions that amazed the adults around her. At first, it sounded funny but soon that battling little girl that provoked her mother's aggressiveness turned out to be distressing.

The first time we met Marina told me straightaway that she could play by herself, but it was interesting that she frequently requested my sharing in her playing. Very "bossy", everything had to be as she determined, comprised the time to get in and out of the consulting room. She would always use some time with her mother in the waiting room, including her in the first part of the session. The fact of having two mothers was a secret between Marina and Ana that gradually could be shared with me. Insofar as Marinas' fantasies of birth and abandonment were worked through, the fantasies of a fateful destiny of the child's aggressiveness stopped tormenting Ana's mind. After about two years of attendance, affective exchanges took the place of the omnipotent defenses, both in the mother and in the child.

I believed I have acted as a continent, occupying the place of a "grandmother" for the child, and I became a kind of "incubator" for Ana to become a mother. Gradually Ana left feeling "inept" as a mother. She could value her maternal capabilities and reinvesting in her profession. She went back to her job, reserving some time for the daughter, the family and herself, and looked for an analysis.

Diana

Very anxious and grieved, this mother arrived asking for help for Vitoria's adaptation in school, believing that her six year old girl was developing a 'panic syndrome'. She was aware of her daughter's suffering and despaired for not being able to help her. So far she had tried to solve the problems by interrupting the adaptation periods in kindergarten, moving the girl to another school, colluding with the teachers, ruling the roost. She felt erring, failing and did not know how to change, extremely wounded in her narcissism

Diana got married against her parents will, needing to prove that she could "get along in life". She made a professional alliance with her husband, and for a long time there were no external or internal conditions for a child's project. Afterwards, nephews arriving and the biological clock running, near her forties she did her best to get pregnant. Still shaken by a first pregnancy very much invested and suffered that did not succeed, Diana worked incessantly during her second pregnancy, ignoring her 'interesting condition'. When the baby was prematurely born the mother sunk in a 'world of cries' and got depressed. Such depression is likely to have been amplified by the pain for the first child she had lost and left adrift this practical and objective woman.

At birth Vitoria cried a lot and expressed in her body her uneasiness through repeated infections, as usually does a distressed baby. Mother and daughter were companions in despair in endless sleepless nights and kept tied together till the school interposed between them. The school rules to promote adaptation were experienced as an attack against which Vitoria defend herself through somatic symptoms: daily vomiting and stomach aches.

Vitoria's treatment was marked by great ambivalence. At first the mother was quite present in the sessions that often took place in the waiting room. As Vitoria started to come into the consulting room by herself, Diana started to call me up more frequently, demanding urgent interviews. In these meetings we worked through her ambivalence since almost every time she would come to 'end it all', but instead of breaking up the treatment, the therapeutic alliance was fortified. Through those interviews I learned that Vitoria lived in overexcitation, keeping several activities without contention or limits and without attention to her sleep and feeding rhythms. She had not a time set to go to sleep or a time to get up, and she could not take a nap in the afternoon even if she felt sleepy. She would eat so many cookies and candies that sometimes they took the place of a meal.

Diana wavered between rivalry and identification with me regarding my capacities to watch, to look for and open a space for Vitoria. She attacked me counting my work as useless and even evil – after all she had never seen her daughter so violent. She wished I could help her, and really tried to change, to set limits, telling the truth, keeping her decisions and developing authority without being authoritarian. She could not think of more intense affective exchanges and of more time spent with her daughter without being jumbled with her, but it came about naturally. Diana used me also to "recharge her batteries", to contain her anxiety , her despair, her hurry in solving problems and her impotence feeling, improving her capacity of 'holding' and 'revêrie' .

Some few interviews with the presence of the father were really tense. Keeping even more the negative aspect of the transference, he would stay in an arrogant and joking attitude, trying to despise my job and ask for concrete and faster results.

The ambivalence showed itself in the countertransference discouraging me and even sometimes making me wish the interruption. I felt dazed, exhausted and impotent as often I recommended psychoanalysis for the mother and counseling for both parents. Interestingly the treatment lasted nine months, the length of a pregnancy with frequent threats of miscarriage and premature birth. The interruption was decided by the mother, pressed by her husband who said that the daughter was fine and they needed the money they were spending. Diana became more motherly, linked to her daughter as someone separated from her and kept a good relationship with me giving me some news a year later.

Finalizing

When parents come they bring us their impotence feelings and lots of guilt. The settling of an initial asymmetry provides an idealization of the analyst and the devaluation of either one parent or both. We usually have more contact with the mother, which is the object of this paper. She presents herself as someone who had failed and needs to accept the rules of whom is supposed to know, submitting to this relentless judge, the analyst, who is invited to embody a severe superego, the tyrannical father or mother from the mother's fantasies.

Since we explain that we are there to try to understand, to clear up and help promoting changes, but that we have no ready answers, we open up a wider space, not only for the child's analytical process but also for the maternal blossoming. It is fundamental that the mother occupies her place, freeing the analyst from this 'impossible mission'. An analyst will never become a mother; her competence is from a different order. She can be continent of projections and anxieties, she can help the child and its mother to play their roles in the family in the healthiest way, clarifying the intricate game of projective identifications and allowing changes in maternal and paternal imagoes. Facilitating the mother to be mother and the father's wife, and the child to be the child of the home, the father's and the mother's child. There are several processes going on during a child's psychoanalytic treatment. I think that although we have a restricted access to the mother's internal world, our job facilitates her 'becoming a mother' at the same time as we 'become' an analyst in every session, which is a fundamental feature.

References

WINNICOTT, D.W. (1960). La théorie de la relation parent-nourisson. In *De la Pédiatrie à la Psychanalyse*. Paris: Payot, 1978 (p.244, 249, 250).

BION, W.R. (1962) Uma teoria sobre o pensar. In *Estudos Psicanalíticos Revisitados (Second Thoughts)* Rio de Janeiro: Imago, 1994 (p.127-137).

4

The Role of the Analyst in Clinical Practice with Patients Under Critical Pregnancy

Luz María Abatangelo de Stürzenbaum

Brief Introduction

Pregnancy is in line with an erotogenic body which accounts for a subject. The expressions of each gestation are singular. The different moments the female goes through: menarche, pregnancy, parturition, and menopause refer to the woman´s relationship with her own mother. Through the present work, some aspects of the analyst´s role with a patient under risk pregnancy will be shown. The analytical work allowed the creation of a space, through which transference clichés have been deployed. Furthermore, the patient, held by this particular "illusion" of the analytical role, could talk about herself, her anxieties and her fears.

Amelia´s case. Disclosing the old lake monster

Amelia is a patient who was 38 years old at the time of consultation. She was referred by her gynecologist. She was in her second pregnancy month, after successive attempts of *in vitro* fertilization. I receive a woman with harmonic features, nice and quite anxious. The reason for consultation was that she suffered from insomnia, she was very irritable, she often quarreled with her husband, and as she expressed, she felt "dread of losing her baby". She commented that she had been married to German for 10 years. At the age of 26, Amelia had undergone surgery due to an ovarian cyst that caused her strong pain. Surgery was satisfactory and without consequences for future maternity. Amelia was a single child; she had lived with her mother until she married German. He father had died due to a heart attack when she was 13 and as she narrated, her mother had entered into an "endless mourning". The relationship with her mother was very difficult: her mother was very dependent and did not have a good relationship with German; according to Amelia, "she did not like him".

While she was historizing, she strongly burst into tears. The relationship with German was good; she remarked that they shared everything related to pregnancy; she felt he took care of and was concerned about her discomforts. During the first three years of marriage, they decided not to have children and when they started to try, without success, they made gynecological consultations. After several studies, they detected endometriosis (presence of endometrial tissue outside the uterus). Surgery was performed, and from then onwards, the road to pregnancy was supposedly open. But this did not happen, and, after one year of attempts, they decided to consult again. Inseminations were performed without any result, until they finally resorted to assisted reproduction.

During the first sessions

Patient: - My body is swollen, my ankles hurt, I am quite afraid of not being able to hold on to my baby, I am afraid of losing my baby. I find it difficult to fall asleep at night, I am nervous, I feel bad, and it is worse because I know that Germán also suffers with all this...

We believe that during pregnancy the essential thing is the connection with the inner body, which forms part of the feminine fantasmatic. Pregnancy implies a transitory regression which updates the own pregnant woman's separation anxiety. I wondered what had happened to the dyadic relation. I thought that Amelia had gone through her adolescence between a melancholized mother and a dead father. During the first sessions, I listened to the narrations in the middle of the burst of tears, narrations related to the body, her fears and discomforts. A situation of real affection and deprivation was perceived. Amelia needed to drain her pain so that, at some time, the conditions could be reestablished for the patient to function at the preponderance of pleasure principle and thus, be able to analyze.

At the beginning, the analyst's role was holding: Amelia found a constant object on which she could transfer her anxieties, fears and pains. As we have already mentioned, the separation anxiety, the fear of mother's attack, as every child is incestuous, had been reactivated. Amelia was a "first-time mother" and "first-time patient" in her therapeutic experience; her manifestations were similar to those of a traumatic neurosis. How had she worked the subjective reception of the embryo in her uterus which she considered "weak"? Anxieties that her psychic apparatus could not deal with had been reactivated.

During the pregnancy second trimester, she started to feel fetal movements; she seemed to have entered into what Green considers "maternal madness", in the sense of omnipotent love and passion, linked to the life-instinct preponderance that allowed her establishing a connection with her baby. Following this thought, that madness was also "therapeutic madness", in the sense of being able to enter into her and understand her states. Amelia sat on the couch; she was lying down with a cushion into her arms, while she talked. Then, in my mind, a countertransference occurrence appeared: an image, a large uterus which wrapped Amelia, the uterus that facilitated her to be a containing uterus?

P: - My baby is in my womb, I start feeling that my baby is moving and it is so wonderful... (She hugs the cushion). It´s very strong, you know?

Her words generated a mental image in me: I listened to her and almost at the same time, I entered into a regressive movement; I saw the thing meant by the image, then, I internally invoked my own inscriptions, trying to find the sensorial representation Amelia conveyed to me; in unison, the elaboration of a creative image occurred, which allowed me to inscribe a new emotional experience with her in my representational field. I think of a metaphor, the Russian dolls, the "*mamushkas*", one into the other, the analyst containing the patient and her baby.

The dream opens the doors...

There was a moment of inflection from the narration of a dream.

P: - I had a dream yesterday. I woke up sad and I want to tell it to you: "I was in a wood, there was a large lake, and I knew something was happening, but I did not know what.... Suddenly, a monster came up, I could not see it, and I just saw its shadow. Everything seemed to be still until the monster appeared. The wood remained deserted". When I woke up, I wanted to cry. Concerning the associations, Amelia says:

P:-The monster´s shadow, my fears come up all of a sudden, quickly, everything was quiet until... (She pauses). When my father died, it was the same; everything was still until he fell down and died... She breaks down and cries. I see a helpless girl. She recovers after a long silence full of tears.

P: - I remember that when I was a child and studied English, we used to read stories about lakes and monsters... in the stories, there was also a Lady of the Lake, who helped the prince to defeat it... and he defeated it... She narrated this childhood memory enthusiastically.

We will focus on some aspects of the dream. I believe it worked as an opening of the unconscious which allowed giving a new sense to the analytical process, as well as widening the representational field. In this transferencial dream, the conflict reactivated by pregnancy appeared: mourning for her father's death. The lake opens as a grave and gives way to the father's phantom, dead-alive, an object in an intermediate metabolization state: it is a shadow that the patient does not want to see. The fetus represented for Amelia, according to the symbolic equation child-penis, the father penis. This is what allowed her, if it was representative of the father penis, to return to the father. This fantasy of nestling a father penis in her womb allowed taking it as a barrier with the mother. Let us remember that her mother was in a melancholic, dependent state; the way to hold her was by identifying herself with the roles that, before, the lost object played for the melancholized object. But that monster is immersed in water, we can relate it to the "oceanic feeling or state", representative of the relationship between her and the fetus, and transferencially with me, as if an invisible umbilical cord joined us. In that manner, Amelia internalized the bond that linked her with me, and which, then, she repeated with the fetus. Let us remember that Amelia was afraid of not being able to contain the fetus. More superficially, it could refer to the melancholized mother who did not let her be contained. This mother was a uterus that let her drop, therefore, a way of survival for Amelia that will probably work as defense: if she could not be nestled, she was going to nestle. At the onset of the treatment, she identified herself with a mother in the transference, able to contain her and consequently, that let her contain.

Amelia associates the dream with a childhood memory which slowly starts to create ties and it is then, when tension decreases, that dread transforms into a smile. It appears the wish to be helped by the analyst to defeat the monsters, and so, she is able to perform the work of mourning process and transmute the internal object. We may wonder what happened with the aggressiveness of that internal persecutory object. It depends on the amount of hatred of the prior ambivalence towards the internal object, now internalized. For the first time, Amelia could talk about her own feelings about the abandonment of her dead-alive and threatening father. Perhaps she could start mourning her father, identify herself with him; having her father's penis inside her let her separate from the mother. The fantasy of separation from the mother is related to the incorporation of the father penis that keeps the fantasy of the eternal mother "under control". Likewise, we find the fear to the mother's punishment. From that perspective, the fetus is polysemous: on the one hand, it represents the monstrous, persecutory mother, and on the other hand, the embryos /fetuses she could not nestle, as a further way of not separating from the mother. Now Amelia "was" not the father penis, she "had it".

Conclusions

I think that as analyst, I allied with the most libidinal aspects the patient had. I could enter into the "therapeutic madness" which allowed me to connect with her, perceive her state and do not destroy myself at making the attempt. During the third trimester, the dreams came back, now more libidinal: she dreamt with the parturition, she could see her baby. The separation anxiety reactivated with the closeness to the parturition time. With birth, a working-off and encounter process started. The mourning for her father's death and the working-through on the mother's thanatic aspects allowed her, in a sense, holding the new life. Her ego remained enriched with an erotic identification and her libido available for the new object.

References

ASLAN, C.M. (1978). Un aporte a la metapsicología del duelo. *Rev. de Psicoanálisis*, XXXV (1), Buenos Aires.

BARANGER, W. (1969). El muerto-vivo, estructura de los objetos en el duelo y los estados depresivos. In *Problemas del campo psicoanalítico*, Buenos Aires: Kargieman.

FREUD, S. (1914). Introducción al narcisismo. In *A.E.* XIV.

FREUD, S. (1917): Duelo y melancolía. In *A.E.* XVI.

FREUD, S. (1920). Más allá del principio del placer. In *A.E.* XVIII.

FREUD, S. (1925). Inhibición, síntoma y angustia. In *A.E.* XX.

FREUD, S. (1933). La femineidad. Nuevas Conferencias de Introducción al psicoanálisis. In *A.E.* XXII.

GREEN, A. (1986).*De locuras privadas*. Translator: José Luis Etcheverry, Buenos Aires: Paidós, 1990.

WINNICOTT, D. (1971). *Realidad y juego*. Translator: Floreal Mazia, Buenos Aires: Gedisa, 1982.

5

Diversity in Voluntary Motherhood:
Between Desire and Biology

Silvia Jadur, Constanza Duhalde and Viviana Wainstein

Motherhood is no longer simply a natural universal occurrence; it is a product of culture and is in permanent transformation. We cannot then subsume women's identity to this genetic function since it is only a potentiality. It is in this way that gender studies have contributed theories that have deconstructed identity constructs, denaturalizing women's maternal functions and disarticulating the male-female binarity. Heteronormative discourses still reproduce a system that encourages "agreed" models as natural, to the extent that sexual reproduction, in heterosexual couples, is seen as an example. Homoparenthood is a different relational prototype that breaks with the triangle of mother-father-child and forces us to rethink and rework the oedipal connection as many times over, as also occurs in the case of women without a partner who decide to become mothers.

According to Foucault, sex has no history, since it is a product of its time and represents the appropriation of the body and its physiological capabilities by an ideological discourse. He states that "it is a set of effects produced in bodies and social relations by the deployment of a complex political technology." Following this line of thinking, it is difficult to conceive, produce and put into practice "new relational models". We might include here procreation without sexuality, motherhood in lesbian couples and in single women, subscribing to the fact that motherhood is fundamentally related to desire.

The new positions occupied by women in production as well as the levels they have reached in intellectual development and in the field of work have meant postponing the possibility of procreation. Today then women can make decisions about their bodies and desires, ranging from contraceptive measures to the termination of a pregnancy, from the desire to have a child and be a mother, to conceiving a child when faced with the impossibility of becoming pregnant, in the absence of a partner or with a homosexual partner. If subjectivity is a part of, and based on, historical processes, let us not forget the western frameworks related to the dissimilar ways of achieving motherhood in Greek and Egyptian mythology and the Old and New Testament. Let us remind ourselves then of Sarah's recourse to surrogacy, Lot's incest, Osiris and Isis' post mortem procreation and Moses' adoption. Regardless of its procreative/genetic origin, a child must be filiated to and included in a symbolic register since its procreators are not always the ones who take on parenthood.

Let's bear in mind that the Romans already distinguished between "children of the family" who were the heirs to a clan, free men, and "children of the land", infants devoid of socio-cultural support who were destined for slavery. Even nowadays the terms "natural child", "legitimate child" or "illegitimate child" still resound, demonstrating the stamp of a community law contrary to nature that has been sustained over time. Let's also take into consideration that from the 19th century onwards, the state operated as an agent of social order, that invaded the privacy of individuals and regulated their emotional, sexual and reproductive relations. Consequently, in the civil marriage contract in which material possessions are legally recorded, children are also registered in the genealogical relation of filiation.

So far we have presented a brief intersection of disciplinary viewpoints which in a way re-edit Marie Langer's proposals to articulate the social with the vicissitudes of women's subjectivity. Langer states that "In the last century women in our civilization have acquired a sexual and social freedom totally unknown just three generations ago. In contrast, cultural and economic circumstances impose serious restrictions on motherhood"...." Our research will focus on the difficulties in women's functions, that is to say in menstruation, conception, fertility, breastfeeding, etc. Thirty years ago this approach would only have been a subject for a treatise on gynecology and obstetrics. Hardly anyone would have thought of tackling it from the psychopathological point of view" (Langer 1964, p. 13). She puts forward a permanent quest to interweave the psychosomatic-biological, calling into question psychoanalytical knowledge, with the Kleinian influences of the time and the intersection with other sciences, within a politico-cultural framework. Langer was a long way from imagining how medical science would change the procreative fate of women.

Louise Brown, the first child born with the help of assisted fertility treatment, using the technique developed by the doctors Patrick Steptoe and Robert Edwards in Great Britain, will soon be 30 years old. Sometime after Louise was born, in France the team of Doctor René Frydman enabled the birth of Amandine. Following the development of these techniques and advances in andrology and biology, including egg donation, sperm banks and ICSI, hundreds of children have been born throughout the world. It is an irreversible reality. The question is how and from what perspective we psychoanalysts listen to the suffering of patients who demand of science a child. How do we build bridges to articulate discourses that ask questions of the different actors involved in this situation which generates polemic and controversy. As psychoanalysts working in the field of mental health and health, we cannot sidestep the prevention aspect of our function. Prevention in health, as seen from the perspective of appealing to a community to generate humanly decent conditions for individuals, who are supporting the uncertainty with regard to a fate that cannot be redressed and confined to inevitable certainties. In response to these dilemmas, I focus particularly and emphatically on the subjectivity of the children who have been born and will be born through these means of reproduction. Just as there is a hegemonic medical model, there is also a hegemonic psychoanalytical one that very often prevents us from putting the pillars of Freud's legacy to work.

It is interesting that this author rethought her writings on motherhood and femininity years later, that she accompanied the evolution of thinking on issues of men and women, in relation to science.

As individuals we are permeated by culture and its productions; our practice also demonstrates the fact that, outside of abstinence, ideology can filter through preventing us from hearing the pain and the secrets of the subconscious. For this reason it is relevant to approach the valuable work of Puget and Wender (1982-2006) on overlapping worlds in which they showed how real events from the external world impact on the personal and on the analytical function.

Langer, rectified some of the formulations of her book *Motherhood and Sex* at a conference entitled "I fell into the trap of idealizing motherhood" saying "It is very difficult to define what the biological disposition for having a child is, because on the one side we have the biological aspects and on the other the social and cultural one. What is certain is that women are different from men, it is absurd to play at being unisex. We have a biological apparatus capable of procreating children and we have a social situation that influences our desires, our possibilities and our ideologies". She went on to say that: "We know that we have a conscious desire and also an unconscious desire. Let's take the example of the conscious decision to have a child and not be able to get pregnant, even though my anatomy permits it. Let's take the example of adopting the alternative of not having a child because I am studying for whatever degree, because it will ruin my work performance. Behind this apparently linear decision there is a long list of issues that cannot be resolved. Since as human beings we are conflictive, since as human beings we are ambivalent, there are no clean, neat decisions, but rather behind a decision there always remains something of the other option."...

In another presentation, she stated, "Oh, mother free me from this thing they call maternal instinct!". She took the topic of women's sexuality and discussed the natural desire to procreate and maternal instinct. Agreeing with Badinter's thinking she said "This discussion would have been unimaginable a few decades ago... She maintained that Freud and his followers, particularly Helene Deutsch, M. Klein and Winnicott, will be the last heirs to the Rousseaunian ideology. She predicted a new era, in which all the responsibility for the care and mental health of children no longer falls to the mother, but which instead would see the emergence of [paternal instinct]." In any case, she proposes that motherhood is not a topic that is exclusive to women, or just for psychoanalysis.

Let's agree that although the driving force for motherhood is the desire for a child, women who do not achieve pregnancy when they give up contraception, women without a partner, with a lesbian partner, or those who need egg donation due to their age, turn to fertility specialists. The medicalization of women's routine experience from menarche to perimenopause, in addition to the scientific advances in human reproduction, generates demands that medical science satisfies without asking questions about their significance. The first consultation is with those deemed to have knowledge about the body, not with a psychoanalyst. Patients arrive at the psychoanalyst after referral by those same doctors, who recognize and accept that they cannot give account of an ailment that exceeds their function and their knowledge, or else because of the suffering that the psychological apparatus cannot metabolize. The analyst's skill will be in seizing this moment to create a demand for a psychoanalysis that establishes questions and marks, even when it is brief.

Clinical vignettes

Rosmaryn

Is 41 years old. She is consulting a fertility specialist because she has not been using contraceptives for almost two years, she has not become pregnant and she wants to have a child. She got divorced three years ago after 16 years of marriage. Her ex husband did not want to have children, at first because they were dedicated to work and his priority was achieving economic wellbeing, then later because having a family was not in his plans their sex life gradually deteriorated. The patient did want to have children. Shortly after the separation she met a man 8 years younger than herself with whom she discovered unknown aspects of her sexuality and who made her feel cared for, protected and loved. They do not live together and only spend time together for a few days a week. Her current partner has a 6 year-old daughter with another woman, but they never lived together. When he found out about the pregnancy he stood by her, recognized the child as his daughter and maintains a relationship with her. He communicates with the mother to agree on certain child care issues but has no other type of contact. Rosmaryn has told him of her desire to be a mother and at first he was afraid she would demand they live together but when she expressed her desire merely for a father (or procreator?)for a child his attitude changed completely. He shares the idea of planning for a child and supports her in the ups and downs of the doctor's appointments. She is diagnosed as having poor egg quality and was therefore unlikely to achieve a pregnancy even with assisted fertilization. The chance of becoming a biological mother depend on IVF with egg donation. This information is decisive in recognizing the possibility of a psychological consultation on the doctor's recommendation. The therapeutic work focuses on relinquishing genetics and the ideal of a family. Her sister, who lives abroad, and her mother are the pillars of her emotional and economic support and they accompany her in the choice she makes. The young man will recognize the child and his parental commitment will be relative. Taking this path to motherhood is a complex intra-subjective process, centered around the subjective construction of a future child. Over a year of analysis that involved unraveling and resignifying relationships and conflicts and unearthing phantoms, she was able to construct a space for words and emotions which preceded the treatment and the possible arrival of a child. The therapy was continued during the pregnancy and puerperium and currently telephone calls take place periodically.

Diana and Gabriela

Come for a consultation because they have decided to have a family. They have also decided that Gabriela, who is 33, will be the first to attempt to become pregnant by insemination from an anonymous donor. Gabriela is a working professional, Diana is 26 and is finishing her university degree. Both their families have accepted their homosexuality and their life as a couple but have not been informed about the desire for motherhood and the treatment. They are finding it difficult to decide when and how to tell them. They are afraid of the reactions of the social milieu with a view to the future, for example when the child starts school. The therapeutic work was the same as for any couple that needs to construct the emotional foundation for a child. It was recommended that they obtain legal information from a lawyer trained in child and family law. They were able to build a support network of friends and very slowly their families came to accept their chosen undertaking. The sessions lasted for about six months at the end of which they made several unsuccessful attempts. A year later, they came to a talk on homoparenthood that we organized at the Association and which was open to the community, in order to renew contact and share with us the news that Gabriela was pregnant. Since then we have kept in contact via e-mail. In this way they ask me for help, since they have created a forum for lesbian couples and would like to have advice available if any situation requires it. This forum also led to the setting up of a small self-managing group of female couples who wanted to become mothers. Felipe was born in February.

It is worth mentioning that artificial insemination is not a modern technology; the first attempts to carry it out date back to the 15th century. It is believed that artificial insemination was attempted on Juana, the wife of King Henry IV of Castile. In the 18th century, the Italian priest and physiologist Spallanzani carried out successful experiments on artificial insemination in animals. In the early 20th century heterologous inseminations were already being carried out in women. In 1949 methods for freezing and unfreezing sperm appeared and in 1950 the idea emerged to add antibiotics to the semen to prevent venereal diseases. Later, in the 1970s and 1980s efficient methods were developed for semen collection and cryopreservation, which was when sperm banks appeared in various countries.

Marisa (34 year-old) **and Juan** (37 year-old)
Come for a consultation after undergoing treatments to stimulate her ovulatory cycles and improve the quality and quantity of his sperm. Finally, following the failure attempts at assisted fertilization and ICSI (intracytoplasmic sperm injection), they are advised to turn to a sperm bank. The specialist considers it a good idea to refer them for consultation. They are both doctors and have been together for 6 years. They know the scientific information but as individuals they need to process the effects of giving up on genetic paternity inter and intra-subjectively and at the same time accept the idea of gestating a child using donor semen.

In individual analysis sessions they are working through the effects on their subjectivity and in addition in couple's therapy they examine any conflicts that have arisen in the relationship, unconscious pacts, the desire for children and for motherhood/fatherhood and the updating of projects.

Marisa, who has had psychoanalysis prior to the reproductive problem, does not want to give up on becoming a biological mother. Adoption is not a path they are ready to consider at this point. I specifically believe it to be essential to mourn biological motherhood and desist from medical treatments in order to access adoption, since it is also a complex choice.

In the case studies presented, one of the core issues to clarify is the relationship with the future child and the account/information they will be given about their procreative origin. This is a nodal topic prior to any treatment since it is interwoven with sexuality and the oedipal trajectory of the procreators – future fathers and/or mothers. If we take up some of Talila Saal's ideas to understand the issues of the body and sex, we must place them in the register of what is real, symbolic and imaginary since when we talk about the erogenous body we do not do so from the point of view of biology. While "Here we are faced with a significant subversion of an apparent natural order, since it is not the organism in its natural functions that supports and underpins the appearance of the desire, but rather it is the other's desire which is essential for the child to live, which ensures and enables its bodily survival"(Saal, p.23).

Let's agree then every individual is talked of before their existence, inhabits projects and fantasies, occupies a space, absorbs libidinal energy and is a promise of being. That space is the desire of the mother's, and is also the effect of castration, which must not and cannot be reduced to the desire for a child as motherhood is not women's only function. According to Saal "The specific thing about this desire, which makes motherhood a fact of culture not of nature, as has sometimes inappropriately been claimed, is the simple expedient each woman has of saying no to motherhood. Within this possibility of saying no a fundamental qualitative leap takes place which transforms it into a matter of choice and not destiny. Giving life is not reduced to giving birth, giving life is separating oneself." Let's bear in mind that different sexualities are organized on the basis of a symbolic order, where the foundational aspect is castration, with the incompleteness of men and women being what drives desire.

In the clinical practice presented, it is essential start from the choice of motherhood that is made by women. At the same time they are planning a family. Let's accept that the family is an ill-fated social structure in constant crisis, which is currently still central in so far as it provides for the normativization of sexuality in relation to the procreation and raising of children. We can talk of legal and legitimate families, whilst gay or lesbian couples do not have a legal character of the same status as heterosexual couples, at least in Argentina. It is then in the family that, subscribing to Althusserian ideas on the family as the producer and reproducer of individuals in a particular community, we separate the functions of child rearing, motherhood and fatherhood from biology. This is an important fact since within family relationships individuals are not just constituted as such, they are filiated to a symbolic genealogical order that is independent from their genetic origin. Lastly, it is of course indisputable that family and culture are subsidiary to the oedipal connection.

Concern about the origin of life, about reproduction, appears in childhood as an epistemic investigation that leads to the construction of childish sexual theories that are tied to parental identifications, with Oedipus, above all with the family story of desire. This has nothing to do with the union of the egg with the sperm. The function of medicine is to cure, to suture the organic wound, to recognize the patient as being a person who is suffering. In these subject areas we psychoanalysts have an extremely wide field in which to reflect, research and listen, as mere facilitators helping the individual to discover their unconscious truths, make the desire speak out, mitigate suffering and generate the best subjective conditions for a new individual to emerge.

References
FERNÁNDEZ GIROLAMI, M, JADUR, S, *ET AL.* (2006). Guías para la intervención Psicológica en tratamientos de alta complejidad. *Rev. Sociedad Argentina de Medicina Reproductiva,* 21 (2).

JADUR, S. (2004). Aborto e infertilidad. *Psicoanálisis y el hospital,* N° 26.

JADUR, S (2006). Sexualidad y trastornos reproductivos. *Rev. Otra Mirada,* N° 5.

JADUR, S, & DUHALDE, C. (2005). Aspectos emocionales y la relación médico-paciente en la consulta por infertilidad. *Rev. Sociedad Argentina de Medicina Reproductiva,* 20 (2).

JADUR, S. & WILLNER, R. (2007). El sostén emocional al servicio de la eficiencia médica en los tratamientos de reproducción asistida. *Rev. Soc. Argentina de Medicina Reproductiva,* 22 (1).

JADUR, S, DUHALDE, C, WAINSTEIN, V. (2008). Concebir la posición analítica en un grupo de pacientes con problemas en la procreación. Encuentro en la comunidad. Premio FEPAL, Psicoanálisis y comunidad.

LANGER, M. (1951). *Maternidad y sexo.* Buenos Aires: Paidós, 1964.

LANGER, M. (1982). Conference: Oh, madre libérame de eso que llaman instinto maternal. "Feminismo y sexualidad". En Seminario: "Feminismo, Política y Movimientos Feministas". 1-3 marzo, Centro de Estudios Económicos y Sociales del Tercer Mundo, México.

LANGER, M (1984). Conference: Caí en idealizar la maternidad. Invitation by H. Kesselman, Madrid.

LANGER, M, PALACIO, J. & GUINSBERG, E. (1983). *Memoria, historia y diálogo psicoanalítico.* Buenos Aires: Folios, 1984.

LANGER, M. *ET AL.* (1971). *Cuestionamos.* Buenos Aires, Granica.

ROUDINESCO, E. (2002). *La familia en desorden.* Buenos Aires: Fondo de Cultura Económica. 2003.

SAAL, F. (1998). *Palabras de analista.* México: Siglo XXI.

VEZZETTI, H. (1996). Marie Langer: psicoanálisis de la maternidad. *Anuario de Investigaciones,* Buenos Aires. 4: 377 - 389.

VOLNOVICH, J.C & WERTHEIN, S. (1989). *Marie Langer. Mujer. Psicoanálisis. Marxismo.* Buenos Aires: Contrapunto.

6

Vicissitudes in the Development of the Male Identity. Relevance of Gender, of the Analyst and the Patient, to the Analytic Process[1]

María Teresa Flores

The primary relationship and the structural basis of the male identity
"Everything is confusing, difficult to grasp, the more I try to understand or make it transparent the more elusive it becomes. I don't know what came first, the tears or the sound of the harmonium. I do remember there were two houses - the one in Eira and the one in Adro. I know the tears and the stars were in the house in Eira and the harmonium music in the house in Adro.

My mother told me that I was born in the house in Adro, and that some time later, the family left Adro and went to live in Eira. They were both small houses at ground level, with two rooms; it was more than enough space for mother and son. A few years ago, I happened to pass by these two small houses where my mother and I began to belong to each other; they looked incredibly small ... An enormous chest sat opposite the front door. I know the poor keep everything they own in these chests: clothing, bread ...

One day, I went over to the chest - perhaps to let my mother know that I wanted some bread - and I saw something on top of it that I had never seen before. Standing on tip-toe, I reached for it and pulled. What happened next was most amazing: from inside this object came a beautiful sound, more beautiful even than my mother's singing voice, for surely I had heard her sing. But perhaps I am mistaken, perhaps I had not heard my mother sing. At the time my mother was feeling sad ...

One morning, I woke up alone in the house. I woke up crying, and I called out - mum, mum - but mother didn't come. Mother wasn't there. The door was locked, I called out again - mum, mum - but the house was empty. I could see the daylight through the cracks in the door. It was a warm sunny morning, in July or August perhaps. There would have been piles of straw in the terrace outside. But I could hardly see, my eyes were filled with tears

1 Translation: José Márques

and anguish. - Mum, mum .... and all of a sudden, in the morning light, I saw little stars falling from the sky, little green, red and gold stars. The tears ran down my cheeks. - Mum, mum ... and through the cracks, nose pressed against the door, eyes wide open, I saw the stars falling, one after another. - Mum, mum ...

No one opened the door so I could catch the stars. Not even you mother, for you were out earning the daily bread to feed your child, the same child that now dedicates this poem to you".

By Eugénio Andrade[2]

"Everything is confusing, difficult to grasp" said the poet and the same can be said of the primary relationship, especially when we are dealing with the mother figure, a figure that is unique, present, and close but also filled with anguish, a figure with which the infant is intimately connected, drawn towards by the impulse for life, whose pain and tears he is closely involved with and confuse with ... as conveyed to us by the verses of Eugénio Andrade and as we shall see, by the clinical vignettes of **João** and **Miguel**.

The constancy and stability of the inner maternal object, the certainty of her love and the creation of an illusory space enable the child, little by little and in accordance with the development of their capacities, to tolerate the introduction of reality and accept the reality of the Other, the third, which is first introduced by the mother, "the father-in-mother". The child gradually begins to follow the gaze of the mother as it moves to the Other, someone other than himself, which stimulates the child to curiosity and exploration of the world around him, or, in the words of the poet "a sound, more beautiful even than my mother's singing voice" and "little stars falling from the sky". The child can then surrender to curiosity about the world around him and explore the space of the third, the space that is not I-not her. The child feels the need to explore this world, under the mother's gaze of acceptance; he draws on her look of pleasure as he goes about discovering the world, on her fascination with and love for him. But it is not always like this, sometimes as the poet says: "No one opened the door so I could catch the stars". "Not even you mother ..."

Miguel was 29 years old when he first came to see me. He had decided to interrupt his career as a fashion designer to protect himself from the

2 From the literary collection "The Poems of Eugénio Andrade" "É todo um mundo confuso" by Paula Mourão, Seara Nova, Ed Comunicação 1981

"*queers*" in the industry who were pursuing him and making fun of him. Right from the start, he felt violated by and at the same time, attracted to the homosexual teachers; this led to severe bouts of anxiety, with numerous somatisations, gastro-intestinal complaints, and sensations of being out-of-breath or feelings of panic from fear of dying. He was a young man of medium height, very thin, and insecure and shy. He related his many complexes about his body; he felt that his "shoulders were too narrow and that his body was underdeveloped" which made him feel effeminate. In coming to see me, he was partly motivated by his hypochondriac and homosexual anxieties; however, he was also afraid that the point of the analysis was to deprive him of his homosexuality.

Miguel is the youngest of the siblings, the one that should have been "*a girl*". His father was absent for long periods and so they grew up in a totally female environment. He described his mother as a very anxious person who was frequently taken to the hospital due to her "*crises*". During childhood, he frequently experienced "*crises of being out-of-breath*", which were diagnosed as anxiety attacks. His mother's presence could neither contain nor alleviate these attacks and from an early age, he himself would ask to be taken to the hospital. "*It was strange ... every other child was afraid of doctors and their white robes, whereas I would ask my mother to take me to the hospital, and as soon as I got there, I would feel better and calm down.*"

Miguel described situations that could be interpreted as hypnagogic hallucinations: as a child, as he was about to fall asleep, he "*saw giant sugar cubes revolving in the air, moving toward him threateningly, as if about to crush him*". These experiences startled him and caused him to panic. Recently, during analysis, he spontaneously associated the giant sugar cubes with the maternal breasts and the characteristic suffocation of the relationship with his mother. The always absent father never functioned as a container for the anxiety of the mother and the son, or as separation and calming object, which would have provided the son with a male identification model. Instead, the anxiety was magnified by collusion and lack of differentiation with the mother, a fact which only recently Miguel has become aware of and which he is able, only at times, to contain and talk about. In Miguel's case, the mother was unable to provide the male identification model. Rather, she made it difficult for him to develop a male identity and on occasions, by allying herself with the oldest boy, caused Miguel to feel humiliated, and as a consequence, feel abandoned and unworthy. Quoting Ogden (1989) "the absence of a firmly established internal object father in the mother's unconscious Oedipal object relations generates an emotional vacuum that robs the little boy of one of the essential ingredients with which to psychologically and interpersonally elaborate the Oedipus complex".

The primary relationship and the formation of the male identity

Freud earlier considered the Oedipus Complex to be a nuclear complex, however, after Freud, authors have tended to treat the primary relationship as crucial in the initial period of female identification, in both boys and girls, through identification with the Primary Female (Stoller, 1968), and the "Primary Maternal and Primary Female" (Guignard, 1996), since the first object of identification, for both sexes, is the mother. As Ogden says, the mother with a secure paternal identification can provide the little boy a so-called "phallic third" that allows him to step away from the maternal dyad and forge an individual primal-scene fantasy, and therefore, create a triangular narrative construction.

The importance of the pre-oedipal states and the male and female identifications during the pre-oedipal period has been acknowledged by several authors. In the first stage of formation of identity, the baby sees the image of himself reflected by the "mother's eyes". By about this age, the baby already knows its gender although it doesn't know what it is to be female or male. This marks the beginning of the formation of core gender identity (Core Gender Identity, Stoller).

In the early stages, the role of the father is essentially mediated by the mother. She is the "container" which ensures the stability of the dyad and the father accepts the almost exclusive attention which she gives to the baby. Winnicott (1956) referred to this as the "primary maternal preoccupation". This preoccupation provides a stable base for the baby's growth, for their psychological and emotional development and feeling of "going on being".

Some mothers are incapable of living in this state of "normal disease" and instead of being preoccupied with their baby and its needs, they look for involvement with activities in the outside world, in what Winnicott called a "flight into health". In other situations, mothers can, due to a depressive state, become incapacitated to look after their baby, giving rise to the "dead mother complex" (Green, 1983), as we shall see happened in João's case.

João, who is now 28 years old, began analysis 8 years ago. At the time, he lived alone and spent very little time with friends because of his panic attacks and his feelings of incapacity, unworthiness and impulsiveness. At the beginning of the analysis, he focused on the fear of losing control of his aggression and violent impulses towards his mother, whom he had stopped speaking to *"as a protective measure"* against her constant criticisms. From an early age, João had a very close relationship with his mother and he experienced severe separation anxiety whenever she left him. When João was for years and his brother was born, his mother became severely depressed; she cut herself off for long periods and asked *"not to be disturbed"*. *"My mother says I was very loved as a child but if that is true, I don't know why I feel so insecure"*. As a child, João idealised his father and he realises now that he was always relying on his father to feel worthy among his friends. *"I felt physically underdeveloped in comparison to others"*.

During his childhood, the father maintained a close relationship with him, not as a father but as an older brother, and this has blurred generational differences between them. João treats his father as an equal. There are times when his father's passivity makes him angry and João threatens to "punch him in the face" or calls him an idiot. At these times, the roles are reversed. This reaction is linked to his despair in seeing the person he idealised, his support, his identification model reveal his fragilities, as if João might lose his bearings because of the father's decline. João had his own business, with a partner. The business became very successful in a short period of time but this was something he wasn't prepared for and he felt panic-stricken. As a result, he sold his share of the business to his partner for a nominal amount. *"I know a lot of things are bad for me, but I do them anyway because this is how I can make my father feel that he is to blame for the suffering in my life"*. At times, this rejection of success and the aggression towards his father lead him to thoughts of suicide.

In João's case, we can consider that his difficulties in constructing a solid male identity and that the presence of strong narcissistic elements result from the period of his mother's depression, when João went without a substitute figure, without an available affectionate father who could have compensated for the loss of his mother, and whom he could have challenged without feeling abandoned and afraid of retaliation. The availability of the father enables the child to experience the object of identification within a close affective relationship and contributes to the consolidation of the male identity. According to the Greenson-Stoller disidentification hypothesis, it is through the presence of the father or the substitute male and disidentification with the mother that the boy can form a healthy sense of maleness. However, this hypothesis has come under question (Diamond, 2006; Reichbart, 2006), as it has been found that boys who repudiate their identification with their mothers in this way tend to present a more fragile, rigid masculine identity.

Gender and the Analytic Relationship

The Transference-Countertransference Relationship

As regards male patients with a fragile male identity, it may be asked whether they would benefit from having a male analyst. Does a female analyst constrain the development of the analytic process through a tendency to maintain the patient in regressive states in order to avoid erotization in the analytic relationship? At the outset, in my relationship with Miguel, I adopted the position of container, and intervened only to contain and diminish the anxiety that took him to the edge of disorganisation. Although this relationship had a calming effect, it was almost immediately rejected due to the appearance of the image of the mother as the idealised form and only trusted object. A Negative Therapeutic Reaction appeared to be developing, as if contact with a caring and calming relationship forced him to confront abandonment and rejection by the mother. By rejecting me, he could avoid this awareness and hold on to the image of the idealised mother.

I was either experienced as the good maternal object, as a container and organizer, or as the Other, the third, in an identification with the father figure, that is, the one who was trying to separate him from the mother and from the homosexual fantasies. I felt that the holding on to the homosexuality, which at the time he did not act upon, was providing him with some feeling of cohesion of the self, which at times appeared on the brink of disintegration due to experiences of depersonalisation and derealisation.

During the holiday periods, Miguel engaged in homosexual activity. At the beginning such a separation confronted him with a state of dependency that wounded him narcissistically and set in motion episodes of compulsive homosexual activity, with no awareness or verbalisation of the rage or intense feelings of abandonment that our separation had provoked. These episodes were also a way to fill the emptiness created by our separation. Currently, our relationship is not yet sufficiently internalised to allow Miguel to feel the separations without anxiety. However, he seems more secure and independent, he is no longer the totally insecure abandoned child that first came to see me.

At the beginning of the analysis, João seemed quite tense, he spoke very fast and gave me little opportunity to speak. A number of sessions went by, during which I did nothing but listen to his many accounts of feelings of rage and aggressiveness towards his mother and others "who did not respect the rules or other people". I felt straight away that the important thing was not my interpretations but my constancy and that of the setting; the slightest change provoked great rage in him, because it was identified with maternal chaos and later, with the father, and I, like the father, "didn't listen to him or consider him worthy". João wavers from an unworthy and fragile self to a grandiose false self who identifies with the superior father. He is already showing some insight about his narcissistic compensation, although unable to overcome it.

Female analyst / male patient

Similarly to what was said in relation to the formation of psychic bisexuality and the capacity of the mother to provide the boy not only with female identification models but also male models by way of the father-in-mother or vice-versa, in the case of the female analyst/male patient, *what is significant is the capacity of the analyst to live with and be flexible about the two aspects of her psychic bisexuality, so that she can respond to the identification needs of the patient.* "The greatest object that the analyst has to face in the session is the fear of his or her own feelings and emotions, together with the defences called upon to elude this fear: it is this fear that can hamper or even prevent empathetic listening" (Bion cited by Bolognini 2004, p.57) and understanding what is going on with the patient.

It is through a state of reverie associated with receptive listening, as well as a deep awareness of the transference and counter-transference relationship and of what is occurring in the inter-subjective relationship between analyst and analysand, that the analyst can become aware of the characters present in the "analytic field", that is, the characters in the internal world of the patient and those that emerge in the analyst-analysand relationship. In the analytic relationship, these female and male aspects make an appearance not only in the several characters that play out the various conflicts being lived by the patient or being relived transferentially in the here and now of the session, but also in the analyst who wavers from a containing, receptive attitude, "without memory or desire" (Bion) to a more active and interpretative stance directed at selected facts, in which the setting can function as the third.

The erotization of the relationship may be more frequent with a female analyst and it may be related to several factors: a defence against the anxieties surrounding the desire to establish a fusional relationship with the analyst and becoming dependant on her, reliving in the transference a past traumatic relationship; or a defence against the feelings of humiliation and unworthiness that would be suffered, principally by a man, in displaying his vulnerabilities and shortcomings before a woman. This situation can be magnified by the narcissistic vulnerabilities of the analyst who, through interpretative activity, may tend to displays of analytical power which will reinforce the typical asymmetry of the analytic relationship, a situation which may be experienced by the patient as humiliating.

The seductive behaviour of the patient during the session, is frequently more related to his child sexuality than to his adult genital sexuality, and is associated with a reactivation of primary relationship experiences of the oedipal and pre-oedipal periods. This is a possible listening vertex for sexuality in the analytic relationship. For A. Ferro (2000), sexuality in the analytic session is "a type and mode of the encounter between the beta element and the alpha function". The "acting" of the analyst in such an encounter may be seen as an expression of the narcissistic vulnerability of the analyst and the projective identification of the patient, which, if not interpreted by the analyst, may sometimes result in a re-enactment of the patient's past traumatic experiences in the here and now of the analytic relationship.

References

BOLOGNINI, S. (2002). *L'empatía psicoanalítica.* Turín: Bollati Boringhieri.

DIAMOND, R.J. (2006). Masculinity Unravelled... *JAPA* 54(4): 1099-1130.

FERRO, A. (2000). *La Psychanalyse comme Oeuvre Ouverte.* Paris: Ed érès.

GREEN, A. (1983). La Mère Morte. En *Narcissisme de Vie, Narcissisme de Mort,* Paris: Ed. Minuit.

GUIGNARD, F. (1996). *Au vif de l'infantile.* Lausanne: Ed Delachaux et Niestlé.

OGDEN, T. (1989). *The primitive edge of experience.* New Jersey USA: Jason Aronson Inc., Reprinted by Ed Karnac, London 1992.

REICHBART, R. (2006). On men crying. *JAPA* 54(4).

STOLLER, R.J. (1968). The Sense of Maleness. In *Sex and Gender*, New York: Aronson.

WINNICOTT, D.W. (1956). Preocupação maternal primária. En *Textos seleccionados: Da Pediatria à Psicanálise*, Río de Janeiro: Ed Francisco Alves 1978, Trad. Collected Papers: Through paediatrics to psycho-analysis.

7

"Women are Copycats! They should be thrown to the Garbage": Phobia to the Feminine Identification in a Five Year Old Boy

Carmen Rosa Zelaya Pflucker

According to a Talmud legend, the Midrash, at birth the child is equipped with universal knowledge; however, it adds that an angel appears, touches his upper lip with his finger and this knowledge immediately fades into oblivion[1]. Apparently, this legend accounts for the elaborative intensity involved in the human psyche going through the laborious process of representing the various basic events of life and thus of sexuality, one such event. At present, it is very difficult to determine the content of this notion. We know that Freud found strong resistance and opposition to his early statements about child sexuality. Addressing his understanding, clearly involves distinguishing the sexual from the genital. The allusion to the archaic as that first moment of instinctual encounter with the psychic environment, in which original fantasies lead the way to the inscription of the first psychic traces, as noted by André Green (1990), opens the perspective to a deeper exploration in the understanding of the first primitive forms of psychic organization.

Joyce McDougall (1998) argues that "In the very beginning, human sexuality is essentially traumatic. The many psychic conflicts that arise from the clash of internal drives and the coercive and ruthless force of the external world start at the first sensual encounter of the baby with the breast" (p. 11). This statement, shared by Green himself, suggests the emotional intensity that is at play in the first body contacts. Anguish will configure a first model of relationship, prompted by the purest instinctual expressions, within a context of total confusion.

Watching a newborn baby, can we consider that the mode of contact with the body of his mother can be a pleasure -oriented sexuality? Or rather an imperative initial need to hold on, of a primary anxiety for survival (Pérez,

---

1 Legend quoted from Janine Chasseguet-Smirgel Freud and female sexuality: the consideration of some blind spots in the exploration of the "dark continent".

1996), or a search for a fusional extension of the fetal status (Bouchart-Godard, 1992; Kristeva, 1980), and that this transforms and progressively leads to the discovery of the sensation of sexual pleasure. The female body, the mother's, with its textures, temperatures and smell is the first reference of pleasure (Aulagnier, 1993), but from which will also emerge, as Sophie de Mijolla (2004) indicates, the phantasy of an archaic mother Goddess, omnipotent and indifferent, representing the *"black continent"*, through which the supreme aberration will be to imagine that she can only desire objects for her own benefit.

Child development would be marked by sequential moments of encounter with reality, which would demand the psyche in its narcissistic state, the difficult and often painful awareness of separation, dependency, sexual inadequacy and incompleteness. Joyce McDougall describes psychic origins based on the experience of the development of "universal trauma of human existence": the existence of the other, the discovery of sexual and generational differences, and the inevitability of death. It is indisputable that it is through the mother that the first identifications are presented and transmitted and demand the child an entire process of metabolism of the effects of these early experiences and events, preparing him to face the following trial: castration anxiety of the Oedipus situation and the identification with the paternal figure.

The step towards the discovery of the father's genitals, comparing them with the child's own, and the recognition of the primal scene, requires a radical departure from the infantile omnipotence to accept limits, incompleteness and the laws that distinguish the generations. While the resolution of the phallic oedipal conflicts are based on the gains obtained in the previous phase, the encounter with the father is a new opportunity for identification, favoring the reduction of castration anxiety and the fear of violent self-destruction or the destruction of the other, leaning on trust of a virile affirmation in affectionate and complementary coexistence with the feminine.

Early childhood is therefore a period of hard trials for the child and his psychic environment. Piera Aulagnier (2003) states that *"It's through the story of the relationship with his objects, that the self constructs its own"* (p. 190), and that within the period of the identification process, the self faces successive results of his encounter with the identifications of others, transmitted through gestures and words, of which neither party is aware (Balint, 2001). In some children we appreciate frustration in their attempts to overcome problems not symbolized by the parental psyche, thus inheriting alienating identifications. I will present excerpts from some sessions with Paul, to illustrate the interference in the development of male identity associated in a first instance with early failure in the relationship with the mother, as well as the transmission of some anxieties about the feminine by his father. These two situations limit his psychic development.

Reason for consultation

Paul's parents are worried about his violent reactions; they confess to feeling powerless to stop him. He attacks his parents, his younger brother and people close to him, beating and insulting them, screaming with rage when he can't get what he wants, *"I want you to die!"*

The father places the beginning of these reactions in the time when the mother became pregnant with her second child; he says the child became fearful, irritable and jealous thereafter. As to himself, he confessed he felt a great rejection to greeting women with a kiss, recalling how he was forced to do so as a child, and therefore, he does not require this from Paul. The mother appears depressed and fearful, both of Paul's and her husband's reactions. She says that he is also very demanding, perfectionist and explosive.

Background

Paul's parents are two young and successful professionals in their respective work. They decided to have Paul after they both ended their postgraduate studies. They shared the joy of pregnancy, prepared themselves by attending courses and reading books on parenting. The mother says she imagined herself being relaxed, being able to proceed with her normal work, traveling and continuing her normal life as before. However, she also wanted to be a mother that was different from her own, whom she remembers as being very anxious and unable to take care of her children, who were raised by their grandparents Both parents idealized the possibility of repairing weaknesses and failures of their own parents, making a commitment to take care of Paul. The pregnancy was very happy for both of them; they used to say "we're pregnant." However, they thought that facing the reality of the intense demands of Paul at birth was traumatic. He cried a lot, breastfeeding was painful; the mother claims that she was full of wounds; Paul did not hold on to the nipple and cried when nursing; they had to stop trying, yet, were full of guilt for not achieving what they had intended. The parents began to fight with each other. The father used to go crazy with the crying child; he would go out in the middle of the night to look for infant formula. The mother says she felt the urge to throw Paul away; she wept with him; she says she did not accept until recently that she had postpartum depression, despite having read on the subject.

She says that her own mother has always worked hard; that she could not help her taking care of Paul at the time, and she had not looked after her own children, she could not even change diapers. She just looked at her helplessly while she was in despair; she did not criticize her, but neither did she stay long. She wanted to be different, to be able to stay and raise her child. However, it was a conflict for her to quit her job, as she aimed to develop professionally.

Before returning to work, when Paul was around three months old, the parents left on a trip for a week and Paul got a urinary tract infection during that time. The mother says she felt guilty because she could not stay with him, even when she returned, because she had to go straight to work. Since then, Paul was raised by a nanny in his maternal grandparents' house, where his parents leave him every morning before going to work and pick him up at night. Paul was very attached to her aunt and her husband as he grew up, until she became pregnant and began to reject him; she even referred to him as "diabolic."

His only brother was born when Paul was about three years old, a period when he presented a temporary constipation and was operated of hydrocele. Since then, his parents identify the persistent occurrence of many fears: of darkness, of going to the bathroom alone, of ridicule, and competition. He begins to get frustrated easily; he reacts with physical and verbal violence.

Some fragments of the therapeutic process

From the beginning I see a very frightened child; he is three and a half years old. Given his initial inability to be separated from his parents, he attends sessions alternately accompanied by either one of them. He usually arrives holding a toy in each hand: horses, dinosaurs or robots. He is very intrigued and very curious about opening and closing *Matriuska* each time he comes to his session. Also from the beginning, he defines a clear division between the toys from the box: he separates and puts aside the zebra, cows, sheep, turtle, giraffe and female dolls from the tigers, leopards, lions and male dolls. He contemptuously says that he rejects the first ones for being *"stupid, slow and quiet"*, while the latter are *"wild and strong"*. He keeps the latter and establishes a repetitive game in which the lion, which he calls *"red-lion"* and paints its face to look wilder, fiercely attacks the giraffe or turtle demanding that they shouldn't not defend themselves. His attack intensifies until he makes sure that he has killed them; he approaches to them and says *"They don't breathe"*. He does not even tolerate the possibility that they might recover; he attacks them repeatedly without leaving room for defensive reactions. The proposed game is to attack by surprise; he specifically asks me to make them sleep, or simulate they were distracted looking in another direction while the lion bursts in violently, beating them mercilessly, while he shouts excitedly, *"They're dead! And they're never going to live!"*.

Sometimes, he is able to associate the violent attack of the chosen animal to the rage he feels when he finds *"mixed up food"* or when someone else eats it; he shouts *"the crocodile is hungry, that's why it attacks"*.

The parents took advantage of lunch time to accompany him to the sessions. However, their fatigue and disconnection was evident. They used to talk to him about school or field trips, but not about the topic of his game. Paul would fly into rage, would make them shut down by screaming, insulted or beat them insensibly, without showing a minimum of guilt. Usually, they were paralyzed by the explosive intensity, and they would end up falling asleep. Later on, he organized a game that he repeated excitedly.

Paul: *She (the baby) was running like crazy around the house and crashed very hard against the wall many times.*

Therapist: Each crash must hurt her a lot.

Paul: *She cried aloud.*

Therapist: Someone must come when they hear her.

Paul: *No one was hearing her.*

Therapist: But where were her parents?

Paul: *They were far away in their offices, they are never going to hear her, also because there's no one else around.*

Later, when Paul was five years old and began to attend his sessions alone, he undressed female dolls and scrawled angrily in their bodies while exclaiming, *"Women are copycats! They should be thrown away into the garbage! And never again pick them up!"* He also expressed deep frustration and anguish when I did not understand him or could not meet any of his desires; he ordered me yelling, *"Don't look at me! Don't blink!*

Don't breathe! ... and I won't control myself! Because my dad also yells at me and at my mom, and he doesn't control himself!" After a year and a half of therapy with Paul and his parents, the father called me very moved to ask for a session for him.

Discussion

Paul's story gives an account of strong disconnection suffered since the beginning of his life, traumatic in its contact with the breast. The evident intensity of his instinctual needs suffered an unbearable frustration when faced with anxious and inexperienced parents and without the environmental support needed by the mother to sustain and respond to Paul's demands at birth. Subsequent experiences of frustration seem to have left in Paul a deep and harrowing embedded feeling of helplessness and incomprehension. In each frustration, he seemed to experience again the pain of early vulnerability, helplessness and anxiety when feeling that his integrity is exposed to the danger of being attacked by those powerful and wild figures that come from his primitive fantasies.

P.L.Assoun (2006) highlights the feelings of impotence and humiliation in situations that activate the castration anxiety as an experience very close to reality. He states: *"The proper phobic way of anxiety, with this experience of being" "trapped" reveals the central fear of feminization ... the fact of being at the mercy of the Other and to no longer "being able to have the power to" makes the person respond through panic"* (p. 75).

Paul was in a deep state of impotence and dread. He was fixated in an archaic mode of object relationship, overwhelmed by the fear of *"running out of food or to have it mixed up"*, as well as being eaten by monsters or being raped by *"the archaic god father and/or the mother crocodile"*. His need to grasp on and his intolerance of separation would be closely related to the successive interferences in the development of *"primary maternal preoccupation"* (Zelaya, 2007), when the mother confesses her inability take care of Paul, and her desire to return to work soon. Paul was identified by the mother as the "aggressor" son (Raphael-Leff, 1995) that should be removed, as he did with his most vulnerable aspects projected on female figures. Throwing them away expressed his despair to eliminate such aspects from his living space. The scenes of violence and cruelty against the female body likewise reflect his need to kill or destroy the woman-mother of early childhood, for fear of being claustrophobically caught in her possession.

Within the context of an object relationship, Perelberg (2003) notes that "passivity" is associated, in terms of the archaic, to the phantasy of a specific position in the situation of seduction of the primal scene. She states that the repudiation of the feminine is the ultimate repudiation of the differences between the sexes and generations, in an attempt to retain a phallic position. A central feature in Paul seems to be castration anxiety, based on the threat posed by the woman's body. Successive pregnancies, the aunt's and then his mother's, would have aroused intense fantasies about female power. The coincidence of his constipation, operation, and the emergence of fears with his mother's pregnancy demonstrate the intimidation that the proximity to the feminine represents. Faced with this reality, then, the masculine emerged as the strong, the wild and especially the dominant, he would need to make sure he can assert defensively in a narcissistic, phallic and actively violent position, fighting actively any situation closely associated with the experience of being passively engulfed by the female figure.

While both parents were trying to get close to Paul, they could not truly connect with him to rescue him from this confusion. Despite the conscious intention not to repeat the lack of support they both experienced from their parents, they could not hear Paul's message. As in the past, Paul continued attacking them, and they, in the midst of impotence, just gave up depressingly. Through the father's story, it is possible to appreciate the difficulty that he himself faced in asserting his manhood. The analysis of Paul's clinical material allows us to appreciate how much of his unconscious conflicts related to male identity were being transmitted, producing in Paul a serious difficulty to advance in his psychosexual development.

The fear and repudiation of the feminine clearly express a defense corresponding to an archaic, pre-genital mode of relating. Paul showed that he had identified with his father, assuming the same defenses and the same aggressive ways of expressing himself. The paternal problem limited his ability to alleviate his child's fears and the possibility of offering him a model of respect, strength, protection and restraint with which to identify.

References

ASSOUN, P.L. (2005). *Lecciones psicoanalíticas sobre Masculino y Femenino*. Trad. Viviana Ackerman, Buenos Aires: Nueva Visión 2006.
AULAGNIER, P. (1993). *La violencia de la interpretación: del pictograma al enunciado*. Buenos Aires: Amorrortu.

AULAGNIER, P. (1984). *El aprendiz de historiador y el maestro-brujo. Del discurso identificante al discurso delirante.* Trad. José Luis Etcheverry, Buenos Aires: Amorrortu 2003.

BALINT, E. (2001). Unconscious communications. In *Where the Wild Things Are in infancy and parenting,* J. Raphael-Leff (ed). London: Psychoanalytic Publications Series.

BOUCHART-GOUDARD, A.(1992). Comment reprendre à son compte la naissance? *Dialogue- recherches cliniques et sociologiques sur la couple et la famille,* 4° Trim:27-32.

CHASSEGUET-SMIRGEL, J. (1975). Freud and female sexuality. The consideration of some blind spots in the exploration of the "dark continent". In *The Gender Conundrum. Contemporary Psychoanalytic perspectives on femininity and masculinity,* D. Breen (ed.), London: Routledge, 1997.

KRISTEVA, J. (1980). *Desire in language.* New York: Columbia Press

GREEN, A . (1990). *La nueva clínica psicoanalítica y la teoría de Freud.* Trad. José Luis Etcheverry, Buenos Aires: Amorrortu.

MIJOLLA-MELLOR, S DE (2004). Femmes, fauces et grands criminels. In *La cruauté au féminin.* S. De Mijolla-Mellor (ed). Paris: Presses Universitaires de France.

MC DOUGALL, J. (1998). *Las mil y una caras de Eros.* Trad. Jorge Piatigorsky, Buenos Aires: Paidós.

PERELBERG, R.J. (1995). A core phantasy in violence. *Int. J. Psycho-Anal.* 76, 1215.

PÉREZ, A. (1996). Vínculo temprano y establecimiento del psiquismo temprano. In *Psicoanálisis de niños y adolescentes en América Latina,* Córdova: FEPAL.

RAPHAEL-LEFF, J. (1995). *Pregnancy.* London: Jason Aronson Inc.

8

Reflections on Masculine Subjectivity: Julian in Pursuit of Masculinization

Johanna Mendoza Talledo

> It's not time to make a change,
> just relax, take it easy.
> you're still young, that's your fault,
> there's so much you have to know.
> Find a girl; settle down,
> if you want you can marry.
> look at me, I am old, but I'm happy.
>
> I was once like you are now, and I know that it's not easy,
> to be calm when you've found something going on.
> but take your time, think a lot,
> why, think of everything you've got.
> for you will still be here tomorrow, but your dreams may not.
> Father and Son (1967)
> **Cat Stevens**

Masculine identity has generally been interpreted in psychoanalysis as travelling a linear path because the male retains the primary object of desire and love, as well as the organ of origin. However, clinical experience shows reality does not fit that statement, but rather raises further questions: How does the male constitute not only his gender identity but his genital potency, giving that dominant feature to sexuation? And understanding the construction of masculinity as a rather complex process that goes from early childhood to further consolidation in adolescence: How does this strengthen, reaffirm or disqualify male sexual identity? Eliminar doble espacio punto y aparte pf

The clinical material on Julian, a 43-year-old professional, allowed me to reflect on the impact of family events that occurred in his teens, on the definition of the characteristics of male gender identity and the role played by models in the transgenerational construction of identity. The material presented also helps understand the acute crisis of jealousy with respect to his wife that brought him to the consulting, and which I understand as the crack in his defensive structure.

The Paths to Masculinity

For the male child, the prehistoric mother, the archaic figure invested with all the attributes of wholeness and grandeur is not the same as the object of desire based on the recognition of anatomical sexual difference. After this recognition, she falls "under the sign of narcissistic defeat that traverses the subject as well as the object" (Bleichmar, 2006: 20). There would not be continuity, but precisely discontinuity marked by ambivalence and the presence of the sexuated father, a figure present since the beginning of his life, but which nonetheless takes on a specific significance at this time in the boy's development.

In the early days there is no father with the function of establishing the law, of the structuring function, there is no father of prohibition, the ego ideal. The presence and proximity of the body of whom we could call the primal father, besides the place he has in the mind of the mother, occupies the place of the third or separator of the initial fusional link with her; Klein (1955) refers to this moment as the function of cutting before highlighting his role of interdictor. These early inscriptions enter as representations that, due to the force of the drives from the primal mother, can be conceptualized as residual representations (Bleichmar, 2006).

Freud (1920) noted in *Beyond the Pleasure Principle* that in the oedipal stage, the effervescence of infantile sexual life is doomed to extinction because a child's wishes are not compatible with reality. "Loss of love and failure leave behind them a permanent injury to self-regard in the form of a narcissistic scar, which in my opinion ... contributes more than anything to the 'sense of inferiority' which is so common in neurotics." (Freud, 1920: 20). Also, Chasseguet-Smirgel (1976) emphasizes the need to consider reality based on the correlative and absolute difference between generations. When the male child realizes the anatomical difference, the reality is that the mother is castrated, but she has a vagina that the child cannot fill or satisfy. The reality is that the father has a penis that the little boy does not have.

Then the boy, due to the state of helplessness with which he is born and the consequent maternal dependence (the Freudian *hilflosigkeit*), and second to the feeling of inferiority generated by the perception of the difference between generations, needs to establish, to organize a sense of masculinity that becomes the support of future genital potency, and that offers him the hope that in future he will have a penis as big as his father's to be able to have a woman like his mother. How should the father come in, in order to provide the attribute that can give him this male potency? What would be the role of the mother at this point in the process?

Bleichmar (2006) proposes considering three stages in male sexual constitution: The first refers to *gender identity*, that which gives the bipartite attributes of identity. In the first stage, in which "what he is" is marked at the very nucleus of the ego—"You are a boy or a girl"—the attributes that the culture considers pertinent to one sex or the other are inscribed, it coexists with the perverse polymorphism that characterizes these early stages. This is a message given by another, an adult. Gender attributions are then the effect of these meanings, inscriptions, identifications made by the subject and through mechanisms of adjudication and assumption they will be consolidated in successive stages.

The second stage coincides with the *discovery of the anatomical differences of the sexes*. In the male child the attribute existing in his body is not sufficient to constitute genital masculinity and phallic potency in general. In this second stage it is necessary for the little boy to go through a process that has two watercourses which have to come together to achieve the feeling of masculinity and later genital phallic potency: "... on one hand, receiving the potency that confirms masculinity and makes its exercise possible through the incorporation of the father's phantom penis, and, on the other, receiving through the mother's gaze the value of the penis of which the infant is bearer" (Bleichmar 2006:30).

And the third stage in which are defined the *secondary identifications which are the base of ideal instances*. In the case of the male child it is the kind of man he should be which articulates with the paternal superego of the oedipal prohibition. These three stages determine the assumption of genitality that comes into play in a specific way at the time of the metamorphosis of puberty and then with the exercise and assumption of the choice of the genital love object in adolescence. The *hypothesis* that is suggested is that the valorized object of anatomical difference for the male child, because of what is involved in the phallic conferral of the penis and its genital function as an organ of potency, is the father; and that "masculine identification in terms of sexual practice is instituted by the introjection of the phantom paternal penis" (Bleichmar, 2006:73). The penis as an offer of completeness underscores precisely the desire to give an object of pleasure and potency.

Clinical Material

The first time I saw Julian, he struck me as a person one would describe as leptosomatic in the Kretschmer typology[1]: low, lean, agile, angular face and alert eyes, walked up the few steps before entering the office and just before greeting me said, *"Sorry, but I have trouble touching women".*

The concerns he brought to the session were described through markedly rational, logical competitive discourse. The content was frequently related to the difficulties encountered in the workplace. Julian expressed the urgent need to "overcome" these obstacles, mainly to others, when they symbolized authority figures, investing much of his time and energy in these "war strategies." This was the way Julian told me how he felt invaded and persecuted through all these issues of competition, struggle, rivalry, and compulsive demonstration of potency, and how in the face of the least frustration he reacted with great effort to control the situation.

With much less frequency, Julian talked about his relationship with his wife and children, this caught my attention because just one of them was in therapy at that time. He presented his wife as the trusted companion, his partner in being committed to "not to repeat the past". With respect to his children, he expressed he "wanted to give them protection, help and support so they lack nothing because they will suffer in the future, I want to be the perfect father while they are children because when they grow up they will be disappointed in me ... as usual ... no?"

The Reason for Consultation and the Cracking of his Psychic Geode

Julian arrived for his appointment because of a sudden profound crisis of jealousy regarding his spouse: *"I am coming here because I began to feel very jealous of my wife", he was furious, irrationally angry, he thought she was coming home late because she was with another man. But in reality there hadn't been the slightest sign of it. "Everything was so intense that I*

---

1 The association with the typology of Kretschmer, the German physician, I understood it later as a contact with the ancient, with the primary, in the sense that I studied the mentioned typology in my early years as a psychology student. This is an example of the contratransferencial associations produces in the therapeutic bond with Julian, which often facilitated understanding content areas or different stages of the process.

wasn't even aware of my anger. One day I asked myself, What's going on? Why am I so upset? And I began to remember some things. My parents are divorced and they separated because my mom was unfaithful to my dad. I thought perhaps my jealousy had to do with this memory and I had carried it into the relationship with my wife. When I realized this, I continued to remember other things. That happened when I was 16 years old. In fact, since even before I realized my mom was going out with another man, several times I heard her talking on the telephone. Once I was with school friends and one said, "Julian, isn't that your car? Isn't that your mom?" She was driving around in our car with this guy. My friends didn't realize what was going on but I felt very embarrassed and humiliated. A few days later I had a huge fight with her at breakfast, I insulted her and I said ... some things, at that point my father realized what was going on. ... The next day they broke up. I have felt very guilty about it. Why did it have to be me!!! Damn it, why wasn't it one of my brothers, or my dad, it was his call to fix everything. I have remembered so many things as if I had wanted to forget them and put them away in a room somewhere. At that moment I felt like an orphan who didn't have any parents to help and support me. I had to take charge of all the dispute of the breakup and dividing up of property ... and they left us so each of had to look out for himself as best we could. There was a point when I said, I am leaving alone, otherwise I'll sink.

Julian fervently devoted himself to making a life of his own, finishing his studies and being a successful professional. I think maybe his presence and participation in his son's therapy put him in touch with this jealously guarded matter of conscience and it was this experience that cracked his "psychic geode". Joan Raphael-Leff (1994) proposed the concept of 'psychic geode' for the sealed compartmentalization sealed in relation to a trauma so deeply disturbing to remove it from memory, while retaining, for example, acute anxiety, repetition and thematic about the lack, trauma, or absence, going beyond comprehension in everyday life. And indeed, the hallmark of the experience of geodic cleaving is the intense live re-entry into the original area of the trauma, complete with physical hyper-arousal, vivid imagery and overwhelming emotion" (Raphael-Leff, 2002:139). After the cracking of Julian's psychic geode, expressed in this crisis of jealousy came the gradual painful recognition of his difficulties.

What did it mean for Julian that his mother had maintained an amorous relationship with another man who was not his father? Why did he feel so embarrassed in front of his peer group and not feel, for example, anger, pain, sorrow or disappointment? Julian perceived himself and perceived his father insufficiently masculine to hold on to/satisfy his mother? Around the second month of therapy, led by the desire to improve his distant relationships with colleagues at work, he took on the task of attending various social gatherings, to share lunch breaks, etc. He was very happy with the good response from everyone and began venturing into making jokes, especially with one of his female colleagues. On one occasion he told her "she should stop grumbling so much because she was getting as ugly as Snow White's stepmother." At the next opportunity she retorted that, with his eagerness to have everything under control and think he was top dog, he was like Lord Farquuad. "She killed me. Do you know who Lord Farquuad is?" he asked me. Those who have seen *Shrek*, will remember Governor Duloc, who is just over a meter tall, clean, orderly, self-centered and longing for power, and to make himself more attractive he wears a suit of armor that has legs that make him look taller.

This image that Julian confided to me allowed me to understand his imperious need for power as compensation for his lack of masculine potency. By the same token, we could interpret the cartoon character's legs /prothetic legs as that which is added that in his fantasy lets him have a potent phallus (that which his father didn't provide?) and the metal armor suggests to us a reference to his own defensive armor that hides the lack, the lack of potency, that which gives sense to his masculinity?

Months later Julian would remember an experience with homosexual content when he was 11 years old. He happened to be in the bathroom with a friend from the neighborhood and they began a dialogue about how to "screw" to which Julan replied "I don't know, I think with this", showing his penis while he urinated; the other adolescent also did the same at the exact moment that the oldest boy of the group entered and he saw them. This led to a series of taunts and insults among the whole group who called them queers, and to get out of this problem the friend implied Julian had made him show him his penis. Julian felt disappointed (by the lie) and slandered (by the insult) and tried in vain to defend himself with explanations. When he arrived home, he told his father what happened and the father answered: *"You only have two alternatives, either you are fucked with the label of queer and you shut up, or you go and smash in his face."* Julian went out the next day to hit the friend but the kid had left the country, so *"blinded by anger"* he impulsively began to fight with the whole group. *"Of course they massacred me, but at least I smashed two mouths."* The next year the friend returned to spend his vacation and when Julian saw him on the street, without thinking twice pounced on him and began to hit him so much that three adults had to stop him. He describes how he left his companion so badly injured that they took him to a clinic he was so furious that if they hadn't stopped him he would have killed him.

In the next session he again recalled the incident that happened when was 16 years old, adding that the day after the argument and his accusation, he saw his mother with signs of having been beaten, he turned to his father to *"take him on"* and his father said: *"are you coming to tell me something, faggot, if you knew what was going happening and didn't do anything."*

Summing up

Julian's story lets us understand how the events in his adolescence were configured as a traumatic experience that led to the formation of male gender identity and special relationship styles: with men through marked, singular competition and rivalry and with women showing strong distrust and repeated avoidance, contenting himself with a compulsive way of demonstrating male potency.

I suggested at the beginning that to understand the complexity of the construction of masculine subjectivity, one had to consider the confluence of two watercourses. In the foreground the maternal gaze that confers value on the organ her male child possesses as representative of masculinity and male genital potency, the organ that marks the difference and offers pleasure. Everything indicates that Julian's mother could not fulfill that function. Rather she reinforced the archaic image of the insensitive, omnipotent, almighty abandoning preoedipal mother, when she repeatedly made him a spectator of her amorous relationship. In Julian's fantasy, this narcissistic injury and neglect seem to have been interpreted as rejection for his lack of virility.

And in the middle distance, at the developmental stage where the child is aware of the anatomical difference between the sexes, the importance of receiving, through the unconscious fantasy, the father's penis and the potency confirming masculinity makes possible its exercise. Julian's father was a distant figure, who drastically disqualified him in his masculinity (*"are you coming to tell me something, faggot, if you knew what was going happening and didn't do anything).* He did not accompany or support Julian so that he could process his anxieties regarding his masculinity. In contrast, he offered messages about masculinity as synonymous with impulsivity, acting out and violence. The association with Lord Farquuad is eloquent, that little man with additional legs to look taller, representing his impoverished and diminished *self,* providing himself with a substitute penis to give/give himself the image of masculine potency, that organ that would confirm his masculinity and which his father was unable to offer him, to be a model.

Insulted and feeling guilty about the accusation he had made, which triggered the collapse of the family, Julian put away, as he himself describes it, "in a room", in a psychic geode, all his helplessness, anger, anxieties and guilt and by means of the mechanism of splitting, separated from his consciousness the fear of the attack, the fear of not being sufficiently masculine and potent, and the threat of the proximity of others, especially women and spent much of his energy in continuing to fight, following the recommendation of his father. In this way Julian built a "private monochromatic world", in his own words. However, he rerouted much of his effort in the therapeutic process. He gradually perceived a world with nuances and color, where about two years into therapy, he expressed that the sound of women's words began to relax him, where he was excited to recognize people's smells and where he did not feel so much fear of hugging other people.

References

ASSOUN, P.L. (2006). *Lecciones Psicoanalíticas sobre Masculino y Femenino.* Buenos Aires: Nueva Visión.

BLEICHMAR, S. (2006). *Paradojas de la sexualidad masculina.* Buenos Aires: Paidós.

CHASEGUETT-SMIRGEL, J. (1976). Freud and Female sexuality: The consideration of some blind spots in the exploration of the 'dark continent'. In *The Gender Conundrum,* D. Breen (ed.), London: Routledge.

KLEIN, M. (1955). *Love, Guilt and Reparation and Others Works 1921-1945.* London: Hogarth Press.

FREUD, S. (1920). *Beyond the Pleasure Principle.* The Standard Edition of the Complete Psychological Works of Sigmund Freud Volume 18. Translated by James Strachey, London: Hogarth Press and the Institute of Psycho-analysis.

RAPHAEL-LEFF, J. (2002). Presence of Absence. *Journey to Motherhood,* F Thomson-Salo (ed.), Melbourne: Stonington Press.

PART 2

THEORETICAL PERSPECTIVES

9

The Body: Castration and Finitude

A. Mariam Alizade

"It is as if words adhered to our skin to make a place
there for all meaning, for all that is signified"
(Raul Sciarreta, 1985)

On the body and subjectivity in Psychoanalysis

Subjectivity may be understood as "the quality of all conscious, psychic phenomena which the subject sees as being related to themselves and which they call their own." The subjective is that "which belongs to the subject" (Abbagnano1969, p.1097).

The body is subjective in its inscription of language and in it subordination to the imaginary and to conscious and unconscious fantasies. In contrast, it is objective in its bodily limits, its flesh and the space it occupies. This creates a paradox in that, on the one hand, a human being is trapped inside a body which has boundaries and yet this body has the power to stimulate fantasies and symbolisations which liberate it from these very constraints, enabling an individual to explore the infinite space of desires and creativity.

The messages which emerge from the body reflect the incorporation and the introjection of praise, ideals and criticism which are received time and again from significant others. We can also include the effects of the first gaze, which Haudenschild (2004) so clearly describes. At the beginning of life, the infans receives the love-violence of the primary objects (Aulagnier 1975) together with the "great gift of the body" (Sciarreta, 1985).

The human body is, to a large extent, governed by the psyche. The subjective dimension of the body subverts anatomy and physiology, transgresses limits and is the organising force of different scenarios. Psychoanalysis focuses its investigations and its clinical practice on the sexuated body, inscribed with psycho-sexual avatars.

Sexuation is bound by laws such as the prohibition of incest and parricide and also constructs private spaces which challenge societal norms. Some psycho sexual variants have emerged which are the expression of both individual erogenous potential and of fantasmatic inscriptions which transgress conventions and go beyond the material body. Otherness affects the body producing submission inhibitions, facilitations, damage, support (Foucault, 1976).

The anatomy of the body, its somatic form and function, is constructed over the course of time by means of interaction with others and "is interpreted at a later stage" (Garcia,1975). The fundamental articulation of the body consists in the articulation between-bodies. Sciarreta (1985) writes, "The word, laden with unconscious desire engages the body...we are an embodied human being."

The corporeal ego, seen as an individual body, even when possessed by identifications which are structuring and/or alienating, does not lose its essential character of uniqueness. Internally fragmented, it sustains a hidden dialogue with its selfness, activating what Merleau-Ponty (1946, p231) called "the life of my eyes, of my hands, of my ears, these being all the other natural egos." This psychic manifestation, which is the result of the sensorial deconstruction of the body, is closely linked to archaic sensuality, (Alizade 1992, 1999, 2006,) the place of primitive phenomena based on primary sensual experiences.

Bleger (1963, pp. 116-134) highlighted the complexity of reciprocal interactions, of different types of causality and determinism in the complemental series. These psychodynamisms intervene in subjectivity. "To give oneself a body" is a vital function where the intersubjectivity of different bodies comes into play. This is linked to erotism, love, friendship and even mere contact. This function enables archaic sensuality, sublime erotism and the direct expression of sexuality to find fertile ground for the development of the emotional and symbolic survival of the human subject. The constitution of the psyche, by means of the inescapable need for contact with another, expresses one of the universals of existence (Alizade, 2009).

The scopic dimension of the body was studied by Lacan, among other authors, (1949) in his text on the mirror stage. Nobody is able to see themselves as a whole entity if it were not for the gaze of another who is looking at them. This image of the body, which is mediated by the gaze of another, is subjected to narcissistic vicissitudes which influence the superego, the ego-ideal, self-esteem and the sense of self (Selbstgefühl).

The unconscious image of the body (Dolto 1984, p.31) "is always a fantasmatic image with potential communicative value. Human solitude is never without the memory of past contact with another human being ..." The mirror reflects different images. These could be bizarre, new, familiar, sinister, beautiful, transformative, etc. The positive visual image of the body in a state of joyousness can be contrasted with the melancholic image of the body in a state of malaise.

Identifications and introjections create "others within oneself" due to the imaginary impregnation of the psycho-corporeal space in a game of inter-corporeal overlaying which configures roles and conducts. Different images may emerge and combine: the body of the mother in the man, the father in the mother, one sibling in another etc. The body is inhabited by different characters and multiple intersubjectivity predominates.

Bodily codes form part of every culture. Anthropologists, sociologists, historians, philosophers and psychoanalysts highlight the importance of how, in any given society, the norms of behaviour and the relational significance of the body are transmitted to its members within a cultural and historical context. Public opinion internalised within the super-ego dictates aesthetic criteria, erotic gestures, courtship rituals and ways of expressing sexual pleasure. Society interprets that which is corporeal and metaverbal, assigning value judgments to specific expressions of the libidinal *soma*.

Castration and Finitude: The transformative and the fragmentary dimension

The body has radiant aspects, which convey emotions within the spectrum of good health and satisfaction. In contrast, it also has opaque aspects, which reflect disharmony and fall within the spectrum of illness and unpleasure. The sexuated body is exposed to the threat of castration-separation, interacts with partial objects and is a body which is bound by language (Sciarreta, 1985). It is a body which is tamed by the desire of the other with or without the symptoms of trauma.

I would like to bring centre stage a different body, a body which is pure *soma*, a body which represents corporeal reality. This is the body of finitude. This body-*soma*-flesh is the body without words, the internal body, single organ and at the same time totality, flesh and blood, material. The representation of this body is difficult, given that the origins of the unconscious sustain its immortality (Freud, 1914). However, this does not mean that psychoanalysis should ignore this hidden inner body, but rather should give value to its existence and the clinical repercussions that stem from it. By looking deep within this body, psychoanalysis can find the existential human dimension which, although often silent, makes its voice heard in analysis.

For this existential body, there is no castration: there is finitude. Moi (2004) invites us, from a philosophical perspective, to replace the term "castration" in psychoanalysis for "finitude". To my way of thinking, this replacement is unnecessary. Castration is inscribed at the level of sexuation in the body whereas finitude exists at the level of existence. Finitude is linked to an ego which is corporeal and asexual, a fleshly body-ego, whose asexuality expresses its condition of complete mortality in a way which is alien to the unconscious psyche. Even so, in those moments of fragility and of vulnerability, the mortal ego can be seen. This body-ego may die at any moment. Its codes are closely bound up with unconscious emotions and with the unrepresentable. It is the holder of the secret of what is to come, silently guiding us to our destiny. This is the body to which psychoanalysis gives words when facing the terror of emptiness and the almost unimaginable real.

I propose considering two levels at which inner bodies overlap, communicate and come to know each other. The first is the transformative dimension, the source of transformations which occur both chronologically, over the course of time, and also psychodynamically when a new period of life opens up. It is during these periods that changes and metamorphoses take place. Chronological changes involve constant, gradual adjustments, which are generally atraumatic. In contrast, metamorphosis involves sudden changes and usually tends to cause a degree of psychic hyperstimulation. This can be observed in puberty and also when a woman faces menopause and the descent into old age. A dramatic distance separates both metamorphoses: the first promise of youth and life-projects are inscribed in puberty whereas the menopause and old age generally signify finitude and decay.

The sexuated body and the body of finitude interact while life unfolds chronologically and significant events, such as traumas, resignifications and experiences, both positive and negative, take place. The fragmentary dimension includes the deconstruction of the body and is almost completely bound up with the sexuated body. Let us remember the primary fantasy of the fragmented body described by Lacan (1948, p. 104).

Fragmentation involves the study of partial features and can be applied to diverse gender issues: transgender, intersex, neosexuality. This is a chaotic space, of deconstructions and of new constructions, of different narratives about the fleshly body. Psychopathology may find many different forms of expression in this fragmentation.

Gender identity becomes mixed up and confused, moving to a psychic dimension: man declares himself a woman, and "queer" individuals claim a special, unique sexuated position for themselves, neither transsexual, nor homosexual, a nameless place which is always new and original. In the same vein, J Butler develops certain concepts in which the body is a sort of "metaphysics of substance". For this gender philosophy, "difference in itself is a cultural interpretation which rests on supposed naturalised norms. The interweaving of the cultural world with the body is an intense process in which each individual is actively involved" (Femenias, 2003, p38). This "queer-isation" (Chasseguet-Smirgel 2005) of society tries to go beyond the binary limits, the aim being that every individual can find their own particular sexuation without necessarily having to comply with the binary man-woman regime.

Psychoanalytic Practice

In the subjective expression of a symptom, whether this be connected to affects, sensations or experiences, there exists a hidden scenario which analysis tries to uncover. Scopic interaction requires "unconscious communication between two individuals". This causes the emergence of different images. The negative image of the self is projected into the gaze of the analyst who tries to remove this projection, offering a new perspective which has a restructuring effect. In place of the destructive, negative *image,* the analyst provides a positive mirror. This leads to an endless game of mirrors where multiple images are reflected, each with different psychical values. The way the analyst uses these imaginary mirrors will change according to the nature of experiences and significations.

Analysis reveals the scenes which are hidden using different psychoanalytical tools. These include unconscious communication, working with the internal setting of the psychoanalyst (Alizade, 2002) and the transference-countertransference. The internal setting consists of a psychic conquest which takes place in the psyche of the analyst while their mind works creatively in the psychoanalytic encounter. The internal setting becomes part of the presence of the analyst. In this interaction between patient and analyst, the ineffable and the metaverbal come into play: the analyst perceives what has not been said, the facial expression, the tone of voice, resistance expressed through a gesture. Corporeal contact, such as a look, the voice, bodily contact when greeting, etc, form a part of this internal setting, which is the space of intimate intersubjectivity.

Final Comments

This brief essay explores some concepts related to the body and subjectivity. It describes the multiplicity of subjectivities, the function of "giving oneself a body", the embodied word, the scopic dimension of the body, both the transformative and fragmentary dimensions, and the effects of culture on sexual differences. Reference is also made to "queer" theories and to the complexity inherent in neosexuality and transgender.

One of the central points of this paper refers to the distinction between castration and finitude. The sexuated body is the body which psychoanalysis, in its strictest sense, has largely been concerned with. The body of finitude is a body which belongs to the existential dimension, a body which is silent, always present, and almost unrepresentable and which deserves to have a place in psychoanalytic theory and clinical practice.

The analyst works with the patient's anxieties at both a psychosexual level and at an existential level. An individual is afraid to lose a part of themselves (castration –the fragmentary level) and to lose their totality (finitude –the transformative level). Psychoanalysis not only deals with symptoms, conflicts and psychopathology but also with many different dimensions of the human being.

References

ABBAGNANO, N. (1961). *Diccionario de Filosofía*. México: Fondo de Cultura Económica, 1996.

ALIZADE, M. (1992). *Feminine Sensuality.* Karnac: London, 1999.

ALIZADE, M. (1999). El sustrato sensual-afectivo y la estructuración psíquica. *Rev. de Psicoanálisis,* LVI: 579-590.

ALIZADE, M. (2002). The internal setting. In *Psychoanalysis and Positivity.* London: Karnac, 2010, pp .95-103.

ALIZADE, M. (2006). "Weibliche Sinnlichkeit und Tod" (Feminine Sensuality and Death) presented in November 2006 at the DPV Congress, Bad-Homburg, Germany.

ALIZADE, M. (2009). *La pareja rota. Ensayo sobre el divorcio.* Buenos Aires: Lumen.

AULAGNIER, P. (1975). *The violence of interpretation.* The New Library of Psychoanalysis, Sussex: Brunner-Routledge, 2001.

BLEGER, J. (1963). *Psicología de la conducta.* Buenos Aires: Eudeba, 1965.

CHASSEGUET-SMIRGEL, J. (2005) Le Queer. *Le Carnet PSY,* Paris, 100: 37-39, Junio.

DOLTO, F. (1984). *La imagen inconsciente del cuerpo.* Barcelona: Paidós Ibérica.

FEMENÍAS, M.L. (2003). *Judith Butler: Introducción a su lectura.* Argentina: Catálogos.

FOUCAULT, M. (1976). *The History of Sexuality. An Introduction.* Vol 1. USA: Vintage Books Edition, 1990.

FREUD, S. (1914). On Narcissism: an Introduction. *SE,* 14.

GARCÍA, G. (1975). La ecuación cuerpo igual falo y su relación con el simbolismo. *Cuadernos Sigmund Freud,* Buenos Aires, 4: 45- 62.

HAUDENSCHILD, T. (2004). La primera mirada. In *La maternidad y sus vicisitudes hoy,* C. Zelaya, J. Mendoza y E. Soto de Dupuy (editors), Perú: Sidea, 2006, pp. 123-135.

LACAN, J. (1949). Le stade du miroir comme formateur de la fonction du Je. In *Écrits,* Paris, Seuil, 1966, pp.93-100.

LACAN, J. (1948). L´aggressivité en psychanalyse. In *Écrits,* Paris, Seuil, pp. 101-124.

MERLEAU-PONTY, M. (1945). *Phenomenology of Perception.* USA: Routledge Classics, 2002.

MOI, T. (2004). From femininity to finitude. Freud, Lacan and feminism, again. In *Dialogues on Sexuality, Gender, and Psychoanalysis,* edited by I. Matthis, London: Karnac, 2004, pp. 93-135.

SCIARRETA, R. (1985). Seminar on the body. Unpublished.

10

The Mythologization of Penis Envy

Alicia Briseño Mendoza

Sigmund Freud first introduced the concept of Penis Envy in *Three Contributions to the Theory of Sex* (1905), considering that the girl's interest towards the boy's penis blends in with primal envy. It seems that the concept was already accepted and used, however, as a psychoanalytic term, when in 1914 it was mentioned to name the manifestations of castration complex in the girl. Based on the external differences of male and female sexual organs, and on this fundamental physiologic fact that leads to the so called Penis Envy, Freud acknowledges, in my opinion, the asymmetrical relationships between men and women. These relationships are determined not only by this physical fact, but also by the culturally-defined differences. Recognizing the existence of the Penis Envy made it evident for Freud that women in the 19th Century lived under conditions of inequality before men. He simply named what he observed. Once the concept was used for the first time, it developed its own function and importance, and contributed to give an already phallocentric society an additional argument to confirm – perversely – that men and women had asymmetrical relationships. It grew into a mythologization. Understanding the transformation of the concept of Penis Envy into a myth requires understanding the origins of our phallocentric society. Eliminar espacios en todo el capítulo por favor

The foundation of cities in Ancient Greece was seen as a command of the Gods. They decided when and where their cities had to be established and they instructed the chosen ones to do so. Thus, the ancient city of Olympia, where the Olympic Games were held, was dedicated to Zeus. Ancient Delphi, the site once considered the navel of the Earth, was dedicated for the worship of the god Apollo. Delphi was the site where the Delphic oracle, the most important oracle in the classical Greek world, 'spoke' to the people about their health, their future and their relationships. Relationships were established in a similar way. Once a very simple distinction, the division between men and women became much more complex in ancient Athens by the 5th Century b.C. In Athenian democracy (different from modern democracy), an Athenian citizen had to be a man, a son of Athenian father and mother, an owner of a debt-free property, an owner of slaves that could ensure a prosperous economic and social status, and a person with enough free time to be able to take part in all the political activities held in the Agora. Evidently, an Athenian citizen also needed a wife devoted to her house, to raising the children and caring for the family. That was the way in which Gods had meant people to be. Western civilization grew upon these foundational concepts and ideas.

Freud (1925) used the term Penis Envy to describe the girl's desire for a penis when she realizes she does not have an organ like the boy's. This produces a narcissistic wound that makes her feel dispossessed. She complains about this with her mother and later despises her for not having this organ herself. The daughter is forced to chance object of her libido, from her mother to her father, in order to obtain the desired organ. In the Oedipal stage, it is stated that Penis Envy will lead to two transformations of the basic desire for a penis: on one hand, it will lead to the desire of incorporating a 'penis' inside her body through the procreation of a child; on the other, in an identification with her mother, the desire to feel pleasure from the man's penis in sexual intercourse (Freud, 1920 and 1933). Karen Horney, Helen Deutsch, Melanie Klein, Marie Langer, Blanca Montevecchio, Emilce Dio and Mariam Alizade – just to mention a few authors – have questioned different aspects of this theory. Although they accept the universal fact of the Penis Envy, they reject the maternity theory as unique and regard Penis Envy as a secondary form of primary envy. Klein, for example, considers the girl's Penis Envy as equivalent to the boy's envy for his mother's breasts. Such envy can, in both cases, be traced back to the oral-sadistic breast envy, through its different anal representations until it is invested on the penis.

According to the Webster's Dictionary, 'mythologization' refers to the 'restatement of a message as a myth'. Jacob Arlow writes: "The myth is a particular kind of communal experience. It is a special form of shared fantasy, and it serves to bring the individual into relationship with members of his cultural group on the basis of certain common needs Accordingly, the myth can be studied from the point of view of its function in psychic integration -how it plays a role in warding off feelings of guilt and anxiety, how it constitutes a form of adaptation to reality and to the group in which the individual lives, and how it influences the crystallization of the individual identity and the formation of the superego. Personal dreams and daydreams are made to be forgotten. Shared daydreams and myths are instruments of socialization. The myth, like the poem, can be, must be, rememberd and repeated". (1961: 375,379). The myth's goal is not to reflect reality. Although it talks *about* reality, it is actually the *unconscious fantasy* of an individual or a group of people. In this article, Mythologization of the Penis Envy is understood as the transformation of a clinical fact into a myth. It is not a myth originated in the transformation of a collectivity or an individuality, but on the observable fact of the Penis Envy that was taken out of proportion in a phallocentric society that was afraid of the signs of independence shown by women at the beginning of the 20th century, and acquired additional strength through several processes of negative identification.

The term Penis Envy was ultimately used to define not only the fact of anatomical differences between men and women, but it also emphasized the symbolic aspect of that difference, to be later taken to the level of the 'absence', or as Lacan called it, of the 'desire for the Phallus', almost as if women were not able to overcome this absence – even worse, as if women were incomplete and thus devalued. According to Erikson, the loss of Identity is expressed as caustic and arrogant hostility against the adequate and desirable roles expressed by the family and the community. Any partial aspect of this role, or all parts of it – either male, female, national, social, political – can become the main target of this disdain. There is a rejection against one's Own and an overestimation of the Other's. In the case of women, if they see themselves as incomplete and devalued, instead of fighting for a reality with acceptable roles that cannot be reached through internal means, they choose a negative identity and feel relieved, since the identification statements provided by society become contradictory for postmodern women. They become double bonds.

In psychoanalysis (Freud, Foucault, Dio Bleichmar, Burín), any relationship can be a relationship of dominance, rooted in the identification with power figures in the family. Foucault points out thet there exists a power that is exerted on the body itself, which truly and materially penetrates the thickness of the body. This power was not previously interiorized in people's psyche, but there is a network he calls 'Biopower' or 'Somato-power': a network that is the origin of sexuality as historic and cultural phenomenon, where we identify and lose ourselves entirely at the same time. In these relationships of dominance, this 'absence' was interpreted from the phallocentric point of view, for men and women, as the designation of power or dominance, such as a non-sexual instinct (Freud, 'dominance instinct' 1905, 1913, 1915) whose goal is to dominate the object at any cost (Alizade, 1992). Sometimes instincts are intertwined, and they result into a combined product, such as an aggressive sexuality or a sexuality that is accompanied by this other instinct of power and dominance.

Sexuality for many women means menstruation, children and the possibility to be abused. They have not discovered that sexuality can be the vehicle of enjoyment that will bring them a more harmonic growth throughout her life, both professionally and personally, but above all, through a process of self-discovery. They know as a fact – which they express in sessions and interviews – that they do not have the same privileges as men, and they express their feelings with comments like 'If I could be born again, I would definitely be a MAN!' Do they really want to become men? Is this a problem of gender identity? A problem of sexual object selection? Not at all. Clinical experience and the works on sexual and gender identity confirm that there is no such problem of gender identity. There is a dynamic of early envy (Klein, 1960, quoted by Segal), a relationship where the subject envies something – the object's penis-phallus – because the woman wanted and still wants to be recognized.

As a result of this phallocentric society, social experiences, religious education and family values, women are educated not to touch: the body is forbidden, it must not be touched. They never manage to know it at all, and thus they never recognize themselves and they are unable to create a whole image of themselves. They are unable to recognize the signals of their bodies, which leads to an artificial dissociation that prevents them from feeling pleasure. Apparently only pain can connect them with their bodies, through menstruation and labor. When a woman knows the secrets of her body, when she is not afraid of them, she empowers herself. She has the power to decide – decide how she wants to be treated, whether she wants to be abused or not, whether she wants to have children or not. Our culture has magnified some expressions in order to make them female qualities: 'women endure all suffering', 'women sacrifice for their loved ones', 'when they are mothers, they give it all up for their children'. Such expressions contribute to creating an image of weakness, tolerance, and low self-esteem. Only the 'Other' is important. She is erased before the needs of others. She learns to tolerate, to be erased, to control others through sacrifice, to give up her sexuality, to betray herself as a thinking being. She is a valuable person as long as she is a man's daughter, wife or mother, and she is told who she is and how she must think.

Blanca Montevecchio (1991) explains – and we are able to see this in our daily practice – that women are forced to place themselves in the dilemma of losing the love of the 'other', in a social context where the roles assigned to her only complement the man's roles and are not prestigious themselves. They also lack exchange value in a world ruled by market laws. Her aspirations must be delayed should she want to play her socially-imposed role of wife and mother. Kurnitzky (1992) mentions social life begins with the wedding ceremony, which annihilates and subjugates female sexuality as a male cultural product, restraining it again to the boundaries of women's reproductive capacity. This author considers sacrifice is the origin of myths and cults that demand sacrifices as guarantees of community cohesion and reproduction. In return for this sacrifice, cults unify and, at the same time, cause the rejection of any imposed restriction by the community or society members. This ambivalence conflict between the mandatory nature of sacrifice and any existing attempt to cancel the related precepts, or prohibitions indeed, motivates all civilizing processes. Any attempt to avoid sacrifice presumes being aware of its existence. The outcomes of the external nature and society, sacrificed in cult ceremonies, are closely related to those sacrifices assumed to be subject to human nature. This is a domestication process no communitarian entity can desist. On the other hand, the dialectics of nature's dominance in support of social life involve an essential requirement: heroes are expected to experience a symbiotic – almost incestuous – relationship with nature. Such a relationship provides mythic heroes the power to be allegedly undefeatable. In the past, the bride's wooer was expected to solve puzzles to marry her. Wedding then was recognized as a sacrifice ritual where the bride's nature is domesticated and made subject to the man's domination regime. Like in all rites of passage, the wedding ritual represents both death and rebirth. In such a case, the wooer kills the free nature of the bride and she is reborn as his dependent wife. Woman then submits to the sacrificial altar and takes on all inner and outer blames and deficiencies, through a derogating pact that pushes her to ignore the origin of man's presumptions, which are lately denied by him ("violent innocence", Bollas).

The feelings of embarrassment and guilt imposed on her derive from such a derogating pact and are subsequently conveyed to daughters. Since those feelings are not conscious, they behave as hereditary traits. However, there remain two contradictory yet parallel messages. The first one can be articulated as follows: 'I hope you can attain what I refrained myself from trying: achieve your full potential as a woman,' whereas the second one involves the petition to repeat this derogating pact. For centuries, woman has received a denigrating and aggressive treatment that outrages and subjugates her. Over time, she has developed the need to defend herself, and has given birth to a muted and unconscious anger. Like other minority groups, women however call for the denial, dissociation, transformation, and change of direction of hostility as a form of protection. (Montevecchio, 2002).

Most women find feminism irrelevant since they consider men play the role of their enemy, devaluate the importance of children, and take on the idea that women represent a homogenous group instead of a diverse one. Most women are driven by neither ambition nor power, but by the moral and emotional consequences of the existing options. Generally, such options include sex, children, and family. The solution is not simple for either gender. As a product of the dominant sexuality of the 19th century and the early 20th century, when psychoanalysis was born, the penis envy – a phenomenon that can be observed in clinical practice – was not only able to remain valid thanks to the permanence of our phallocentric society, but also seems to have grown notorious as it triggered the 'phallic castrating' female response that pretends to discard the 'frightening yet desired' man while empowering and mythologizing the 'penis-phallus'. Men thus feel terrified for the possibility of losing their sexual power and ability – represented by his penis – since they would not be relevant as persons. On the other hand, this has prevented women from looking at themselves and acknowledging their own valuable objects, their breasts, their vagina, and their reproductive capacity as life creators. In addition, society has not embraced the idea that, despite sexuality and anatomy issues, both genders are valuable, as both woman and man are thinking, affective, and creative beings.

It is possible, nevertheless, that the fear to recognize the value of the only thing women and men really possess, their bodies, pushes them to experience a permanent anxiety that leads them to seek different forms to relieve such a feeling. For women, this is not an easy task. Surrounded by a society governed by the Big Phallus, women's pursuit for growth, independence, and identity, along with their reaction to the underlying changes, involves the decision of incorporating new ideals and the narcissist tension this produces or maintaining all previous values and remain subjugated and devalued. As perceiving the conflict between remaining subjugated or gaining independence is painful, women's ego undergoes fissions so as to repress or deny such a conflict. Therefore, as they find it impossible to deal with and process contradictions, they cannot find a creative solution to the problem.

Kaës (1991) states every society organizes positively based on mutual structures, common identifications, a community of ideals and beliefs, a narcissist agreement, and tolerable forms of wish fulfillment. They are also organized negatively based on a set of resignations, sacrifices, deletions, repressions, and discriminations. Free and independent women see themselves reflected in others' eyes and identify with the disqualifications they are subject to, as consequence of the pact that derives from social agreements. The values they acquire become negative and demand a long process characterized by ambivalence and the strong need to reduce the distance they have experienced socially. Once women are able to identify themselves positively with the values of culture and build awareness of the fact they are not expected to sacrifice by being dominated and subordinated, but to succeed in developing an egalitarian concept of men as their complement, reaching creative agreements, and taking on new roles by integrating and enjoying them, envy will then become gratitude.

References

ALIZADE, M. (1992). *La sensualidad femenina*. Buenos Aires: Amorrotu.

APPIGNANESI, R. & FORRESTER, J. (2000). *Freud's Women*. New York: Other Press, First Patines.

BENJAMÍN, J. (1988). *Sujetos iguales, objetos de amor.* Barcelona: GEDISA.

BRISEÑO, A. (2004). Códigos del Amor. *El amor desvirtuado... O de cómo Quetzalcóatl perdió su reino por un amor incestuoso*. México: Editores de Textos Mexicanos, pp. 119 -123.

BRISEÑO, A. (2005). Psicoanálisis y Mito. Una revisión teórica. Trabajo presentado en el pleno de la Sociedad Psicoanalítica de México, A.C. el 2 de diciembre del 2005 para el cambio de Miembro Asociado a Miembro Titular.

FOUCAULT, M. Entrevista. *Las relaciones de poder penetran los cuerpos*. Recuperada el 10 de marzo del 2005 en: http://www.identidades.org/fundamentos/foucault_cuerpos.htm.

FREUD, S. (1905). Tres Ensayos de Teoría Sexual. In *Obras completas*. Trad. José L. Etcheverry, Buenos Aires: Amorrortu, Vol. VII.

FREUD, S. (1914). Introducción al Narcisismo. In Obras completas, Vol. VII.

FREUD, S. (1915). Pulsiones y destinos de pulsión. In Obras completas, Vol. XIV.

FREUD, S. (1931). La sexualidad femenina. In Obras completas, Vol. XXI.

FREUD, S. (1933-32). 33ª Conferencia: La feminidad. In Obras completas, Vol. XXII.

KAËS, R. (1991). El pacto denegativo en los conjuntos trans-subjetivos. In *Lo negativo. Figuras y modalidades,* Buenos Aires: Amorrortu.

KURNITZKY, H. (1992). *La estructura libidinal del dinero.* México: Siglo XXI.

MCDOUGALL, J. (1996). *Alegato por una cierta anormalidad.* Buenos Aires: Paidós.

MONTEVECHIO, B. (1991). Metáfora de la conquista. In *La identidad negativa,* Buenos Aires: Ediciones Kargieman.

MONTEVECHIO, B. (2002). *Más allá de narciso: la problemática de las identidades.* Buenos Aires: Lumen.

SEGAL, H. (1992). *Introducción a la obra de Melanie Klein.* México: Paidós.

1 1

Emotional Repercussions from the Abortion on Men

Dolores Montilla Bravo

"Its not hard being a father, neither is getting to be one"
Wilhelm Busch

Abortion has traditionally been considered a feminine subject and this is so in relation to it's physical aspect, however not much has been studied about the living experiences, fantasies and emotional reactions in men before and after an abortion. This is why the finality of this work is to show and make an impact of what little investigation there is about this subject and from my own clinical experience.

It caught my attention that in predominantly young patients whose partners had aborted, when I inquired how it had happened, they said that they weren't aware they had stopped using contraceptives or blamed their partners for whatever went wrong. This made me think that men should be more aware of the mutual and personal responsibility of contraception, this applies to all age groups, from young to mature men. In relation to this issue and abortion, several questions came to my mind: Does experiencing abortion affect the attitude and commitment to use contraceptive methods?' 'How does an abortion impact the development of intimate relations?' 'Are there any negative emotional effects?' 'Is self-esteem altered after an abortion; are some ages more sensitive than others?' 'Is the academic performance altered in teenagers?' 'Is sexuality modified after an abortion?' There are many questions and probably I won't achieve to elucidate some of the answers, nevertheless, I hope to stimulate the study of this psychosocial phenomenon in some colleagues and give some psychoanalytical answers to the questions on this matter.

Even though there's little research on the emotional effects from abortion on men, in the psychoanalytic and psychotherapeutic clinic, the grief for abortion, as much in men as in women, is frequent and occasionally takes extended periods of treatment, it might be direct or through indirect manifestations of second hand perturbations due to grief's failure.

In one of Freud's classical works *Mourning and Melancholy*, he defines what a mourning is; he differentiates it from a pathological mourning and details the process in which the individual transits along its way. However, the mourning over an abortion has proper characteristics that aren't shown in any other type of duel, this is because within the loss of the object (the aborted fetus) there is concrete, simultaneous and concomitantly loss of the corporal and psychological self. According to Rascovsky and Aray, we can determine certain factors that perturb the process of abortion's duel.

The previous relation with the dead object. Firstly, there's the ambivalence between giving and taking a fetus' life. We must acknowledge not only the individual balance between life and death's drive, but also the ego aspects in which judgment of reality and social pressure take part. The aspects of concrete reality in a well-balanced person may help to elaborate the mourning adequately. Secondly, the lack of vision of the object, that favors negation's mechanism.

The mourning over the object. It is worth reminding that the aborted fetus is like the patients "double", it's a part of his personality that dies, because there are vital projected fantasies in him. One characteristic of the object that makes the duel difficult is the object's defenselessness, which makes the handling of guilt more difficult. In more extreme cases, the hate towards the object and the fact of making a harmless object of death's instinct a victim, generates more feelings of guilt and persecution as well.

The damage to the corporal and psychological self. When a pregnancy takes place, there is a whole preparation of the mechanism, in a way that psychosomatic modifications affect completely. With an abortion there's an abrupt modification of these processes, for that reason it is also necessary to have a mourning over this loss, as well as by all those fantasies and psychological expectations that are abruptly interrupted with the procedure, including the narcissist's identification with the parental pair's fetus.

The quality and intensity of guilt. According to the individual's level of psychological integration there can be a bigger pathological guilt of persecutory kind that is reflected by resentment, fear, pain, self-reproach, desperation, and hopelessness. It isn't strange that these people have serious accidents after an abortion. However, in better-integrated individuals, another type of culpability occurs, more depressive, which at the same time makes the reparation, the mechanisms of sublimation and the duel easier.

The mobilization of primitive fantasies. These can reactivate a filicide parental *imago*. These images which in the incontinence represent the "bad" parents, threaten life itself of the patient and obliges abortion as the only solution.

Which would be some risk factors in masculine psychodynamics that would make them prone to a lack of planning a pregnancy and then aborting? In the clinics different scenarios can be seen: those individuals who had "regretted abortions" and with this, they felt consistently aborted of the affective relation with both parents, these individuals have more inclination of repeating the same story (specially those men who refuse to acknowledge a son as theirs, where the father is vivid as a fetus and the relation must be aborted through getting rid of the fetus-father. Its worth to remember that the endopsychic configuration parts from the external experiences with the real parents, and the emerged experiences of the frustration and instinct of death, dominate the projective mechanism); masochist personalities, that have the need for punishment and to destroy the good object in a consistent way; men who have been identified with a devaluated father, which at the same time has made his masculinity questionable and the need to constantly get women pregnant to verify his virility; when adolescents haven't been able to reveal to their parents, in many occasions they do it in a undercover and passive way through a non desired pregnancy and/or an abortion; men with a borderline structure of personality, where the bad use of impulses can't allow tolerance to frustration, nor the capacity of deferment.

In an investigation made in Sweden in 2002 (Kero & Laos, 2004) with 250 men of an average age of 32, whose partners have had aborted, a study was performed on them according to their reactions at four and twelve months. Immediately after the abortion, 60% had a sensation of relief due to this decision, along with sadness, anguish, feelings of impotence and exclusion, emptiness, ethic and crisis conflicts. A 30% only experienced a sensation of relief and 10% only negative feelings. Of the whole sample group, 89% went with their partners to the clinic and all of the above-mentioned felt franc feelings of rejection from the staff, which in some cases, heightened guilty feelings they already felt and in others, aggravated frustration. At four months, 90% of men described the abortion like an act of responsibility, that satisfied the pair's needs, of the guys and girls as individuals, of the children that existed and from the one's yet to be born. However, they didn't exclude that the decision of aborting was something "sad". 10% continued with very ambivalent feelings, mostly feelings of guilt also adding couple problems, breakups and sexual dysfunctions (precocious ejaculation). At twelve months, 97% of men said that aborting had been a positive experience in such a way that it had given them maturity and more profound partner relationships. They also showed a forceful desire in promoting that men should participate actively when making the decision and accompanying their partners during the abortion. Three percent continued in a situation of unresolved duel that had affected their academic/ sexual/familiar and working performance. All of them had already gone to some kind of psychological support. However, the most significant data was that 30% of the men's sample continued having sexual relations without using any kind of contraceptive method or condom because they were still putting the contraceptive responsibility on women. From there that 40% of abortions done in women are previous to other abortions.

In the last few years, in the United States of America and England some investigations were made (Coleman & Nelson 1998; Zolese & Blacker, 1992) on teenage males in high school and college kids. The authors reported that teenage/young students particularly and generally men, had been essentially ignored in investigations related with the emotional effects after an abortion. Their intention has been doubled; determine the risk factors that can take pathological states of anxiety and depression, as well as evaluating if the experiences of an abortion modified the contraceptive practices, favorably or not, in the use of condom. Between the risk factors that have been found are: previous abortions, abortions in the third trimester of pregnancy, more intense maternal orientation, unsolved previous traumas, borderline personalities, age in which the abortion is lived, the environment's response (family/parents) and the level of ambivalence before the abortion.

Ambivalence among the decision of abortion comes as much from the internal events (beliefs, affections, attitudes, conscious and unconscious fantasies towards the fetus and one), as external circumstances (relationship status, social support, economical security and the mother's age). These factors' combination, along with the level psychic integration will give as a result the degree of previous and post abortion conflict. On the other hand, its important to take into account, that those teenagers/young men that achieve to deal successfully with the duel, in a great majority (80%) take contraceptive measures that involve them (specifically the condom), and lean more towards attitudes in favor of life. However, those teenagers/young men who had a longer and higher number of depressive/anxious episodes tend to fall in the same non-responsible contraceptive conducts, therefore to non-desired nor foreseen pregnancy situations. Holmes (2004), as a way of conclusion to his study, points out that if it's true that 95% of the men who have lived an abortion experience (when there's a loving bond) have immediate effects of relief and even get to live it as a crisis that allowed them to mature; also feel negatively impacted and say they'd rather avoid or not being part of that experience. He also mentions that many men don't seek social or professional support after an abortion by considering that doing it can be considered a "weakness" that exacerbates discomfort and the pairs duel. However, its common that they respond with somatic disorder, insomnia, a decrease in the academic and/or professional performance, which if extended, these could cause true repercussions in the personal, familiar, and finally in the professional and health areas. That's why the author recommends that in our clinical work (in cases of abortion), men should always be valued and special attention should be given to the verbal aspects and, conscious of their religious and spiritual ideologies, just as much to the non-verbal and unconscious hints that allow the understanding of their internal struggles in order to be able to communicate this to them so they can achieve a greater comprehension of themselves.

Conclusion

From my point of view, the important conclusions of all these investigations that can be used as a starting point of our work here in Mexico would be.

-The investigation of masculinity shouldn't be despised in those activities where both sexes intervene in a sharing way and that traditionally have been evaluated as uniquely feminine matters. I now specifically refer to contraception, pregnancy, abortion, diseases' transmission and the raising of the children.

-For men who have an affective bond with their partners, there are important emotional effects in its psychic sphere that could be transitory or permanent that could cause important damage to its personality, pairs dynamic, to the family and society.

-At a clinical level, those of us who work with children (boys and girls), teenagers and adults, have the professional obligation of evaluating attentively the trans-generational story, the familiar dynamic, the relationship with the real and internalized parents, the balance that exists between acting to reflect the conscious and unconscious aspect of the world of ideals, to be aware of and put into consideration these subjects in a way that they have

the possibility of taking a more responsible and healthier attitude towards sexuality, being that the reason for the necessity for the use of the condom in conjunction with other contraceptive methods in the prevention of unwished and unforeseen pregnancies, abortions and sexually transmitted diseases is well established. These considerations also apply to girls and women.
-To promote a gender's investigation that clarifies the preferences in the election of a contraceptive method.
-Finally, in the classrooms with our students (men and women), and in the health and scholar institutions we should keep promoting sexual education with more efficient methods, by convincing PARENTS of its importance.

References

ARAY, J. (1967). *Aborto: Un Estudio Psicoanalítico*. Buenos Aires: Paidós (Capítulos I,II y III).

COLEMAN, P.K & NELSON, E.S. (1998). The Quality of Abortion Decisions and College Student's Reports of Post-Abortion Emotional Sequale and Abortion Attitudes. *Journal of Social and Clinical Psychology*, 17 (4): 425-442.

FREUD, S. (1917). Duelo y melancolía. In *Obras Completas*, Traducción José L. Etcheverry, Buenos Aires: Amorrortu, Vol. XIV: 237-258.

HOLMES, M.C. (2004). Reconsidering a "Woman's Issue:" Psychotherapy and One Man's Postabortion Experiences. *American Journal of Psychotherapy*, 58(1): 103-115.

KERO, A. & LALOS, A. (2004). Reactions and Reflections in Men, 4 and 12 Months Post-Abortion. *Journal of Psychosomatic Obstetrics and Gynecology*, 25(2): 135-143.

RASCOVSKY, M.W. (1967). Notas clínicas sobre el aborto y su trascendencia en cl progenitor masculino. In *Aborto: Un Estudio Psicoanalítico*, J. Aray (ed) Buenos Aires: Paidós, pp. 143-165.

ZOLESE,G. & BLACKER,C.V.R.(1992). The Psychological Complications of Therapeutic Abortion. *British J. of Psychiatry*, 160: 742-749.

12

Anna Freud,
Unconscious Ties for the Construction of a Psychoanalyst

Joséphine-Astrid Quallenberg

The big question that has never been answered and which I have not yet been able to answer in spite of my thirty years of research on the feminine soul is: What does a woman want? (Sigmund Freud). We are celebrating the first 10 years of the creation of COWAP, of women and their relationship to this wonderful discipline of psychoanalysis, of women and their infinitely intricate contribution to what is human and, fortunately, subverted in this field of knowledge in our present culture. What establishes the link between psychoanalysis and the feminine? We have examples of this when we approach the analysis of the early women psychoanalysts, when we try to understand the unconscious motivations of the evolving of psychoanalysis, when we investigate the thinking of those who, on one hand, suppress the question of the feminine, like Anna Freud, who we shall discuss in a moment, and of those who, on the other hand, like Marie Langer, can explore the question of femininity with profound freedom, and who have been the subject of several papers.

Who is this Anna Freud, unknown and somehow excluded from some circles in France and the United States? Who is this nonconformist Anna Freud who weaves her story, a form of legend since her early *childhood*, to construct a psychoanalytic identity interested in *Childhood*, in her childhood, but also in the *Childhood* of humankind? What are her ties with the *feminine*, with her *multiple mothers*, with her father, with the psychoanalytical?

Several "Anna Freud" exist in our current psychoanalytic universe. Her father's daughter obviously exists, the youngest girl in the family, the Antigone who will do two analyses with Freud. The daughter of a cold and distant mother, who was tired of maternity, refused to nurse her and abandoned the small child for several months after her birth. Finally, who is that Anna Freud who was kept, cared for and protected by her nanny Josephine Cihlarz? But, who is Anna Freud, the psychoanalyst, the theorist who has a vision of Freudianism centered on the "self"? Anna, the princess of psychoanalysis, heiress to a vision that challenged Victorian morality with a proposal for sexual liberation, was never married. She became the *Athena-Antigone* of the Freudian empire, the intellectual and institutional legatee of this new discipline in those repressive times.

In the early seventies, a new reading is established in the psychoanalytic world, through the post-structural thought of Jacques Lacan and Luce Irigaray. For many feminist theorists, the Freudian unconscious is a repository of patriarchal structural relationships. However, Sigmund Freud not only worked with women, with disciples such as Marie Bonaparte, Sabina Spielrein, Melanie Klein, and evidently with Anna, but his work was extensively studied by theorists of feminist literature such as Teresa de Lauretis, amongst others.

Like the amazons that emerge in the community's boundaries (Wladimir Granoff, p. 551.), de Lauretis goes in search of an Anna Freud that extracts, that removes the invisibility in which she was confined, not a traditional invisibility, but one of identity. De Lauretis does not search for her in *The Ego and the Mechanisms of Defense* but in her insertion point in the analysts' community, at the point of group identification. And this point of inclusion is Anna's word, spoken before the traditional analysts, her request to be admitted into the Viennese Psychoanalytic Society, where she presents herself as a character of her own case study. What about her relationship between flagellation fantasies and a daydreaming? Anyway, she creates ties, composes a mixture of life and fiction before a *voyeuristic* audience, an obscene game of a life story, of her life story. *Anna-Athena-Antigone* provokes and challenges their Society. She is the symbol *par excellence* of a dubious virginity. Was she rejected by her mother? Was she a virgin? Or a woman centered in masturbation? Or phallic oriented? Was she Athena-Antigone for her father? And what can we say of her life beside Dorothy Burlingham?

Anna was born in Vienna on December 3rd, 1895. She was the sixth and last child of the marriage of Sigmund Freud and Martha Bernays. Her birth left her mother physically and mentally exhausted, so she was quickly handed over to the care of her governess Josephine Cihlarz, a woman with whom she maintained a privileged relationship throughout all of her life. Later on Anna referred to Josephine as "the oldest and most genuine relationship of her childhood"; this bond with her inspired her later concepts of "psychological mother" and the contents of the article *"About losing and being lost"*. She kept a distant relationship with her mother and feelings of great ambivalence toward her sister Sophie, Martha's favorite and the prettiest of the daughters, which Anna tried to compensate for with her intellectual development.

Furthermore, it is interesting to include other biographical information on Anna Freud that is important in explaining the phenomenon of this father who deposits the legacy of a theory on his youngest daughter, which she receives and protects with reverence and effort. As the youngest and unwanted daughter of the Freud marriage, Anna arouses little interest in the midst of this large family and from this particular father. However, Anna's love and admiration for her father go back to her childhood and this profound identification leads her to want to study medicine, to be formed as a psychoanalyst. The family opinion discourages this choice and for six years she studies for a degree in education. Later she works as a teacher. As in every bourgeois family of the time, it is expected that only the boys study in universities. However, Anna persists and is analyzed by her father for three years at age 23 and again a year later. Volnovich highlights the fact that Anna's analysis was performed after Freud published very precise specifications in one of his technical writings (Freud, 1912).

Interestingly, at the time of his daughter's analysis, Freud writes *On Narcissism* (1914) and in this text explains the narcissistic aspect of parental love. "They must fulfill the dreams, the unattained desires of their parents; the boy will be a great man and a hero instead of his father, and the girl will marry a prince as a belated reward for the mother. The thorniest point of the narcissistic system, the immortality of the self that is harshly besieged by reality, has gained security by seeking refuge in the child. The poignant paternal love, so childish at heart, is nothing other than the revived narcissism of the parents, which in its transmutation to object love, unequivocally reveals its pristine nature as Freud said in 1914:88.

Freud never denied the narcissistic nature of his love for Anna, and rather, gave frequent testimonies to that effect. To support this narcissistic aspect of his love for Anna, Volnovich (1999) recovers several expressions from Freud's abundant correspondence: "Anna is my Antigone, who in Oedipus at Colonus guides the blind father by the hand. Anna is my Cordelia, the devout younger daughter of King Lear. Anna is the most talented and most complete of my children. Anna is my only true child. Anna is stronger than I am. The only luminous spot in my life is due to my daughter Anna's psychoanalytic discoveries". And he publicly states: "I rejoice in being able to say that at least my daughter Anna Freud has set this work as her life mission, thus repairing my oversight". His "oversight" was in reference to the application of psychoanalysis to education.

On the other hand, Elizabeth Young-Bruehl, in her biography of Anna Freud, says: "she was the mother of psychoanalysis, and the responsibility to preserve its spirit, to ensure its future, was passed on to her (...). Zealous of psychoanalysis, she became not only her father's successor in her own right, with her precise scientific theoretical and clinical contributions, but also a woman whose life was entirely devoted to psychoanalytic theory". What about her own mother?

Freud considers a girl's maternal identification as a way out of mourning the hope of touching masculinity. Beyond narcissistic identification, the feminine is based on the conscious and unconscious representation between mother and daughter. The girl that identifies narcissistically with her mother, failing to keep up this illusion, in frustration turns to the object of her desire, that is, her father. This triangulation movement leads her to a process of symbolization that will allow her to rest her femininity on her father's femininity, and that will allow him to recognize and value his daughter's femininity, to invest her narcissistically and at a libidinal level.

Anna Freud, as we mentioned above, had a difficult and distant relationship with her mother, and an overly close one with her father, which was a disadvantage for her development. She appeared to be a mature woman, but remained in the illusion without developing a true mourning of the narcissistically fusional and incestuous relationship to her father. Her first reactions towards femininity were not well elaborated because of the early difficulties she had with the mother-daughter dyad in the initial stages of her childhood. She compensated by turning to her father and idealizing him, which at the time preserved her from any kind of decompensation. But later on, as this idealization was perpetrated, it became a source of obstacles to her complete psychosexual development. In this sense Young-Bruehl (1991) traces this line of development by going over all of Anna's correspondence, poetry and professional writings: the text of "*About Losing and Being Lost*", the altruistic submission, the "fantasies of being beaten" and the daydreams are issues that were worked on in her analysis with her father and in her self-analysis.

The description of Anna during the analysis on her father's couch, points to the transformation of a jealous, depressed, masochistic and almost anorexic young woman, a teenager with latent homosexuality, into a woman who will become, to her father, the cornerstone of the analytical institution of the time, who will become the Anna-Athena-Antigone of the Freudian psychoanalytic world. The unconscious communicating vessels of Anna Freud's transformation toward the psychoanalytic world and her history as the future heiress to the Freudian throne were being woven since her mother's fourth month of pregnancy. According to Young-Bruehl (1991), the pregnancy of Freud's wife is represented as a "specimen dream" of July 1895 and is one of the many explanations for the disturbing symptoms of "Irma"/Emma/Mathilde/Martha/Anna.

As an example of the type of relationship that Freud had with his daughter, Young-Bruehl (1991) describes, in Anna Freud's biography, the illusory elaboration of a fantasy that Anna describes in a notebook, where she imagines she is married to her father. Freud states that her erotic interest is aroused by this. And following: "Father, she says in one of her letters in 1925, always makes it clear that he would like to know that I was much more rational and lucid than the young women and women he knows... I would also like to be the way he thinks I should be... because I love him... and do not want to be a burden... and a worry for others".

How to understand the undertones of Anna-Athena-Antigone relative to the unusual bond that Anna had with her father? Athena's character occupies a space between the masculine and the feminine. As a virgin deity, her heart is inaccessible to the passion of love, she vehemently rejects marriage. Athena Parthenos, "Athena the virgin", emerges, like Anna, from her father's head. She is thought without a body. Her voice is powerful, only her voice. Anna carries, like Athena, the phallus of wisdom, and this becomes the scepter of Anna-Athena-Antigone, the psychoanalytic authority after the death of Freud. Her father applauds her for going further than him. Anna-Athena never had children, but was the triumphant mother of the intellectual offspring of her great father.

Antigone's character is the embodiment of the indispensable helper to her father, the guardian of his welfare. Her self-definition is linked only to the fact that she is her father's daughter. She retrieves meaning and ego strength by intrapsychically representing herself as the possessor and reincarnation of paternal power, of the all-powerful fantasy of a profoundly idealized father, as is clearly expressed by the mythical figure of Athena. In contrast, Antigone is the one that, with closed eyes and her heart on her sleeve, guarantees without any doubt the triumphant posterity of the almighty father that Athena has already kept on the summit for years.

Antigone does not feel favored by the paternal power. She is simply the guardian, the custodian of the fire of past glories. Antigone, daughter of the incestuous union of Oedipus and his mother Jocasta, suffers her destiny without contesting it, without objecting to its severity (I am not speaking of Jean Anouilh's Antigone, the Antigone that opposes and confronts the family with the state). She becomes the *sine qua non* companion to an old blind father and she supports her father until his death. She mothers and cares for him as if he were her own son, just as in Greek the word Antigone means *in place of the mother*. She accompanies him in his decline, as a sacrificial figure, just like Antigone, she watches over him in his fall towards undeniable death, always, in spite of the setbacks and difficulties, always and forever her father's daughter, under a subtle denigration of her womanhood.

On the other hand, the "Athena Complex" represents woman's triumphant denial of castration by choosing to identify phallically with the father. Phallic idealization and the devaluation of femininity exemplify the theory of feminine castration and of the masculinity complex. The two analyses that Anna underwent played a significant role in the construction of the Freudian theory on the development of normal sexuality. In the position of Antigone, maternal meaning is denied and all that matters and has meaning, all the libido is directed toward an impotent father, who has lost his phallic powers and relies entirely on his daughter until his death. Using the Anna-Freudian terminology, Athena can be seen as the one who identifies with the aggressor and Antigone as the one who submits altruistically (1936:128). She describes herself as the Governess, that is, if we analyze it from Antigone's position, Anna Freud lives her life without sexual life and at a man's service.

What would Freud say *"après la lettre"* about the femininity of his faithful heiress? For Freud (1931:234) there are three possible ways to resolve the Oedipus complex in women. The first is to turn your back to all sexuality like Antigone did. The second is to persist with self-assertion regarding the threatened masculinity, that is, to have the fantasy of being truly a man, which has similarities to Athena. And the third is a more tortuous path which ends in a normal feminine attitude to the Oedipus complex in its feminine form.

In the Athena complex, the mother is completely absent since the early years. The masculinity complex is generated from these early conflicts with the primal mother. In the Athenaic position, the woman feels protected from her feelings of jealousy, revenge and inferiority, thanks to her manic fantasy, the fantasy of sharing her father's phallus and his omnipotence. The mother is perceived as insignificant, powerless and worthless. Martha Freud was seen by her daughter as an unimportant woman. She had a distant and cold relationship with her. She did not feel the passion she felt for her father. Whereas, in the Antigone complex, the mother is absent in two ways: one as a source of love and empathy, understanding and listening, and the second as a rival for paternal affection. What is idealized in the Antigone complex is not the actual relationship between father and daughter, but rather the fantasy of being the surrogate wife and displacing the mother. What is difficult to mourn is not the lost childhood, but the impossibility of accepting the parents as a couple, the primal scene and its interdiction. An ethereal woman, distant from her femininity and vehemently passionate toward who was always her role model, Anna Freud devoted her life to her love for psychoanalysis and in 1971 received from the IPA a medal at the Congress of Vienna to commemorate her return to Vienna. Athena's head is represented on the medal, with an inscription that says: *Auf meine treue Anna-Antigone gestützt*. S.F. (Rangell. 1984:39).

Finally, Octavio Paz describes that he was always intrigued by the enigmas of Sor Juana, by her personality, her life choice and her passions, a woman who was ahead of her time, who surprisingly withdrew from the world and became a nun. Like Paz, using his voice, one could ask: Why did Anna Freud, a woman who also rebelled against her time, become the Athena-Antigone of the God-Father-Freud? She had to live so many resignations, so many confrontations. Confrontations and resignations that were both painful and at the same time gave her the power to draw away from the feminine objectification into which her era submerged her: a time when women were submitted to the masculine absolute, to the ideological forces of the phallocratic dominant society. Anna Freud, her life and her writings are a time of struggle for feminine individuality, for the autonomous expression of thoughts that were criticized as subversive and yet were authentic in their rebellious legitimacy, and a voice toward the future of psychoanalysis as the creation of an understanding of humanity in its innermost space, the unconscious.

References

BEHLING, K. (2006). *Martha Freud.* London: Éditions Albin Michel.

DE LAURETIS, T. (1994). *The Practice of Love.* Bloomington: Indiana University Press.

ETCHEGOYEN, A & TROWEL, J. (2001). *The importance of fathers.* London: Routledge.

FREUD, A. (1936). *El yo y los mecanismos de defensa.* Buenos Aires: Paidós.

FREUD S. (1914). Introducción al narcisismo. In *Obras completas,* Eliade electronic edition.

FREUD, S. (1931). La sexualidad femenina. In *Obras completas,* Eliade electronic edition.

GRANOFF, W. (1974). *La Pensée et le Féminin.* Paris: Éditions de Minuit.

VOLNOVICH, J. C. (2000). Nenas de papá. La relación de los varones con sus hijas. www.etatsgenerauxpsychanalyse.net/mag/archives/paris2000/texte79.html.

RANGELL, L. (1984). The Anna Freud Experience. *Psychoanal. St. Child,* 39:29-43.

YOUNG-BRUEHL, E. (1991). *Anna Freud.* Paris: Éditions Payot.

13

Julia Kristeva: a Thinker in the Limits

Olga Varela Tello

Born in the city of Sofia in 1942, moves to France at 23, where she adopted the land and language, to graduate from her PhD in Linguistics at the École des Hautes Études. She joined the group Tel Quel where she met her future husband Philippe Sollers. Kristeva´s articles began to appear published by Tel Quel and by the newspaper "The Critic". Her research in linguistics including her interest in Lacan seminars, gave place at the same year to "The text of Rome" and to "Semiotics search for the semánalisis". Julia Kristeva is an emigrant in the ample sense of the term, traveler in permanent moving and change, provoker until the limits. After finishing her PhD she started to study psychoanalysis and made out this discipline no longer an articulation for its readings but a clinical practice, her laboratory research on the subject is the main source of theoretic reflection. Ends her training as psychoanalyst in 1979. In 1976 she started to travel regularly to USA to teach as a permanent visiting Professor in the French department of the University of Columbia. Many of the pages of *"Love Story"* (1983), *"Black Sun" (1987)*, *"Depression and melancholy" (1987)* are inheritance of the Northamerican experience written in EUA. In her novel, *"The Samurais"* the life style and the particular way of living of the American universities were shown.

In the evolution of her thinking, the *psi* occupies a center that radiates the great range of concepts that introduces the work. Critics first the Freudian bases, then turns in a renovated and lucid way to the source of the psychoanalysis knowledge of Sigmund Freud, Kristeva insists in a key concept for psychoanalysis: re- birth. The power of anamnesis and the psychic reconstruction means that the unconscious work governs this notion. And she expresses it like this: "If an acquisition in the history of psychoanalysis exists, is precisely this complexity of the psychic apparatus where Freud established the milestones and which were enriched by the contributions of its successors: Kleinianos, Lacanianos, Winnicottianos and others" (Paris, 2003, p.14). To her, psychoanalysis is a loving adventure that adjusts the anguish, encourages re-birth and believes in the creative incessant re-commence. All those novels deprived to the public, those of the patients, open up a psychoanalytical experience to the possibility of hearing the words, the enjoyment, the drive, the disturbances, the silences. The analyst builds its theory of the subject as an on-process-being and of the subjectivity as the loving and revolted language.

Julia Kristeva (*ibidem*) points out that: "is in the image of the feminine and maternal suffering that resumes the difficulty of being a woman, in which I have put much of my personal experience". It could be said that Kristeva does not consider herself or her writings as one of a feminist, although many of these have been used by feminists. She indicates that, Simone de Beauvoir functions as a paradigm of a voice that managed to be heard in a patriarchal and monological culture (although she criticized her because of her rejection to motherhood). Kristeva, did not adhere for that reason to the feminism in foreseeable terms: she argued with her au-pairs installed in the speech of the falocentric dialog the same way she differed with the feminists. She got interested in the feminine condition because of mother/son relationships and because of the linguistic conditions that these relations matter for the construction of the subjectivity. Insisted on the power of a culture dominated by men that represses the voice of women, maintained that: woman is never defined, the woman as a concept stops being a real flesh and bone subject and is treated as an ideology identity crossed by the concept of gender and position, than by biological determinations. She insists that identity and difference must be recognized. The claiming movements of the feminism, are not libertarians, the modern feminism is only going to be a moment in the endless process of the coming of a consciousness on the implacable violence (separation castration) that supposes all symbolic contracts. The feminine exploitation is still too large and the traditional prejudices against women too violent for this phenomenon to be analyzed with sufficient distance.

In contrast to Freud and Lacan, Kristeva accentuates the importance of the maternal function in the development of subjectivity and the access to the culture and language. Instead of maintaining with her two teachers that the child enters in the social universe, in the identification, in the language and in the law in virtue of the paternal function, locates this process in the Jorá semiotics, the maternal. The semiotics defined as the pre-edipical, pre-verbal, drive, corporal, the semiotic is the space where the pre-linguistic libidinal charge meets. Is the reign of the Jorá that is detected in the somatic aspects of the language (from which the representation of the meaning in a symbolic way is excluded), rhythms, silence, and gestures. The passage towards the meaning that marks the exit of the semiotic order is realized through the Law of the Father: However semiotics does not give in completely. The maternal kristeviano is a function; it does not refer to one gender, the feminine carrying on the mother role, is previous to the gender division and as such includes the feminine and masculine. There is no woman but it becomes one. Maintains that the struggle of the subject woman is to separate of the obligation to be the Other of the man. She describes the maternal function as: a function in which the encounter of the mother and the baby´s needs for love and desire does not separate. As a woman and as a mother, a woman loves and desires since she is firstly a social being and a language being. As a woman and a mother, she is always sexual. Her analysis suggests that the mother function, in some cases, can be filled, as much as by the man than by the woman. She insists that the maternal body operates in between nature and culture. Adopts expressions like its two in one, to situate the process that constitutes subjectivity and the relation with the maternal body, which will be a model for future relations of the object.

In the book, *The powers of Perversion*, terms as impurity and stain are attributed to the woman. She thinks that in the nourishing abomination is found a parallel to less, that being his foundation, in the abomination, is provoked by the fertilizable feminine body (menstruation, birth). It will try to separate from the phantasmal potency of the archaic mother, phantasmal mother that constitutes that abyss necessary to constitute in an independent place (and none invading) and in a different significant object, learn to talk. The evocation of the maternal stain registers the logic of the nourishing abominations as a limit of a frontier, of a border between genders, of a separation between feminine and masculine, as a fundament of the own organization, individual and meaningful, subjected to the law and moral. The total acceptance of the satisfying and archaic relation with the mother, prolific and protective, is the condition of another opening, opening to the symbolic relation, true culmination of the route. For an elaboration of the archaic relationship with the parents, especially with the oral relationship with the mother, the human being is conducted to introject the drive linked to the archaic objects. Without this introjections, the pre-objects, the abjects, are threaten from the outside like impurity, stain. Abomination that in the long, run triggers the persecutory machine. Describes the abjection as an operation of the psique through which the identity of a subject constitutes when anything threatening its frontiers is excluded. The biggest threat will be the dependence of the maternal body. The *Black Sun*, points out that the maternal body, even when is vital to become a subject, is later due to abject. But, because the women cannot abject the body of the mother with whom also they identify as women, they develop what Kristeva calls a depressive sexuality. Her analysis in the *Black Sun* suggests that a new speech is needed, one that does not prohibit love between women since it is in this love in which the feminine subjectivity is born. In patriarchal cultures, women have been seen reduced to the maternal function, which is they have been reduced only to reproduction.

In the book *The new diseases of the soul* explains that before wanting to surpass Freud, to propose one more righter vision of women, it is necessary to try to understand his notion of castration. Freud, explains, states the anguish or fear before the castration and a subsequent envy of the penis: it's about imaginary formations, proper of the neurotic speeches of genders, man or woman. The fantasy of the original scene and the fantasy of the castration, although nothing makes them present in reality, are needed hypothesis that allow us to situate the fundamentals of the neurotic speeches of the man and the woman. Freud texts, mainly those about the second topic, los met psychological and its prolongations, especially Lacan allows to understand that the castration is the imaginary construction supported in a psychic mechanism that constitutes the symbolic field and all those subjects that register in it. Ii is about the coming of the language as a separation of a state, pleasant fusion, so the restoration of the difference, sent to separate subjects of the object, constitutes the common sense, for both genders. Some family relations lead some women (especially those who are hysterical) to deny this separation and the language derived from it, this is what the Freudian discovery says about this point. For this operation, constituent of the symbolic and the social, may appear with all its truth, and both genders understand that it will be fair to register in it too, all the series of depravations and exclusions that accompany the anguish of losing the penis and that reflect the lost of complete and the totality. The castration appears then, as the set of necessary cuts for the symbolic advent.

Women like men, will be able to have access to the symbolic order through the father, being trapped in the classic double tie; if the woman identifies herself with the mother, is placed in the place of exclusion and marginalization of the patriarchal order. If, on the other hand, identifies with the father, makes her and her image a masculine figure that brings out the same exclusion of the patriarchal order. Reason why the women must refuse this dilemma, accept the Law and the sexual difference in the form of the patrilineal and refuse to become one of them. From her marginal position she cannot enter the symbolic chain. Reason why, women should not refuse the symbolic order and also shouldn't adopt the masculine role as a femininity model.

Kristeva develops the term "Feminine Genius" through the life and work of three splendid and scrutinizing women of the XX century, original in their expositions, overcoming (each one in her field) of what feminine subjectivity means; Hanna Arendt-Melanie Klein-Colette. For Kristeva, the common characteristics of these three women, is that being a woman defended a certain phallic affirmation; they were not pale mirrors of men, or masculine women. They were woman in the splendor of term: they didn´t merge with the male power, but they did with their phallic affirmation make the possibility of advancing in their singularity, showing the overcoming of the binary dichotomy of the genders. The psychic bisexuality is a human experience that only some subjects are attentive to discover and she expresses this in her work and her thoughts. Thus, each subject invents in its intimacy a specific gender and in this is where it genius resides, is simply its creativity, is what it's called Feminine Genius.

It could be defined genius, from the kristevian point of view, as the capacity of opening a way through and beyond a situation that is considered close, as the determination moved by an intimate force that knows how to deconstruct the condition of something already crystallized: the history, being a woman, the way of loving, and the art. Unlike the automated existence, a memorable life is for Julia Kristeva that one worthy to be told, because it contributes a novelty, a creative singularity able to encourage an advent, a re-birth or a revolt. It was and it is persuaded that the last achievement of the men and woman rights is the dedicated care to the total development of their singularity and the genius is the more complex version of the singularity. Each one must liberate the feminine condition of the biological, social, circumstantial restrictions, assessing the initiative of breaking those cultural programs oppressing the individuality.

Conscious or not of the mutations that are produced or accompanied its awakenings, the question presented to women could be formulated like this: What place do we occupy in the social contract? Not wanting to be excluded again and not happy with the function that always have been adjudged to us to maintain, to order, How can we point out the place we occupy, the legacy by tradition and that we want to transform? From this evidence, some women are trying to contribute a new glance (new objects, new analysis) in the inside of the human exploratory sciences: anthropology, psychoanalysis, linguistics. The woman that feels the shortage of gratification tries a revolt that does; they have the sense of a resurrection. However, for the social setting, this revolt is a rejection, that can conduct to violence between genders: deadly hatred, dispersion of the family couple, or a cultural innovation, and probably both things at the same time. The challenge is there and is bound to a time. Struggling against evil, reproducing evil but in the heart of the bond man-woman, when a woman is separated with too much brutality, when sees her affections and her social condition of social being ignored by a speech of power, struggles her frustration with arms that feel disproportioned, but they are not in respect to the narcissistic suffering in which they originate. The external debt to the mother makes the woman more vulnerable in the symbolic order, more fragile when she suffers it, more virulent when defending from it. The belief in the absolute power of an archaic mother, full, total, evolving, without frustration, separation, symbolic cut (symbolic castration), is what allows us to understand that is impossible to deactivate mobilized violence without questioning this archaic mother myth, the invasion of the feminine movements by the paranoia has been put on relief, and is well known the scandalous phrase of Lacan: "The Woman does not exists. Does not exists as she soothes of a mythical fullness, supreme power, on which the terror of power and terrorism as a desire of power supports".

The desire of being a mother, considered alienates or reactionary by the previous feminist generation, has not become the flag for the present generation. It increases the number of women that consider their maternity compatible with their professional life. Also, they consider it indispensable for the complexity of the feminine experience, with its joys and sorrows. This tendency has an end: lesbian mothers or some single mothers that reject the paternal values, with the consequent violence that the child and the man are object of. Accepting in these cases, the Freudian affirmation according to which the desire of a son is the desire of the penis, and in that sense, a substitute of the phallic power, we have to pay attention to the words of the modern women on this experience.

The pregnancy is a species of instituted psychosis, natural. The arrival of a son, on the other hand, introduces the mother into the labyrinths of an unusual experience, the love for another. Not for oneself, nor an identical being, far from it, for another with whom I'll fuse together (loving passion or sexual). Is a slow, difficult and delicious learning of the attention, sweetness and forgetting about one. Realize this journey without masochism and without annihilation of the affective personality, intellectual, professional, seems to be the challenge of a maternity without guilt. It becomes a creation, in the most powerful sense of the word, but neglected at the moment. The father has to identify with the journey of labor and childbirth, with the maternal experience, becoming maternal and feminine before adding its own part of indispensable and radical distance. We should think that it is allowed to find another me if, and only if, we, men and women are capable of this maternal experience that postpones eroticism in the tenderness and makes out of an object, another me.

The idea of Kristeva is that the woman comes back to motherhood, a different motherhood, since their role as mothers will be the key of a true social change. She sees maternity as a model of love, as is, the transference in psychoanalysis. Unconditional love, directed to the final separation between two people trapped in a loving relationship. The idea is that both, mother and psychoanalyst have to help produce ||free subjects, capable of situate themselves inside the Law, that allows them to build provisional identities, subjects in process, inside the symbolic order. She sees the love as an agency that gives the subject permission to act.

References

CLÉMENT, C. & KRISTEVA, J. (2000). *The feminine and the sacred.* España: Ediciones Cátedra.

KRISTEVA, J. (1989). *Powers of Perversion.* México: Siglo XXI editores, 2ª spanish edition.

KRISTEVA, J. (1995). *The new diseases of the soul.* España: Cátedra Teorema.

KRISTEVA, J. (1997a). *Love Histories.* México: Siglo XXI editores, 6ª edition.

KRISTEVA, J. (1997b). *Black sun. Depression and melancholy.* Venezuela: Monte Ávila Editores.

KRISTEVA, J. (2000). *The femenine genius. 1. Hannah Arendt.* Argentina: Paidós

KRISTEVA J., MANNONI O., ORTIGUES E., SCHNEIDER M. & HAAG G. (1994). *(The) Work of The Metaphore. Identificación/Interpretación*. España: Gedisa, 2ª ed.

PARIS, D. (2003). *Julia Kristeva and the gramar of subjectivity*. Madrid: Campo de Ideas.

PART 3

RESEARCH PERSPECTIVES

14

Violence Prevention through the Recovery of the Parenting Function in São Paulo

Cândida Sé Holovko and Edoarda Paron Radvany

"Everybody is conscious of the cruelties that can strike one's life without striking one's body. They are the ones that deprive people from certain nourishments necessary for the life of the soul" (Weil, S. 1949)

Introduction

In the anguishing dilemmas of present-day society – in which people go through intense migrations, rapid changes of social values and a strong tendency towards globalization – geographical borders are hazy, especially those that mark the identities formed by the set of cultural values of a certain community. This uprooting brings grave consequences to the mental health of the individuals, who sometimes see themselves forced to face unfamiliar situations, and whose past tradition is often inadequate, if not frowned upon (e.g. the north-eastern Brazilians within the rest of the country and the Muslim immigrants within Europe).

In this brief text, which could also have been entitled "The psychoanalytical listening of a NGO from the periphery of São Paulo, Brazil", we intend to approach the experience of working with a population that lives in social exclusion. It is about people whose basic necessities (need of truth, order, security, equality, private property, collective property – as stated by the philosopher Weil, in 1949), apart from not being contemplated, are continually violated. Deprived of these essential necessities, many of these people (mostly north-eastern immigrants uprooted from their lands, their families, their habits) find the worst conditions of development in the big metropolis.

According to Weil, uprooted beings would have only two options of behaviour: "either falling in an inertia of the soul almost equivalent to death, as most of the slaves of the Roman Empire, or throwing themselves into an activity that tends to uproot, frequently through the most violent methods, those who haven't yet been or are but in part" (p. 46).

The psychic experience of this population is in general of strong resentment, feelings of unworthiness, loss of dignity, all of which often lead to serious psychopathological disorders, such as anti-social behaviour and acute depression. Having their basic necessities denied, these people are often seriously disturbed in the constitution of their *self* and *psyche*. Anti-social conducts, as Winnicott signalled, still express an attempt to find rescue from a meaningless existence, of recovering that of which one was deprived. "The understanding that the anti-social act is the expression of hope is vital when treating children that present anti-social tendency (...) The anti-social tendency is characterized by an element in itself that compels the environment to be important. The patient, through his unconscious drives, compels someone to be in charge of taking care of him (...) When there is anti-social tendency, there has been a true dispossessment (not a simple lack of care)..." (Winnicott 1984, pp. 139-140).

Given a situation of such human precariousness, in what would consist the role of the psychoanalyst? We think one of the roles is to discriminate the meaning of violence for them and, if possible, to offer destructivity another place beyond that of simple drive discharge: a place of transformation and metabolization, so that it can come to be symbolic language. These are people that lived the experience of violence, were affected by it, yet were not able to transform it and symbolize it to break free from the vicious cycle. For them, only further gestures of violence were left: the perpetuation of this tragic reality.

We believe the work with this population should be of double orientation: on the one hand recognizing the suffering they experienced, witnessing and legitimating their indignation in relation to the aggressions and injustices encountered; and on the other creating the conditions so that these people can once again feel worthy of finding a place of pertaining and hope in life (ego and ideal of ego strengthened).

The work in the NGO
The following lines tell of the experience we have had, for two years, as members of the Committee of Women and Psychoanalysis (COWAP – IPA) and the Setor de Parcerias e Convênios da Sociedade Brasileira de Psicanálise de São Paulo working with a Non-Governmental Organization. This NGO helps 1100 children and adolescents from a suburban community

in São Paulo and has been working with this population for 40 years. They offer alphabetizing programs, complementary school activities and lessons such as: sports, arts, cooking, music, computer, fashion workshops, environmental consciousness. They also act as a multiplier source, preparing teachers and instructors, and spreading their knowledge to other similar organizations. One of their main objectives is to prepare teenagers for the labour market, creating conditions for a healthier emotional, social and intellectual development. As secondary gain, they help remove these adolescents from the streets, where a life of violence and drug trafficking would almost certainly follow; thus making a significant contribution towards decreasing local urban violence.

We began our work with an extended study of the institution, investigating the population's data with the educators, those who deal directly with the youths and their families. This initial work of institutional diagnosis with the educators (caregivers) revealed, over time, a true therapeutic effectiveness. It created a demand for the continuation of the meetings, which not only contributed to having more information about the Institutional functioning and the young people's problems, but also exposed their urgent need of a proper listening context for elaborating the anguishes and the emotional overload that usually arises when dealing with this population. Thus originated an opportunity for reflecting upon their experiences and elaborating the conflicts that hinder the intervention and weakens its functions (authority conflicts, hierarchy issues, the *setting* of limits with these difficult children, rivalry problems, coexisting with tragic life stories, etc.)

As the meetings went on, we could observe relevant changes in the educators group: they were more able to contain anxiety, impulsivity and were more available to listen and deal with children and teenagers. There was a clear transformation in the educator's attitude that went from a passive posture to more solicitous behaviours towards the organization, becoming more thoughtful and creative. They revealed in time to be more united as a group and less distressed (the complaints about the fantasy of depression amongst the educators virtually disappeared if compared to the beginning of the sessions). The rate of personnel replacement also decreased considerably. The experience proved so rewarding that it reached the group of coordinators and even the presidency of the NGO, who also came to have a place of psychoanalytical listening and elaboration of institutional matters, substantially broadening the channels of communication that were quite obstructed.

A year later, we started the mother group project, simultaneously maintaining the work with the educators and coordinators. The women that were part of the group were selected amongst the mothers of children that had the most difficulty in being placed in the NGO. The major complaints were connected to aggressive, anti-social behaviour and learning difficulties: they were defying children, rebel, and often violent with the other NGO youths, including the educators. Some of them would steal and it was feared that they would resort to (or continue) a criminal life, in partnership with the drug traffickers. We organized groups of mothers every two weeks, 9 mothers in each one, over a one year period (2007). As for the children's treatment, we succeeded in forming a partnership with IPPIA (Institute of Psychiatry and Psychotherapy of Infancy and Adolescence), for tending to their psychodiagnosis and occasional psychotherapy. From the beginning, we tried to establish with the groups of the institution (educators, coordinators, etc.) as well as with the mothers group some defined spatio-temporal limits: a fixed 1h30 session for both, in the same location (one of the buildings of the Brazilian Psychoanalytical Society of São Paulo). The meetings were coordinated by a duo of psychoanalysts, constant for each group.

Considering the differences from a classical psychoanalytical situation, we felt that the *setting* needed to be revised, that is: not handling the transference, not encouraging regression, presenting the main affect to the group to give them an exit through action, avoiding unnecessary setting changes (especially because they are marginalized communities whose main characteristics are abandon, exclusion and emigration); preventing the acting-out through the handling of phantasies, and encouraging internalization processes. We didn't work with transference or regression directly, but instead we used it, as for our counter-transference, to understand the transferential phenomena that could aid in our interventions. The method used is very similar to the one called "Psicocomunidad", created in the 70's by Cueli and Carlos Biro in Mexico and described by Lartigue (2005). This method uses psychoanalysis for the exploration and investigation of group situations in marginalized communities, and aims at integrating three aspects: investigation, educating and a specific work on a theme of interest, in our case, violence (within the institution and within family relationships).

A report of the experience with one group of parents

"Equality is a vital necessity of the human soul. It consists in the public acknowledgement – general and effective, truthfully expressed by the institutions and traditions – that the same amount of respect and attention is owed to every human being, because respect is owed to the human being as such and not in degrees"
(Weil 1949, p. 19)

During the first session with the mothers, we realised that only one of the children didn't have a violence complaint. The mothers were very distressed and without much hope of finding solutions for the difficulties they had been facing. They felt powerless to deal with the aggressiveness of their rebel children and, in desperation, frequently ended up beating them violently; creating a vicious cycle of violence that perpetuated itself. The caring and understanding atmosphere in the group rapidly allowed the mothers to emotionally narrate their own traumatic childhood experiences of being constantly hit, in a brutal way and often without any given motive, which caused an enormous sentiment of revolt and humiliation. Paradoxically, they realised that they were using the same strategy with their children, generating a large amount of anxiety and guilt. It was evident that there was a transgenerational transmission of violence as a result of the uncountable traumas experienced by many generations and that were made present in the form of identification with the aggressor.

Gradually, it was possible to recognize with the mothers the different motivations for their children's anti-social behaviour (see Perelberg, 1999). Sometimes the aggressiveness could be seen as a form of approaching and communicating; other times as an expression of frustration, resulted from the various depriving situations or difficulties to answer the environment's expectations; also as a means to create a distance (separation-individuation) in the relationship with parents who tended to interact in a symbiotic and asphyxiating way with their children. The possibility to examine, with the mothers, these various situations by naming them, allowed these women to identify, also within themselves, many of this motivations and it was very useful when they saw themselves in the narrative of the other participants.

There were various opportunities in which we were able to help the mothers understand the distinction between authority and authoritarianism. It became apparent that when they felt helpless and impotent in face of their children's aggressiveness, they chose to use brute strength in order to control the situation, but in time it became apparent that this only generated more violence. The necessity was, therefore, to strengthen the maternal function so that they wouldn't have to resort to such authoritarian and aggressive alternatives.

Quotes from mothers during the last session of the semester

"I was destroyed when I got here, I couldn't imagine I was able to have peaceful moments with my daughter... I stopped receiving complaints of stealing from the NGO and I found out that I was living only for her and that attitude was suffocating us".
"My son told me yesterday: Mom, how funny, now you're my friend!'
"I've never been in a place where I felt so taken care of and not judged, now I feel stronger to take care of my children".
"I want to be able to listen to my son like you listen to me here".

Final Comments

We observed that the mothers group created a truly rich space for the emergence of emotional experiences that couldn't be symbolized and named in the past. The violence suffered and repeated by the mothers, when dealing with their children, was a result of that which remained without a meaning and was thus reproduced by a repetition compulsion that expressed itself transgenerationally. Uprooted, they tended to reproduce the violence experienced, in a vicious cycle that perpetuated the uprooting.

The psychoanalytical listening of these people, deprived of the most basic necessities of the soul, define a setting different from that of the traditional practice, focusing less on the transference of past experiences and more on the transference for the future. Safra (2006:87) states: "Usually, in our work, we are conscious of how the transference is affected by the meanings of the past. Nevertheless, the transferential situation is also signified by the future. In this case the analyst is put in the place the patient aspires to find and fulfil".

The importance of being a mother, for this group of women deprived of various goods (material, physical and psychic), is often misunderstood by the social and public mental health services. We realised that, for many of them, to give birth and raise children was what dignified and motivated them to keep on living, often in search of repairing their own wounds. On that account, we think that working towards a recovery of the maternal function in these conditions is extreme valuable. Helping mothers to think about their realities, being able to contain the emotional turbulence caused by such an oppressive reality and creating a space to discover the values they want to cultivate with their children, can be a way to contribute to the reduction, at least in part, of the terrible threats that emerge from urban violence and help at least some children and teenagers to find a little bit more hope. Hope to believe in a future with less violence, in an environment with more psychic quality, encouraging their cognitive/affective/emotional development.

> *"This has to be done immediately. It is indescribably urgent. Losing the moment would be incurring a responsibility almost equivalent to a crime"*
> (Weil, p.194)

References

CUELI, J. & BIRO, C: (1975). *Psicocomunidad*. México: Prentice Hall Int.

LARTIGUE, T. (2005). Psicocomunidad. Un método para el desarrollo de comunidades marginadas. In *Modelo de desarrollo humano comunitario*, R. Serrano *et al.*, Mexico: Plaza y Valdés, pp. 215-264.

PERELBERG, R. J. (1999). *Psychoanalytic understanding of violence and suicide*: a review of the literature and some new formulations. In Psychoanalytic Understanding of Violence and Suicide; R.J. Perelberg (ed.), London: New Library of Psychoanalysis, 33.

SAFRA, G. (2006). *Hermenêutica na situação clínica. O desvelar da singularidade pelo idioma pessoa.* [Hermeneutics in the clinical situation. The unveiling of singularity through the *person idiom*] Sao Paulo: Sobornost.

SOLÍS-PONTÓN, L., LARTIGUE, T. Y MALDONADO DURÁN, J.M. (2006). *La Cultura de la Parentalidad: Antídoto contra la violencia y la barbarie.* Mexico: El Manual Moderno.

WEIL, S. (2001). *O Enraizamento*. Translated by María Leonor Loureiro-Bauru, Sao Paulo: EDUSC.

WINNICOTT, D.W. (1956). *Privação e delinqüência/D.W.Winnicott.* Translated by Álvaro Cabral, Sao Paulo: Martins Fontes, 2005, 4a edition.

15

Transitional Space, Transition to Modernity and Experience of Madness in a Women's Group of Canas Province, Cusco, Perú

Elizabeth Haworth

This paper is part of an ongoing systematization, from a psychoanalytical perspective, of a group intervention, with groups composed of women leaders of the Community Defense Offices from the cities of Cusco and Yanaoca, capital of the province of Altiva Canas. These Community Defense Offices of Cusco are part of a project sponsored by the National Legal Institute (IDL by its Spanish acronym). The *defensoras* offer orientation and care to women who are victims of family violence or other forms of violence. They constitute the first step of the justice administration ladder and are certified by the Ministry of Women and Human Development (MIMDES). After spending some time listening, counseling and even "resolving" cases of violence -due to the lack of someone responsible for this function- they demanded a *psychological space* for themselves because "*it is very rough for us, violence is among us*". We had already carried out a previous intervention with a group of *defensoras* in Cusco, which served as background.

Through a brief presentation of group work, I would like to discuss how the experience of feeling mad is linked to images, conceptions and cultural models about two ways of being women that could be interpreted as non elaborated conflicts about "modernity" and "tradition"[1], in the context of a project that aims to eradicate violence against women and children through a transformation of daily life practices (Certeau). Also, they imply different conceptions about the self and about the relationship with others; and, of madness associated to disruption of the world, extensively studied in Andean worldview by many disciplines, in particular by Anthropology. In relation to this point, Winnicott's ideas help us to understand: i) the notion of "group" as a transitional space that functions as a "holding" that allows

---

1 The quotation marks are because we do not believe that in this context modern is "better" than traditional, but some debates describe it as such.

for the elaboration or reelaboration of different and conflictive cultural experiences; ii) his notion of culture as a "potential space" that allows for the meeting of different experiences and of "language games", as developed by the philosopher Wittgenstein, that can be used in a discussion about ways of life in communities as well as in the debates about cultural diversity in Peru and of development projects. We conclude with general ideas about this work perspective.

Group process

Yanaoca, capital of the Province of Altiva *Canas* is situated at 3,800 meters above sea level and is at four hours by bus from Cusco. Yanaoca was the place where the ancient canas indigenous peoples lived, before they were conquered by the Inca Empire. Once an important city, it is nowadays a quiet place except on Saturdays (fair day) and on holidays. The Community Defense Office is two blocks from the Main Square whose main attraction is the wonderful highland blue sky. Poverty and isolation make a contrast with the natural beauty of the place. There are some modern buildings: Internet booth, hotel.

One of the initial problems some psychologists from Cusco mentioned was the language barrier. *You have to speak the same language; affection is transmitted through language.* All this with the aim of justifying that we had to be Quechua-speaking and local. In spite of this, women themselves said they wanted to work with us. We had an interpreter who was very warm and quickly understood the work methodology and was well known by them. Seven peasant women, living in Yanaoca and one man that stopped showing up after a few meetings, formed the group. They were asked to speak openly about what they wanted, what they felt, without a specific issue. The rule of confidentiality was established as well as the number of meetings, every two weeks, which was then extended upon their request. The initial settings underwent some changes due to a lack of coordination and to seasonal events (crop cycle). We had 10 two hour meetings. Psychoanalyst Cecilia Martínez supervised the sessions.

Women leaders from Yanaoca, who are part of different Peasant Communities, constitute the group. The demand arose due to a conflict between the two main leaders: Micaela, who came from Chumbivilcas, a province close to Canas, spoke mainly in Quechua, and permanently made reference to a mythological –religious universe, and Tomasa, who was a land owner, single mother, a widow and one of the main leaders of the

Peasants Federation, an important organization in the area

We could say that this conflict can be read as a conflict between tradition and modernity, between permanence and change. The rest of the group took sides with one of the other. Bernarda, the oldest of the group spoke fluid Spanish; she had been raised by Catholic priests and worked in Lima. She was treated very respectfully and was considered a "wise woman". She was not married but had an adopted child. Grimanesa was very young; she recalled having suffered a lot when she was a child and married a "very nice" teacher. Carmen, her relative, owned a piece of land and was also married. Peregrina's husband was a well-known leader from a left party who had been a victim of a military raid in the war against Shining Path. His vision was impaired due to this attack. He advised her in the community defense work. During the violent years of Shining Path, Canas was a transit area but it was not a terrorist zone *per se*. Arminda is also from Canas. Thus, we have a group of women leaders, some of them move around different worlds and others remain anchored to their community. Many of them have children who study or work in Cusco; they are very active, and they work hard. Some of them walk for over an hour to attend the sessions. This expresses the community's dynamics: they use Internet, they are becoming familiar with e-mail, they go to their celebrations and they are realizing that something is not well in their community, so they become *defensoras*.

Madness: Noqanchis soqqa warmis: we are mad women

The experience of their own madness moves them to ask for help. From the beginning of the group process, there are plenty of references to madness and death. As an anecdote, just before starting the first session, a *Taparaco*[2] was lying in the front door. They were alarmed and scared because it means that death is around the house. I say that maybe "something bad is going to die" (maybe I said this to calm myself also). Micaela says: *me*. Micaela is the spokesperson that constantly denounces madness and death. So much violence is turning the community and them mad. It is difficult to express the tension, fear of breaking down, as well as an astounding strength and care to ameliorate the suffering of others. Their main problems are expressed in terms of persecution; they are persecuted by authorities, leaders, but also by themselves. They seem to live all their lives at once, with no pauses, no

---

2 Insect similar to a large butterfly with black wings but body of a mouse. It is like a bat, unsightly.

milestones. Deaths are perceived as all the same: it doesn't matter if ageing causes it, if it is sudden, or is due to an accident or to violence. Most of them link madness to childhood traumas, others to mythical reasons: *from the moment I removed the vase with yellow powder, bones for sure, I felt faint, I lost control. I felt dead, I couldn't respond. Since then, I am very nervous, I want to strike...* This event occurs after her husband was violent to her and she denies the consequences, displacing the affect to the *tapado[3]*. Despite moments of deep depression and anxiety, there was a real commitment to listen and to be heard.

This madness is understood by them as the appearance or re-appearance of terrifying experiences of violence and retaliation that threatens them with tearing them into pieces. Somehow, a traumatic historical-community experience[4] is recreated and is becoming a permanent reference in daily life. These contents refer to what Winnicot calls *unthinkable anxiety,* meaning the realm of experience that cannot be integrated, tolerated and that falls into the repetition compulsion. The fear of breakdown is due to the return to an early subjective experience that was unbearable for the individual who is forced to repeat it endlessly. Therefore, there is a need for a different experience that restores the previous deficit of maternal or environmental holding, which will help to overcome these early traumas. The return to this experience implies going back to a state of temporary madness, of re-elaboration and re-experience of that early stage, which is different from psychosis. It is to experience a mad state of mind in order to obtain mental health.

Initially, they talked about the early madness they experienced and as the group process went on, they began speaking about the madness around them, with which they live as if it were natural: corrupt authorities that do not comply with their role as legislators, of protecting citizens; on the contrary, they are violent and destructive; incest between fathers and daughters; teachers that rape their pupils; *el mundo al revés* - the world turned upside down. They constantly portray a world without law, not only the father's law but also the mother's: love. Micaela says: *the girl, loquita, mad she was, abandoned, nobody gave her love, I felt sorry for her, I started*

3 In Spanish tapado means covered, concealed. The term refers to valuable things that were buried by the Indians during the Spanish domination
4 The provinces of Canchis and Quispicanchis were the sites of Tupac Amaru's rebellion, which ended with his death, dismembered by four horses pulling in four different directions.

feeding her and I talked to her; first she barely talked but once she told me that she was all alone and slowly she became normal. She was crazy for not having mother or father.

But madness is also related to changes within themselves as women. Armandina is a woman that was part of the *defensoras* and fought with them violently, madly, insulting and slandering them. She is a widow, lives alone, without children, *she is crazy, no one controls her.* Another reference in this respect is when they say that *now that women's rights are trendy, women are defiant; they make me angry; they go to parties and leave the children alone.* This concern goes alongside a strong criticism of *machismo* and with the pain of not being able to finish their studies. In one of the sessions, all of them said that they were going to go back to school, some of them at the primary level, a few others at the high school level. This conflict is present: they want to be like Armandina who travels alone on her own, is not accountable to anyone, but they are afraid of being alone, without the holding of their community, mad women. They are conscious that a good part of the bonds and of the holding rest on them. Last, acting as crazy women is also a resource to defend themselves from external as well as internal attacks: to talk in a confused manner, to go from Quechua to Spanish, to conceal their ideas instead of communicating them, sometimes are ways of protection.

The group as a holding and transitional space

Their demand was clear from the first session: *we are hurting ourselves too much, I feel a negative force;* expressing also their distrust of me because as one of them said: *ultimately you are a stranger, how do we know what you will do with what we say, you can harm us.* From the viewpoint of operative groups, developed by Pichón Riviere, the group entered into the task phase very quickly. It was very clear for them that they wanted to talk about themselves and resolve their conflicts. In the first session, the issue of suspicion towards me also emerged when I asked them to allow me to record the sessions since they spoke in both languages, Quechua and Spanish. Micaela was against because she was not sure how I would use the recording: *lawyers told us not to do it.* Also, there is a misunderstanding: she sees that I am smiling and she thinks I'm mocking her. This allowed us to understand how sometimes we believe that we understand something and it is not so. *Difficult to understand our problem of confidence, waqmanta.* They were bringing dreams and fears. Slowly, they began recalling their close as well as distant relationship with their mothers, their terrors when they were children because of alcohol consumption in the communities. The group process was marked by discontinuities due to their living conditions and to important events referring to deaths, some of them violent, of relatives as well as to daily life cultural practices that go against what they are learning and what they are realizing.

Anzieu (1998) takes the term illusion developed by Winnicott and applies it to the group. Every group creates a group illusion. *From a dynamic point of view, group illusion is an attempt to solve the conflict between a wish of security and unity and an anxiety of having a body dismembered and the feeling of being threatened by the loss of personal identity within the group situation [my translation].* The individual child requires the illusion in order to build an external world that is represented as an extension of maternal omnipotence. Within the group, says Anzieu, group illusion allows the constitution of the being of the group itself as a transitional object.

The proposal of a group of this nature is totally new for them as there is no specific issue or method. The intervention was designed to target what was boycotting the task: to offer a holding to a very intense anxiety of disintegration. In this sense, we tried not to remain in mythical constructions or in collective images but treat them as if they were dreams that condense their affects. In this way, the *tapados*, the dream with the *apus*, the *karkachas*, the mad woman of the town, even Tupac Amaru were interpreted as images that were revealing something about them related to something hidden (*tapado*), the forgotten, the incestuous, sexuality, and to the experience of a dismembered body. In this way, we offer them new meanings that come precisely from the encounter of two views: one, that of peasant women, and the other, a *gringa* psychologist who would not give them money but would listen and where a cultural space is re-created in an intersubjective manner where they can be listened to and recognized in a different way.

They value the group as a space of quietness and reflection: *coming is like a medicine for me, we have recovered trust in ourselves, and we have had an awakening though we have fought also.* They differentiate this space from other sorts of project meetings and even their families are involved: my husband tells me 'run quickly to the meeting, the car is coming'.

Culture: We are from Tupac Amaru's land but we are not strong
In the first session they bring Tupac Amaru into the conversation. He is

present in the streets, official meetings, parties, in the schools' names, etc., as a symbol of resistance to the conqueror. He was torn apart by four horses in the main square because according to the history, he did not die. His wife Micaela Bastidas was killed after they cut her tongue. Behind the official speech of having to be strong, proud as the revolutionary Kunturkanqui and Micaela Bastidas, hides the image of dismemberment. Change, rebellion may lead to death.

Winnicott does not provide a definition of culture but he speaks about a *cultural experience* as an extension of the idea of transitional phenomena and of play, with emphasis on experience. In using the word culture, Winnicott also refers to inherited tradition, which is in the common pool of humanity within which individuals and groups can contribute and from which we start *if we have any place where to put what we found*. Winnicott stresses that he does not know the meaning of the word culture, but that the interplay between originality and the acceptance of tradition as the basis for inventiveness is a very exciting example of the interplay between separation and union. It involves renewing tradition based on the uniqueness of the individual, returning to the paradox: to create something new while maintaining the previous.

Posing culture as a relational experience, as interplay between separation and union, that is, as a general framework, allows us to go beyond other conceptions that propose culture as a closed or semi-enclosed space of practices, ways of life, customs and values that emphasize the difference. We think this is the case with some approaches to our cultures: these are thought to be backward cultures, which must be transposed to modern capitalist development. They offered Internet to the people but not markets or agricultural development, neither there are meeting spaces to process fears and distrust from receiving these. In this case, despite the differences, as the philosopher Wittgenstein would say, there are shared language games (being female, Peruvian, knowing about violence, psychotherapist) that made possible a shared potential space that opened the possibility to re-create our own cultures. Since in that encounter, the group's unthinkable anxiety is reactivated, so does what Saul Peña poses, based on Winnicott, as the therapist's suppressed or repressed madness. At various points, we considered what we were doing there, what was our unconscious motivation. Maybe it had to do with our own experience of coming from different cultural experiences that were also connected in some way with how do they feel, and that was one thing in common. It is not necessary to belong to the same culture; it is the respect to the people what makes the encounter possible. Winnicott proposes to consider cultural experience as an encounter that transcends personal existence and is in close relationship with the interplay prior to the structured interplay.

Some final thoughts

When we talk about the cultural experience of a rural Andean community affected by poverty, exclusion and constant gender violence, we think about the impoverishment of the people themselves. However, this does not allow us to glimpse the richness of the connection. Winnicott spoke of madness in the early stages of the baby as *the breakdown of what exists at the time of personal continuity of existence*[5]. When the mother cannot be there to relieve or repair the damage, primitive defenses are organized to defend against a repetition of unthinkable anxiety or to a return of the acute confusional state that belongs to disintegration of a nascent ego structure (Winnicott p.114). The problem is when cultural experience also cannot become a consistent holding for people and then these terrifying images of their childhood correspond to the present reality. And this is where we come to our central point. The project or the proposal is that their task as Communal Defenders is to "resolve", that is, to guide people, mostly women like themselves, who go through situations of family violence. These situations, "cases" as they call them, are very intense, the magnitude of the violence produces horror in them/us and involves not only physical violence but also especially, neglect and abandonment. In many ways, they are the others, and the difficulty to take a distance also invades them and they do not differentiate those images from their own, over-identifying with them. From this perspective, the project has an impact, clearly unintentionally, in the promotion of "insanity": it gives them a task which is to de-naturalize the existing links, their daily and ancestral practices are not "good", among other things because they produce pain and suffering. The subjugation of women and child abuse are not "natural" as some of them mentioned talking about change. The aim of the project offers hope that things can be different but also places them in a situation between two forms of cultural practice, understood according to Michel de Certeau, as the practice of everyday life. The initial conflict is between terror of breaking with tradition and maintaining it, changing what hurts.

---

5 The stress is by Winnicott himself

At first, this change, being advocates and becoming a sort of authority in their communities, brings problems within their communities. The prevailing *machismo* is discouraging; they are criticized for being women who walk the hills alone, in clear reference to an unbridled sexuality. These rumors are spread and become unbearable. However, continuing to work to end violence makes them feel strong, useful and important. But they also generate conflicts over where do they belong: the world proposed by the project, Lima, relationships between separate individuals, each with the capacity to make decisions, independent women models or theirs, a world of relations, collective, broad, with much envy but also solidarity. At one point, they experience this as a betrayal to their community but are aware that the community must change their approach towards women. This experience has allowed them to meet and move between two cultures without losing their own.

In this moment, when discussions on programs and activities at the state level are reopened, it is commonplace to say that Peru is highly fragmented, that we do not recognize ourselves in others and them in us. Enterprises and international cooperation agencies are proposing interesting initiatives but sometimes they do not seek to generate a meeting space to allow mutual listening. The urgency, the rush to meet quantitative targets do not allow us to stop to consider how the terms are understood; it is generating mistrust and fear of losing what was achieved, anguish in the face of chaos and confusion. Perhaps many of these initiatives could be less contentious if we took some time to get in touch with our own anxieties and those of others. In this context, Winnicott's proposal aims to create an experience of cultural encounter, shared holding that could lead to individual and cultural change. Winnicott says that he is not always doing psychoanalysis, understood in the orthodox way, and teaches us how to generate spaces that, holding each other by way of a network, will allow the emergence of new experiences and people with sense, which recreate their culture again and again.

References

ANZIEU, D. (1993). *El grupo y el Inconsciente. El imaginario grupal.* Madrid: Biblioteca Nueva, 1998.

WINNICOTT, D.W. (1971). *Playing and Reality.* USA: Penguin Books, 2005.

16

Pre-natal Depression: Risk Factors in a Sample of Mexican Women[1]

*Teresa Lartigue, Delia de la Cerda, Itzel González
and Martha Pérez Calderón*

At the beginning of the 20th century Kraepelin, in his *Introduction to clinical psychiatry*, considered melancholia as the morbid expression of an inadequate feeling where women have more propensity towards the illness[2]. Regarding the aetiology he postulated that "certain external influences played a primordial role, standing out from these the emotional shocks produced by the death of close relatives" (Kraepelin, 1905, p.26 our translation). Along the same line, Freud (1915-1917) thought that the aetiology of melancholia was similar to that of normal mourning[3], that is, the consecutive loss of the object (of a loved person), later on he extended this concept to include the loss of a loved object, or of an abstraction which has taken the place of one, such as one's country, liberty or an ideal. He pointed out that in melancholia, even though the subject knows that a loss has occurred, he does not know *what* it is that has been lost, since the object-loss is withdrawn from consciousness.

1 Research study, sponsored by the Health Secretariat, the National Council of Science and Technology, the Research Committee of the International Psychoanalytical Association, The National Institute of Perinatology, the Mexican Psychoanalytical Association, and the University of Mexico City. Project number MO252-9911 CONACYT; 212250-50021 INPer; 01-10 y 01-11 APM. Translation: Martha Pérez Calderón.

2 Our italics in this phrase and in others further on; it is important to note that a century later, it has been confirmed that depressive episodes, major depressive disorder and bipolar disorder II appear twice as frequent in women than in men (DSM-IV, 1994).

3 The following symptoms are present both in mourning, as in melancholia: profoundly painful dejection, cessation of interest in the outside world; loss of the capacity to love and inhibition of creativity. In melancholia, we can also find: a lowering of the self-regarding feelings and/or impoverishment of the ego that finds utterance in self-reproaches and self-revilings, and culminates in a delusional expectation of punishment, the loss of self-regard. This syndrome of worthlessness can be accompanied by insomnia, refusal of food, decline of the libido or sexual desire, tendency towards mania (where the ego, instead of being subjugated by the object, dominates it) and propensity to suicide (Freud, 1915-17).

Freud's first discernment, that distinguishes him from the psychiatry of his time, is the conceptualisation that all self-reproaches are in reality, directed against a loved object, which have been shifted away from it on to the own ego - where complaints are in reality quarrels. The process that took place is the following: a) the free libido, instead of being displaced onto another object, as it would be the case in normal mourning, was withdrawn into the ego and an identification with the abandoned object was established. Thus, the well-known phrase "the shadow of the object fell upon the ego" (p.247) the latter could henceforth be judged by a special agency, as though it were the forsaken object; b) an external conflict became internal, a double vicissitude or split of the ego took place, part of it was altered by identification (in the modality of incorporation or devouring of the object, due to a regression to the cannibalistic oral phase, therefore the refusal of food) and the other part was transformed into a critical agency[4]; c) the existing precondition for the libido to be withdrawn into the ego is that the object-choice had been effected on a narcissistic basis, therefore facilitating its' return to the ego; d) this narcissistic object-choice was coloured by an intense ambivalence, resulting either from a profound disappointment by the object, or by a constitutional factor and; e) there was also a disposition to obsessional neurosis, that triggered a regression to the stage of sadism and anal erotism where hate enrages against the ego, and therefore the propensity towards suicide and the danger of this syndrome.

In this way, it can be elucidated that in the unconscious dynamic the what that was subtracted from the consciousness in melancholia has to do firstly, with the fact that the unconscious (thing-) presentation of the object had been abandoned by the libido; secondly, with the countless separate struggles carried out over the object, which take place in the system Unconscious, linked to the ambivalence: love and hate; and thirdly, that the path from the system Unconscious to the system Preconscious-Conscious is blocked due to the combination of two factors: a constitutional one and the one caused by *current traumatic experiences that reactivate those experienced in the first years of life.*

Abraham (1948) points out that melancholia is the result of a high quantity of erotism and/or constitutional moral sadism. The factors needed to produce a melancholic "syndrome" are: a constitutional over-accentuation of oral erotism; a fixation of the libido at this level; a severe injury to

---

4 Later known as super-ego.

infantile narcissism before the Oedipus-wishes have been overcome, and the repetition of the primary disappointment in later life. Abraham demonstrates that the narcissistic injury is a consequence of the insatiable demands of love of these types of personalities, and that for this same reason, they end up in frustration, in the narcissistic injury. Therefore, the main issue in its psychogenesis is circumscribed to the over-accentuation of oral erotism and to a fixation of the libido at this stage, and as a consequence of which the other factors emerge (Dio Bleichmar, 1987, p. 150).[5]

Following the same line of thought as Freud, H. Bleichmar (1976) postulates that depression (may it be narcissistic, guilt, mixed, or of normal mourning or simple) corresponds to one condition: the loss of the object. He also adds that it constitutes a state in which a desire is experienced as unattainable, desire to which one is intensely fixated. Narcissistic and guilt depression are likewise, dependent on the structure and pathology of the super-ego, it is only the type of ideal at play that differentiates them: narcissistic perfection or well-being of the object, as well as the intention of aggression, it is that which allows to understand why it is so frequent to find both modalities coexisting in the same individual. When the super-ego is characterised by the tendency to construct high ideals, or by the sadism of the critical conscience, this severe super-ego could take one or both of the types of ideals mentioned above, as a foundation for the demand concerning the ego; however, in simple loss the aggressiveness of the critical conscience or super-ego does not exist.

Besides the loss of the object, or of the love of the object, or of an ideal, the loss of the corporal integrity has also been considered as a cause of depression; the pain and/or the physical disability that results from an injury to the body transforms itself into psychical pain, that once anchored to the unconscious reappears, transformed into unpleasant events of everyday life (Nasio, 1996). To suffer form an organic disease constitutes a serious injury to narcissism, furthermore, when this is terminal it affects the subject to a greater degree, creating chaos in the area of the drives, breaking their rhythm and cadence. Nowadays, there is enough evidence to support that people infected with the human immunodeficiency virus are at higher risk of presenting a major depressive disorder (Ciesla & Roberts, 2001); it is

---

5 Melanie Klein, follower of Abraham's ideas includes early ego and super-ego organizations as other fixation or regression points; however, such structures will be modeled by the amount of constitutional envy in the system; the emphasis on the genetic role of the drive is evident (*ibid*).

possible that AIDS may represent some of the sinister "disturbing, gloomy, suspicious, a bad omen, secret, occult, that provokes an atrocious terror, spectral, horrifying", that inevitably confronts us with our relationship to death (Schutz, 1995, p.152, our translation).

Parting from a gender perspective[6], besides considering the different stages of the female reproductive cycle, in which depression can or cannot be present, such as pregnancy, childbirth, postpartum, and the climacteric, several hypothesis arise, that relate depression with life conditions and subjective characteristics in women, such as gender and domestic violence, this external violence brings us to the psychoanalytic concept of trauma, to that violent invasion of energy that disorganises the ego (Freud, 1926). It is suggested that the stereotype of femininity plays a part in the aetiology of depression in women; that is why it is important to study and establish an connection existing between the conditions that predispose them to depression, as well as the current femininity and masculinity models. The main traits that describe the femininity model are: "sensitivity, seeking to pleases others, sweetness (lack of aggression and competition), passiveness, obedience, need of affective contact, dependence, fragility; whereas masculinity is characterised by: activity, firmness, the capacity to cope with risk, autonomy, decision, self-confidence, strength" (Dio Bleichmar, 1991, p.64, our translation). The highest risk profile for developing depression is the one in which the following traits converge: a) Stereotype of femininity with lack of positive masculinity traits (such as the desire to excel and self-confidence); b) presence of the most negative femininity traits such as dependence and submission and; c) lack of positive feminine attributes such as congeniality and willingness to please.

Dio Bleichmar also mentions the following psychosocial factors in women who are mothers: d) death of the mother in infancy; e) conditions of social isolation due to migration, change of residence, etc.; f) having to care for more than two small children and; g) the lack of a support network. Amongst the psychological factors the following stand out: h) problems

---

6 Parting from a holistic and social framework, the sex/gender systems are defined as "the array of conducts and practices, symbols, representations, norms, and social values that societies elaborate, rooted in sexual annatto-physiologic difference, and that give sense to sexual drive satisfaction, human reproduction and in general to the way people establish relationships" (De Barbieri, 1992, p.151, our translation). The gender/sex systems constitute the broadest object of study to explain and comprehend the dyad female subordination-male dominance, which is joint to other ways of social inequality: ethnic, social and generational.

in the couple; i) establishment of addictive bonds; j) self-esteem disorders and; k) vulnerability towards loss. He calls for attention upon a monumental paradox: the maternal role contains the essential components for the body- of a new-born- to be transformed into a thinking being, a human being; however this role, along with its functions has not been to the service of the women's own development. This paradox makes us think of the creator of psychoanalysis, when he distinguishes three types of masochism, one of them refereed to as "an expression of feminine nature", where "the masochist is obliged to do inappropriate things, to work against his own benefit, to destroy the perspectives that open themselves to him in the real world and, eventually, to annihilate his own real existence (Freud, 1924b, p.175 our translation).

Domestic and/or gender violence has certain influence over health, that can be observed in different ways; "female gender pathologies" have been identified, referring mainly to depressive states[7] as a pragmatic way to express emotional distress, that also results in chronic diseases (Burín, 1990). In the same way, the sum of stressful events, that in the long run surpass the ego's resistance threshold, transforms itself into chronic stress, producing physical and psychological exhaustion, associated to diseases like hypertension, obesity, and asthma (Riquer et al., 1996). Studies on conjugal violence point out that feelings of guilt and low self-esteem are characteristic traits in mistreated women, where besides the physical effects, constant aggression can alter their behaviour through sensations of: confusion, inability to concentrate, lack of communication, shyness, rage, prolonged fears, as well as disorders in their life, sleep, depressive, and feeding habits. "In the same way, sexual disorders can be produced due to fear of intimacy, failure of response or lack of interest, and often due to a feeling of 'filthiness' or humiliation" (ibid., p.286, our translation). It is important to note that more or less a third of mistreated women suffer from a significant depression, and some of them become addicted to drugs and alcohol; the risk to try to commit suicide is five times higher that in women who have not been abused (Heise, 1994; 1999).

It would be important to ask ourselves if we could gain new light by taking again Freud's theory of seduction in consideration, that primitive notion of sexual seduction (extended to include the different forms of abuse

---

7 Generally treated with psychotropic medication, that far from resolving the problem, make it worse, what is know as " prescribed tranquility" (Burín, 1987, our translation).

and/or mistreatment that can happen in the home, either as a direct victim or as a witness of it) that lead to the concept of trauma and to understand psychopathology in terms of traumatic experiences that took place in specific stages of development, assigning a great weight to the external factors, or objective reality and to its mental representation inscribed in the psychism, that will later on be given a new meaning; *A child is being beaten* (Freud, 1919) constitutes the best example of what is mentioned above. Without stopping to recognise the great importance of the field of unconscious phantasy, we think that in the vast majority of cases of mistreated women and children, the reversion of sadism towards the own self, central characteristic of masochism, "regularly occurs due to the cultural suffocation of the drives, thanks to which the person abstains him/herself from using a good part of these destructive elements of the drives in their lives" (Freud, 1924b, p.175 our translation). Sadism, cruelty, filicide, violence, hostility (widely documented in recent literature as a serious public health problem[8]), as well as differential socialisation processes for men and women, oblige us on the one hand, to break the conspiracy of silence and take again the concept of trauma, closely related to repetition compulsion and to the death drive. On the other hand, it obliges us to consider why when faced upon one same fact: violence (domestic and/or gender), some women develop a depressive disorder while others develop a borderline personality disorder[9], others an eating disorder, etc. or a disorganised attachment (Fonagy, 2001).

Maybe the answer to this question is directed towards an in-depth study of the diverse factors that incite and determine the degree and quality of the organisation and development, both of the drives and their derivatives, as well as of the psychical agencies that constitute the subject in his/her maturation process. To achieve this, it is important to take into account a) the object that imparts the traumatic stimuli (which can be external or internal); b) the time in which a certain stimuli is imparted and how long it lasts (or the sum effect that implies its reiterative application); c) regarding the intensity of the traumatic experience (quantitative factor); d) the quality of the interaction (qualitative factor); e) the subject's participation in the experience (activity/passivity) and; f) how the experience was symbolised *a posteriori*. Taking into account these considerations, we venture into an interdisciplinary and inter-institutional project, in order to start showing

---

8 Federal District Alliance in favour of women, Mexico: Secretariat de Gobernación, 1996
9 See Lartigue, 1999; 2001.

some light into these interrogations, for which, we've selected a critical stage in the female life cycle, the gestation of a new being.

Research design

With the objective of generating hypothesis and explanatory models of psychopathology and its' relation to sexually transmitted infections, as well as developing preventive measures that will allow to interrupt its trans-generational and/or vertical transmission -measures that may also be used during pregnancy- we started a case-control research in the National Institute of Perinatology[10]. One of the specific objectives was to deepen into the risk factors that characterise both borderline personality disorder as well as depressive-melancholic syndrome in a group of pregnant women. Afterwards, the existing association between this pathologies will be looked into, through the new-born's behavioural organisation, motor and mental development, the quality of the mother-infant affective interactions, and the type of attachment.

The research model, is the one denominated action-research, that is characterised by simultaneously carrying out the expansion of scientific knowledge and the solution of a problem (Martínez, 1997). Both qualitative and quantitative methodologies where used in the research; it was divided in two phases, in the first one, the group of researchers, selected and trained the co-researchers (CONACYT scholarship workers) in order to do the psychological diagnosis studies, as well as to implement preventive interventions and/or of brief psychotherapy, and/or referrals to other institutions.

In the first stage of the study -during gestation- 392 women freely gave their informed consented to participate in this research, of which 113 abandoned the project; that is why the final sample was constituted by 279 women[11] that gathered the following inclusion criteria: to be in the age range of 18 to 43, to be between 16 and 35 weeks of gestation, that they knew how to read and write, that they had a partner and that they didn't have a

---

10 Protocol that forms part of the bigger scale study, in which the association between personality disorders and the risk factors involved in acquiring a sexually transmitted infection, HIV/AIDS will be closely looked into, through the study of pregnant women and their partners (150 with the diagnosis of a sexually transmitted infection and 150 without it) (Lartigue et al., 2000b).

11 Of which, up to April 2002, 101 women have abandoned the study due to problems regarding lack of time, transport difficulties, lack of childcare, pain and tiredness associated to pregnancy, etc.

psychotic personality organisation. The following psychometric tests were applied to them: Goldberg's General Health Questionnaire GHQ (1972); Edinburgh Perinatal Depression Scale EPDS (Cox *et al.*, 1987; Ortega *et al.*, 2001); the Beta-II R test of Kellogg & Morton (1974); the Inventory of Personality Organisation IPO of Kernberg & Clarkin (1995); and the Personality Questionnaire of First *et al.* (1997c). In the same way, Structured Interviews, the SCID I and SCID II (First *et al.* 1997a, 1997b) were applied and recorded, as well as a Clinical History (following the model elaborated by Parres, 1964 for the Clinic of the Mexican Psychoanalytical Association[12]). A General Questionnaire was also applied, , conformed by three surveys , the first one was to track down Sexual Networks (UNAIDS, 1998), modified to our population by Alma Nava and Héctor Avila; the second, regarding a History of Risk for HIV (American Academy Association), and the third, was a socio-demographic and health survey called Reproductive History Census (Arroyo *et al.* 1983; Casanueva *et al.*, 1983). It is important to point out that we also pretended to study their partners, however, a very small number of men accepted to participate in the research (181). It is worthwhile noting that given the case of finding indicators of an emotional disorder, or of an emergency situation, it was recommended to the patients to receive some modality of therapeutic intervention.

Later on, The Adult Attachment Interview AAI[13] of George *et al.* (1996) was also applied and recorded in a subgroup of 105 women, who accepted to participate in the second phase of the study, what we call "the IPA/London Project". This project intends to consolidate a group of 30 women with a diagnosis of borderline personality disorder, according to the criteria of the DSM-IV (1994), the so called "cases", will be compared with two control groups, one of them formed by 30 women with an Axis I diagnosis for mood disorders (depressive episode, major depressive disorder, dysthymic disorder, depressive disorder not otherwise specified); or on Axis II depressive disorder without the presence of a borderline, narcissistic and/or antisocial personality disorder on the same Axis. The second control group is integrated by 30 women without a diagnosis for Axis I and II of the DSM-IV (Lartigue *et al.*, 2000a).

---

12 It's important to point out that Dr. Miguel Angel Solano, a psychiatrist specialised in psychoanalysis, listens to the recordings of the SCID I and II, and of the Clinical History independently, with the intent of confirming or modifying the diagnosis made by the scholarship workers hired by the study.
13 This task is in charge of Dr. Armando Córdova who's currently in process of being certified.

The second phase of the research implies a follow-up of the women and their children though-out the first year of life of the child; the babies are evaluated through-out the first month[14] with the Neonatal Behavioural Assessment Scale of Brazelton (1984) and at six months with the use of the Bayley Scales of Infant Development (1969). The type and quality of the mother-baby affective interactions are appraised through the method of face-to-face interaction, in a situation of reunion/separation at three and nine months of age (Brazelton et al, 1975; Tronick et al, 1978; Lewis y Feiring, 1989; Spangler *et al.*, 1996; Lemche *et al.*, 1999; De la Cerda *et al.*,2000; Lopez *et al*, 2000) and the type of attachment with the mother at one year of age through the method of Strange Situation of Ainsworth *et al.*, (1978). It's worth noting that the GHQ and the EPDS is applied again to the postpartum women (at 1, 3, 6 and 9 months), and at twelve months.

The objective the present paper is to identify the risk factors belonging to the melancholic depressive syndrome[15], that can be found in the aetiology or genesis of depression, through their examination (presence or absence) in the clinical histories of the group of women that constitute the first control group. These factors were derived from the theoretical concepts, with the goal of determining the way in which they interact.

The analysis of the case histories will provide us with elements to respond to our initial question: Can depression and feminine masochism be correlated or can it not? Or, what type of association is there between these two pathologies? In the formation of a depressive syndrome, what are the most important factors: the ones related to object-loss, loss of the love of the object, the loss of corporal integrity, the feelings of humiliation, guilt, hate and psychical pain that are manifested in the chaos of the drives, as a consequence of a traumatic event or a series of micro-traumas (domestic and/or gender violence)? what specifications could be made to the papers of *Mourning and Melancholia, A child is being beaten, The Economic Problem of Masochism, and Inhibitions, Symptoms and Anxiety*?

Preliminary Results

The National Institute of Perinathology is a third level hospital of medical attention, dedicated to reproductive health. In general terms, it is identified as a specialised institution in the attention of high risk pregnancies; it's characterised for attending women without social security, whose partners

---

14 Two evaluations: on the first and forth week after birth
15 Conceptualised in this way by Kristeva (1987).

or even themselves do not hold a steady job, that is why the care giving to people with severe social and emotional disadvantages is a common denominator, even though, some of the do have a professional level education.

Pregnancy, probably like no other experience, announces the start of dramatic changes in different spheres of women's life, in the relationship to her body, to her partner, to her significant others, to her culture and to herself. On an intrapsychic level, four modalities of regression that women go through in this stage have been systematised: 1) regression of the libido, predominantly object libido, towards a narcissistic catexis; 2) regression to object relations characterised by dependence; 3) ego regression, that is why women feel overwhelmed by sensations of omnipotence and grandiosity, and finally; 4) super-ego regression that provokes a tendency towards previous phases of sadism and idealisation. The alteration of the previous existing balance between the libidinal and aggressive drives that can provoke important fluctuations in mood and in behavioural patterns also takes place, as well as in the use of her talents and capacities, it may also cause profound alterations of the body image, that provoke rearrangements in the identity structure, with consequent modifications in the balance between the id, ego and super-ego. These regressive fluctuations with their progressive and re-alternative movements, in which the different developmental stages are recapitulated, establish the condition of a possible object-loss and/or of ideals which are impossible to reach; losses subtracted from consciousness, specific condition for depression in which gestation functions as a precipitating factor; that is why it is considered to be a critical period thanks to the interrelation of the profound physiological and psychical changes, in which weakness or the vulnerability of the ego are the highlighted (Bibring et al., 1961;Cohen y Slade, 2000; Pines, 1972; Lartigue y Vives, 1992; Vives y Lartigue, 1991; 1994; 2001). Therefore, the integral attention of women during the gestational period is of great importance, that is why it's recommended to attend prenatal care, if possible, since the first month of the pregnancy

It is worth noting that out of the 105 women in the protocol STD-HIV/ AIDS that agreed to take part in the second phase of the study (IPA/London Project), 22 have a confirmed diagnosis of a mood disorder on Axis I of the DSM-IV and one woman has a depressive disorder on Axis II. It is also important to point out that the group of women with depression (23 up to date), in comparison to the group of "normal" women, manifested a greater number of emotional distress symptoms during pregnancy; in the same way, they manifested a social inhibition pattern, with feelings of inferiority and hypersensitivity towards negative evaluation, accompanied by attitudes of opposition and passivity towards the different tasks demanded, as well as feelings of impotence, inability, guilt, discouragement, disillusion, and unhappiness[16].

While examining the clinical histories, regarding the risk factors that can be found in the aetiology of depression, we found that these could be grouped in four subgroups, according to the type of loss or traumatic event. Of these 23 completed cases, we transcribed the clinical vignettes that exemplify with greater clarity the genesis of the depression and its course through out the life of these women.

Perinatal losses or congenital defects

This group is constituted by five women, two of which lost their previous baby and two more suffered from the painful impact of loosing two babies. The fifth woman has procreated two children with congenital defects, out of five pregnancies; the birth of child with a congenital malformation has been conceptualised as a perinatal loss. Both scenarios share the common denominator of a real loss of the representation of the expected child; both maternity and paternity are frustrated therefore, generating a very intense work of mourning that can be prolonged, and that can have as a consequence, an alteration in the way the personality functions and/or a crisis in the couple and in the extended family system (López et al., 1997; Lartigue y Vives, 1994).

VIGNETTE 1. Currently, M. is 37 years old, she's a career woman, married, going through her third pregnancy at the time of the study. She comes from a family of teenage parents that got married as soon as the birth of their first child takes place. M's describes her family of origin as traditional and conservative, it's constituted by her parents and 6 siblings, one of them died recently, M. is the youngest.

M. gets married at the age of 25 according to her "not very much in love", regretting profoundly the loss of her freedom, since she was used to decide over her free time; since her marriage she had to restrict her activities

16 Significant differences were obtained on the GHQ, and on three disorders of the SCID-II Questionnaire: avoidant, passive-aggressive and depressive, women with depression obtained the higher scores (p .037; .002; .014; .014 respectively).

and interests. M. has experienced two perinatal losses, the first one was a miscarriage in week 18 of gestation, the doctor informed them that the foetus was lifeless since week 15, the cause was unknown. She had a second miscarriage in week eight of gestation. As a consequence of this second miscarriage M. has presented several urinary and vaginal infections; as well as intense feelings of guilt. During the current pregnancy she lives in fear that her child might be born with something wrong, M mentions that she could not withstand another loss[17].

VIGNETTE 2. A. is a 38 year old woman that finished junior high school, she is married and is going through her fourth pregnancy; she comes from a very large family, A. is the fourth of 10 siblings; she states how since she was young she helped with the house chores. She started attending primary school when she was 9 years old and finished middle schooling when she was 18 years old. At this age she got married "without any previous information". She describes the relationship with her mother as one with little trust, distant; even though she complied with the feminine role assigned (according to her cultural group of reference) she didn't feel identified with the feminine prototype, expressing that she "would have liked to be a man". She describes her sexual relations as being "used", she doesn't like it, and in every pregnancy she has thought that she is going to die. A. has two teenage daughters, two years ago she lost a son during childbirth; nowadays she experiments great fear in loosing this baby, she wishes it to be a boy, like the one that died (our fear is that this child could suffer from the replacement child syndrome). It is clear that she assigns more value to her sons than to her daughters, she mentions that since the first pregnancy she wanted to have a boy. A. feels guilty about the death of her baby "for not helping him". Her depression seems to correspond to a guilt depression, as described by Bleichmar[18].

---

17 Axis I Dysthymic Disorder.
Axis II None.
Axis III Urinary tract infections, candidiasis and high risk pregnancy.
Axis IV Depressive symptoms due to her pregnancy and discomfort consecutive to the infection.
Axis V 85.
18 Axis I Dysthymic Disorder.
 Axis II Schizoid.
 Axis III Motherhood (advanced age).
 Axis IV Miscarriage (two years ago due to rupture of the placenta).
 Axis V GAF 50.

Organic diseases with or without domestic violence

In this subgroup, eight women that presented physical illnesses were included, this element alone conditioned the depressive syndrome; in some cases suffering form a physical disease was accompanied by several traumatic events, related to intrafamily violence.

VIGNETTE 3. M.A. is 40 years old, she finished a university degree, lives with her partner without being married and is currently going through her first pregnancy. She comes form a home in which the father, besides being a good provider, is present and emotionally linked to his children. She describes her mother as more nervous and a little more violent, she has worked half time since M.A. can remember. She is the eldest and only woman of three siblings. M.A. suffered from non-convulsive seizures when she was four years old, the diagnosis for epilepsy was given when she was five. She had learning problems in primary school, where she found support in her mother. In junior high the convulsive crisis started, therefore, she thought that she was never going to be able to get married or have children; in this period, she remembers that the relationship with her mother was very difficult. In adolescence, even though she had male and female friends, she would have convulsions everywhere that is why, she considers this stage of her life as the worse one she has ever experienced. After concluding her university degree and holding successful jobs, she establishes a relationship with a partner who had a "temporary" addiction to cocaine and suffers form a Bipolar disorder. The couple thought that they were unable to have children [19].

VIGNETTE 4. H. is 22 years old, she finished a technical career, is married and pregnant for the first time. Her mother had a child already when she met H's father; there was never a good conjugal relationship, he would beat up her mother constantly, as a consequence, they separated when H. was born. The patient describes her father as very irresponsible, and her mother as distant, and negligent regarding her education. She had a godmother that lived with them, who would always scold them, while her mother and her godmother worked, she and her brother would take care of themselves.

19 Axis I Dysthymic Disorder.
 Axis II None.
 Axis III Epilepsy, under medical treatment.
 Axis IV Fear to harm the baby as a consequence of her illness. Partner addicted to cocaine, and Bipolar disorder.

M. experiences profound spite towards her mother, since besides being an absent mother, was not very affectionate.

H. describes herself during adolescence, as rebellious, she would get bad grades, se would play hooky quite often that is the reason why the conflicts with her mother got worse she got married again when H. was 13 years old. At 16 she had her first sexual relation, with a 30 year old married man, this relationship lasted for a year, afterwards she constantly dated several men, until she met the one that would be her husband, whom is divorced. H. started her relationship with him when he was still married.

At 18 while they were still dating, he hits her and becomes extremely jealous, she presents a major depressive episode; stops eating, and this is why she is hospitalised at the National Institute of Nutrition, for anorexia nervosa (she lost 14kgs in weight). After these events, that repeat themselves constantly, she lives in fear and anxiety, however, she gets pregnant and marries him 5 months ago. She describes her husband as very unstable at work and with serious interpersonal problems; H. has not been battered lately, however, she lives in fear that at any given moment the conjugal cycle of violence might start again[20].

Gender and domestic violence

This group was characterised according to the definition of violence against women "every act of verbal or physical force, coercion or threatening deprivation of life directed against the individual, woman or girl, that causes physical or psychological damage, humiliation or arbitrary deprivation of liberty and perpetuates female subordination" (Heise y cols, 1994, our translation); it is important to point out that every time it is more evident that girls and women are more exposed to the risk of violence in their own homes than in any other place. This group is the larger, constituted by seven women.

VIGNETTE 5. L. is 40 years old, studied a career in commerce, she is going through her second pregnancy, she has a six year old son. She comes from a family of teenage parent (they got married at 18), that procreated

20 Axis I Dysthymic Disorder. History of a Major Depressive Episode.
  Axis II None.
  Axis III 25 week pregnancy.
  Axis IV Stressors: Fear and anxiety caused by the couple's relationship, and a possible change of residency.
  Axis V 85.

nine children, being L. the fourth. Her family of origin has low income, her parents worked as labourers to support the family.

Her mother worked almost all day, when she got home she didn't have the emotional availability to interact affectively with her children, manifesting little empathy towards L. as a consequence she feels that she "did not cover her basic affectional needs". Her father had a drinking problem, which made it difficult for him to keep a job; L. feels and felt very distant, she doesn't keep pleasant memories of him. The father used to beat up the mother, he would argue and they had a very bad relationship, on one occasion he hit her very hard and threatened with killing her, while trying to choke her, L. was a witness to this conjugal violence.

She describes her childhood as an isolated girl, her grandmother cared for her, and dies when she was 15, she experiences a severe depression since her grandmother was the only person to be affectionate with her, L. states "I felt that the world was ending for me".

As a girl she was teased by her classmates because she "had crooked teeth", and she was beaten by her older brother. At 23 thanks to her job, she is able to fix her teeth, achieving more self-confidence, and getting a boyfriend. At the age of 29 she has her first sexual relationship, she gets married two years later, she narrates that when she remembers her childhood "it generates in her strong feelings of sadness".

She comments on the fact that her husband has been unfaithful to her on two occasions, due to "drinking sprees", but L. forgives him "because that is the way men are". Nowadays L. feels anxious by the possibility that her child might have Down's syndrome, due to her age[21].

VIGNETTE 6. V. is 27 years old, she finished junior high school, she's married, is going through her fourth pregnancy, and has three sons. V. is a woman that suffered from domestic violence since a very young age, she was strongly battered by her father. Her mother never took care of her since she worked everyday, leaving V. to care for the house and her brothers.

When V. is approximately six years old, her nuclear family breaks relations with her father's side of the family due to the fact that her grandfather sexually harassed his granddaughters, including the patient.

---

21 Axis I None.
  Axis II Personality Disorder Not Otherwise Specified, Depressive type.
  Axis III Vaginal infection.
  Axis IV High risk pregnancy due to age.
  Axis V 80.

V. describes her childhood as happy, because in that time "there were just punches, blows", her real disgrace started when she was approximately 12 years old. At this age, she has her first boyfriend, reason for which her father takes her out of school, locks her up and sexually abuses her, this situation lasted form the time she was 12 till the time she was 18. During this time, her father keeps on hitting her and her siblings, he wouldn't let her go anywhere, she wasn't even allowed to peek through windows or doors, V. dedicated herself all day to the household chores, she also helped her father in his bakery, which was located in the same house.

At the age of 18, her father hits her because she danced with a teenager at a party, her grandparents protect her and take her to their home, V. files a law suit against her father for sexual abuse, which she withdraws it due to fear.

V. has a boyfriend with whom she goes out on a trip once, when she gets back, the boyfriend's family makes her marry him, she didn't want to and neither did the boyfriend. V. is insulted constantly by her new husband, he screams at her that he didn't want to get married. Short after, when she finds out that she's expecting her firstborn, her husband screams at her, this time saying that he didn't want to have the child. V. gets married to a perverse man, a fetishist that, in words of V. "has incestuous relations with his mother". Currently V. lives in her parent's house with her husband and her three sons. V. is the one in charge of the household chores, she is constantly insulted by her family because she doesn't do things properly. There is conflict in the family dynamics because V's husband spies on his mother-in-law, he also steals her undergarments to masturbate. The patient is worried because her 6 year old son is also starting to spy on his grandmother[22].

HIV-AIDS

The last group is constituted by three women that contracted HIV-AIDS, they got pregnant without knowing that they were infected with the human immunodeficiency virus.

VIGNETTE 7. O. currently is 27 years old, she's a doctor, she's going through her first pregnancy and lives with her partner without being married.

---

22 Axis I Dysthymic Disorder.
   Axis II None.
   Axis III None.
   Axis IV Primary group problems.
   Axis V 50.

She comes from a very low income family, in which she is the eldest of six children that were witnesses and victims of their father's violence, they describe him as demanding, not so flexible and intolerant. The relationship with her brothers was always coloured by conflict, because they were her responsibility, being the eldest daughter. Since she was a child, for her there was only school and work. Three years ago one of her sisters was raped, while she was coming out of the cinema with her boyfriend. Two years ago, another one of her sisters has a psychotic crisis. That same year, O. was performing her social service in Chiapas and came back home with a confirmed HIV positive diagnosis. It calls to our attention that the traumatic events that this family has gone through have happened to three women, it would seem like there is an incapacity to defend and take care of themselves, as if all the violence that they experienced as children by the hand of their father would materialise itself in an external sadism reverted upon the ego. The latter is related to the illnesses that O has suffered since she was a little girl: tonsils, rheumatic fever diagnosed at the age of 18, associated to pernicious anaemia, consequence of which she had to have a blood transfusion. During the last year she has suffered four times from typhoid fever, facial paralysis due to excess workload, dermatitis on the face and dengue, besides strong headaches. In Chiapas she was hospitalised due to high temperatures and nausea, thoracic pain, HIV diagnosis and later on they let her know that she is pregnant. She comes back to Mexico with her partner, who is also HIV positive, to have her baby[23].

VIGNETTE 8. Z. is 24 years old, holds a university degree, is married and this is her first pregnancy. Z. comes form a functional and integrated home, she's the youngest of four siblings, she describes her father as exigent, strict, excessive hard-worker, and of old-fashioned ideas, but affectionate; she has felt her mother to be a bit closer emotionally, but reserved regarding the instruction of her children in the area of sexuality. Z. was taken care of by her siblings, due to her parent's work, she's always had a good relationship with them. Her life had taken place uneventfully until she gets married after finishing her degree. Suddenly her husband fell ill and they did some tests from which it was concluded that he was HIV positive. They did the tests on her as well, and they came back positive; in the forth month

23 Axis 1 Mood Disorder Due to HIV positive.
   Axis II None.
   Axis III HIV positive, typhoid fever, lupus, dermatitis post AZT medication.
   Axis IV Financial problems.
   Axis 65.

of her pregnancy, she accepts to participate in the study. After the initial shock, they look for therapeutic help as a couple, however, the emotional explosions present themselves on and off[24], finding themselves extremely worried about the well-being of their soon to be born child.

Discussion

In spite of the synthesis that had to be done with each one of the cases put forward, we can see, in vignette 1, that Mrs. M's losses (the two previous pregnancies that resulted in miscarriages) have been summed to a series of previous losses- as usually happens. The loss of freedom and the restriction of her interests, when she got married, in reality are covering up something fundamental, of a narcissistic type: the loss of the hopes to get married "out of love" and of her adolescent phantasies. Therefore, the guilt resulting from the miscarriages has to do with the sensation that a part of her rejects the undesired maternity –together with her husband and the products of her pregnancies- hence, she feels that she played and active part as a promoter of the losses, the latter re-edits old phantasies of castration. The oedipal guilt manifested in the phrase "I do not deserve to have children" has its roots in a desire to not have children. The repetitive urinary and vaginal infections can –besides the pathogenic agents at play- point at a deficiency in the capacity to symbolise guilt, and so this conflict is directly derived to the body, giving rise to a somatisation of the conflicts. Probably, this deficit started in early infancy, since it's possible that her mother, married during adolescence, wasn't able to fully develop her capacity to transmit such capacities of symbolic thinking to her children, nor to provide the adequate libidinal charge to her while she was a baby –this could have produced a depression in the infant that deprives her from its relational and affective desires and leaves her empty (Lebovici, 1995). In this way, the current losses have been increased by earlier ones. Regarding the passive and resigned way in which she has lived her marriage and the restriction of her interests, as well as her losses (that are probably experienced as deserved punishments), we could infer that in her, a masochistic character structure underlies- the so called feminine masochism.

Regarding vignette 2, we can observe that Mrs. A. is a woman that comes

---

24 Axis I Major Depressive Episode.
   Axis II None.
   Axis III Pregnancy and HIV positive.
   Axis IV Anxiety and Depression due to HIV positive.
   Axis V 60.

from a large family (she's the third of ten siblings), that has a distant mother with whom she didn't develop a relationship built on trust or intimacy. Given the devaluated role through which she experienced her mother, she had problems in the area of psychosexual identification- manifested by the desire to have been a man. On top of this, there is a lack of information regarding her tasks as wife, and her sexual role within the marriage, that is why she experiences sexual relations as "being used", and at the same time, with an enormous guilt, since she fantasises about the possibility of dying in every pregnancy as a result of a talionic need for punishment -for practising a forbidden sexuality, and for the lack of elaboration of rejecting aspects against the products of her gestations (hence, the guilt experienced with the loss of the baby in her third pregnancy, many years after her daughters were born, now teenagers, as the result of the desire to have a son). At the present time, during her fourth pregnancy, a typical replacement child syndrome could manifest itself, that is why the new baby boy waiting to be born, could access existence from a false place, from the desire of the other and form the place left vacant by the death of his brother -along with the sequels that are derived from the circumstance of coming to occupy the place *of the other.* Even though Mrs. A. fulfils in the eyes of her social group, the expected feminine stereotype, we warn of the lack of positive attributes, and the presence of the most negative ones in her condition as a woman. Therefore, her situation of low self-worth related to gender -probably experienced since her family of origin, by growing up amongst so many siblings, and also by feeling and experiencing sexual relations with her husband as *being used,* that is, as humiliating, as something that *doesn't interest her,* but that she has to agree to because it is her *duty as a wife* to do so. It is not surprising that currently Mrs. A. perpetuates in her own daughters this situation of low self-worth, and that she would rather have sons -event though she doesn't have them yet. Thereupon, her depression, since, as she states, *sacred disease*

Regarding vignette 3, M.A. is a 40 year old woman that is going through her first pregnancy. She comes from a family in which she is the eldest and the only daughter, after whom, three brothers were born. Even though she had learning difficulties and conduct problems, she had a high level of scholastic accomplishment. Regardless of that, the early onset of her illness -four years of age- and the appearance of convulsive crisis since early adolescence, caused a serious infantile narcissistic injury -let us remember the stigma that still nowadays, is imposed on people suffering with epilepsy, the *sacred disease* of the pre-Hippocratic times- and the problems surrounding lack of control (both muscular and bowel) that frequently feeds the fears associated with madness. We believe that is not a coincidence that she married a person suffering from manic-depressive psychosis, on top of his cocaine addiction, as a way to place, through projection, the madness of the other. Her illness also made her fear the possibility to transmit her terrible disease to her descendants, this phantasy was materialised in her fears of inadequacy towards marriage and motherhood. It is also important to consider that epilepsy was an obstacle in the possibility to accomplish or fulfil maternal expectations, the Ego Ideal that forces her *to be the best*, resulting in psychic pain, that once resignifed in adolescence as negation *-the impossibility of getting married and having children-* re-emerges as something sinister in terms of *not transcending*. Regardless of her accomplishments in several successful jobs, after finishing her degree, M.A. suffers from financial problems, since her current partner doesn't help her a lot. Linked to the above, being pregnant at 40, and the ghosts surrounding the possibility of Down's syndrome or the transmission of epilepsy to her child, make her desire almost unattainable.

With respect to vignette 4, we can observe that Mrs. H., who lost her father since birth -she's been told he was irresponsible and used to beat up her mother- and was taken care of by a mother described as distant, not very affectionate, and negligent regarding education, H. manifests a considerable resentment against her. Despite the presence of a godmother in the home, H. holds on to the sensation that, both her older brother (the result of the mother's previous relationship) and her, had to *grow up alone* -given the fact that both the mother and the godmother worked outside the home. In fact, this is a constant pattern in our milieu, since the absence of the father- who never again remembers his descendants- provokes a double lack: that of the first, that disappears, and the one of the mother, that has to leave the home to earn a living. This picture of resentment gets complicated by the fact that the mother remarries when H. enters adolescence (thirteen years old). Confronted with this new situation of exclusion that makes the low self-esteem that always tormented her worse, H. is becomes sexually active, and far form passing through a satisfactory re-edition of the Oedipus situation, this gets complicated: at sixteen she had her first sexual experience with a 30 year old married man, in an attempt to displace the mother and access a paternal figure that may rescue her. When she started dating her current husband, he was also married, therefore this relationship could represent an Oedipal triumph, along with its resulting guilt and recriminations -this explains H's tolerance to being beaten, which her husband does since they were dating. As an answer to her boyfriend's physical and emotional violence -who, as well, presented a pattern of pathological jealousy- H. developed a type of melancholic illness, a manifestation of which was displaced to the body, causing a severe form of anorexia nervosa, and had to be hospitalised. Later on, when they realise her pregnancy, the couple decide to get married, however, H's anxiety makes her fear the repetition of her infantile history, that is, a crisis coinciding with the birth of her baby.

Regarding vignette 5, it is noticeable that a great number of early depravation factors are present in Mrs. L. -who is the forth daughter of nine siblings, resulting from a adolescent marriage- as well as diverse risk factors, such as: financial, educational and cultural poverty; a distant mother preoccupied by work and a number of children, an alcoholic and unstable father; a parental marriage with a lot of problems, frequent episodes of physical, verbal and psychological violence among them -including death threats towards her mother-; a childhood marked by isolation, taken care of by her grandmother, that dies during L's adolescence, and that left her profoundly depressed. Her self-esteem problems were focused on a dental problem -where her castration complex and low self- worth were projected- but it had its origin in severe parental flaws and in her older brother's mistreatment. Once the dental problem was corrected, at 23, she could put aside part of her devaluation conflicts, get to met young men, have sexual relations at the age of 29 and get married two years later. However, the masochist conflict persists, and takes the form of tolerance and resignation before an unfaithful husband -who frequently gets drunk- as well as when confronted with the possibility of a baby with Down's Syndrome, given the age in which she got pregnant this second time.

In vignette 6, it is work pointing out that V. was the victim of constant sexual violence since infancy, at the hand of her own grandfather and father, as well as physical abuse by the latter. The mother, an absent woman due to her work out side the home, was never able to rescue her form this situation , on the contrary, she imposed on her un-proportional responsibilities taking into account her age. As a consequence of the sexual harassment by the grandfather at the age of 6, episode that fills her with guilt over the breaking up of the paternal side of the family; and of the sexual abuse that takes place later on, at the hand of a paranoid and tyrant father that prohibits her form exogamy, and sentences her to the traumatic effect of consummated incest (form the age of 12 to 18, that is, during the whole period of adolescence), V. cannot escape a destiny in which repetition compulsion throws her into the hands of a perverse partner who, has sexual relations with his mother, and spies on his mother-in-law while she showers, what definitely closes the circle of perversion, violence and madness in the family. We can observe in Mrs. V., an extended version of the concept of trauma -psychical politraumatism- in the different ways of abuse and mistreatment in the domestic domain, as a victim -and witness- of different modalities of domestic violence. The incest, consummated in external reality, determined the need to choose a perverse partner that she cannot separate from, in a perverse relationship, that sometimes takes the form of a *folié á deux*. As it could be expected, a representative of the fourth generation, her 6 year old son, has started spying her grandmother.

The main group of the study is made out of women who have been infected with the human immunodeficiency virus; in vignette 7, we can observe the phenomenon described as "poverty feminisation"[25]. Mrs. O. lacked of the basic elements during infancy, and suffered form physical violence at the hand of her father, as well as frequent illnesses, including tonsils, rheumatic fever and pernicious anaemia -this is why she had to have a blood transfusion. Since she was the eldest of six siblings, she turned out to be the parental daughter, who had to take care of the younger siblings and take on responsibilities that surpassed her capacities, therefore, she developed an obsessive type character, with strong masochistic traits. O. grew up in a family with an important psychopathological load, in which women lack the psychical ability to defend themselves from aggressions coming form the outside (a sister raped, another one presenting a psychotic episode, and O. infected with HIV). The obsessive defences made it possible for O. to finish her medical training, however, her history of need and mistreatment might have provoked the reversal of sadism to herself, provoking the formation of a personality structure centred around masochism -since she hasn't been able to use a good part of the destructive components of the drives in positive aspects that would allow her to defend herself against the threats coming from the environment. The HIV infection incremented the depression, that runs parallel to her first pregnancy.

---

25 Unobjectable reality in which women form the poorest countries are the ones "to pay the highest tribute to the disease. In fact, poverty, the particularly insalubrious life conditions in certain neighborhoods, and drugs help the propagation of the virus" (Urrutia, 1992, p. 9 our translation).

In vignette 8, Mrs. Z. is the youngest of four siblings, coming form an integrated home. When she finds out that she has contracted HIV form her husband, a severe reactive depressive episode takes places, this event is experienced as a severe narcissistic injury, since this illness puts her life and existing projects at risk, including her first pregnancy. It's an injury to her physical integrity, that comes form the external world, attacking and placing her corporal integrity in danger, it also confronts her with death, at an age -24 years old- in which all her plans and life projects are truncated -since its a life threatening illness.

Conclusions

Pregnancy leads to the creation of a life, that will change the place of women, in their own world, forever. It involves tremendous physical transformation, as well as alterations in basic physiological processes, such as sleep, digestion, appetite, and hormonal changes that regularly affect the affective state, as well as cognition. In the cases that we've just described, it is important to point out that even though the women's development is within the normal range, the depressive symptoms are mild, and the global assessment functioning is fairly good (85-80); dysphoria is transitory as well as the sadness universally experienced. Luthar *et al.* (1993) have demonstrated that depressive traits can exist in people that confronted adversity with success, nevertheless, they maintain a high level of functioning, which is a sign of the continuity of vulnerability even in the climax of a successful adaptation.

It can also be appreciated in the case histories reviewed that the higher the number of risk factors experienced through out the lifespan, the more it affects development, making it more and more deviant, as well as the severity of the depressive symptoms, how long they last, and their recurrence.

We have seen how the objects that were the source of the traumatic stimuli are, generally, the father, step-father, or an older brother. The time in which such a traumatic stimuli occurred was prolonged to six years, in one of the cases of sexual abuse by the father.

One of the most important aspects, once we've managed to put together the required number of cases, will be the possibility to compare case histories of "normal" women with those that have a borderline personally organisation; we will also be in conditions to document –or not- the way in which development can be distorted during the first year of life.

One of the conclusions of this study has to do with the need to implement preventive services that take care of gestational women, services destined to diminish the prevalence of chronic disabilities or depressive relapses, and therefore, reduce to the minimum the consequently functional limitations; but at the same time, that they can function as services directed to the early prevention, that can stop the chain of trans-generational transmission of depressive pathology. Pregnancy, with its psychological challenges, constitutes a wonderful opportunity to grow and integrate, but also represents a great risk to develop psychopathologies that can have long term effects on the mother-infant relationship.

References

ABRAHAM, K. (1948). Un breve estudio de la evolución de la libido considerada a la luz de los trastornos mentales. En *Psicoanálisis clínico.* Buenos Aires: Hormé, Capítulo XXVI, pp.319-65.

AINSWORTH, M.D., BLEHAR, C.M., WATERS, E. & WALL, S. (1978). *Patterns of attachment: A psychological study of the strange situation.* Hillsdale, NJ: Erlbaum.

AMERICAN PSYCHIATRIC ASSOCIATION (1994). *Diagnostic and Statistical Manual of Mental Disorders.* (4th Ed), Washington DC.

BAYLEY, N. (1969). *Bayley Scales of Infant Development.* New York: The Psychological Corporation.

BIBRING, G.; DWYER, T. F.; HUNTINGTON, D. S. & VALENSTEIN, A. F. (1961). A study of the psychological processes in pregnancy and of the earliest mother-child relationship. *The Psychoanalytic Study of the Child,* XVI: 9-72.

BLEICHMAR, H. (1976). *La depresión: un estudio psicoanalítico.* Buenos Aires: Nueva Visión. 2ª ed. 1978.

BRAZELTON, T.B: (1984). *Neonatal Behavioral Assessment Scale.* Philadelphia JB: Lippincott.

BRAZELTON, T., TRONICK, E., ADAMSON, L., ALS, H. & WISE, S. (1975). Early mother-infant reciprocity. In *The parent-infant relationship,* MA Hofer (ed.), London: Ciba, pp. 137-155.

BURÍN, M., (1987). *El malestar de las mujeres. La tranquilidad recetada.* Buenos Aires: Paidós, 1ª reimp. 1991.

BURÍN, M. (1990). Otros deseos constitutivos de la subjetividad femenina. In *Estudios sobre la subjetividad femenina. Mujeres y salud mental.* Buenos Aires: Grupo Editorial Latinoamericano, colección controversia.

CIESA, J.A. & ROBERTS, J. E. (2001). Meta-analysis of the relationship between HIV infection and risk for depressive disorders, *Am J Psychiatry*, 158 (5): 725-730.

COHEN, L & SLADE, A. (2000). The Psychology and Psychopathology of Pregnancy: Reorganization and Transformation. In *Handbook of Infant Mental Health*, Ch. Zeanah, (ed.). New York: Basic Books, Cap. 2, pp 20-36.

COX, L., HOLDEN, JM & SAGOVSKY, R. (1987). Detection of postnatal depression: Development of the Edinburgh Postnatal Depression Scale. *British Journal of Psychiatry*, 150: 782-786.

DIO BLEICHMAR, E. (1976). La teoría de la libido, el pensamiento analógico en la teoría psicoanalítica. In *La depresión un estudio psicoanalítico*, H. Bleichmar, Buenos Aires: Nueva Visión, pp.150-66.

DIO BLEICHMAR, E. (1991). *La depresión en la mujer*. España: Temas de Hoy.

FIRST, M., SPITZER, R., GIBBON, M. & WILLIAMS, JBW. (1997a). *Guía del usuario para la entrevista clínica estructurada para los trastornos del Eje I del DSM-IV. Versión clínica SCID-I*. Barcelona: Masson, 1999

FIRST, M., GIBBON, M., SPITZER, R., WILLIAMS, JBW & BENJAMIN LS. (1997b). *Guía del usuario para l entrevista clínica estructurada para los trastornos de personalidad del Eje II del DSM-IV. Versión clínica SCID-II*. Barcelona: Masson, 1999.

FIRST MB, GIBBON M., SPITZER RL, WILLIAMS JBW & BENJAMIN LS. (1997c). SCID-II *Cuestionario de Personalidad*. Barcelona: Masson, 1999

FONAGY, P. (2001). *Attachment and psychoanalysis*. New YorK: Other Press.

FREUD, S. (1915-17). Duelo y melancolía. In *Obras Completas*, trad. J.L. Etcheverry, Volumen XV.

FREUD, S. (1919). Pegan a un niño. Contribución al conocimiento de la génesis de las perversiones sexuales. In *Obras Completas*, trad. J.L. Etcheverry, Volumen XVII.

FREUD, S (1923). El Yo y el Ello. In *Obras Completas*. Trad J.L. Etcheverry, Buenos Aires, Paidós, Vol. XIX.

FREUD, S. (1924a). Breve informe sobre el psicoanálisis. In *Obras Completas*, trad. J.L. Etcheverry, Volumen XIX.

FREUD, S. (1924b). El problema económico del masoquismo. In *Obras Completas*, trad. J.L. Etcheverry, Volumen XIX.

FREUD, S. (1926) Inhibición, síntoma y angustia. In *Obras Completas*, trad. J.L. Etcheverry, Volumen XX.

GEORGE, C., KAPLAN, N. & MAIN, M. (1996). Adult Attachment Interview. Unpublished manuscript, Department of Psychology, University of California, Berkeley (third edition).

GOLDBERG, D.P. (1972). *The detection of psychiatric illness by questionnaire*. London: Oxford University Press.

HEISE, L., PITANGUY, J. & GERMAIN, A. (1994). Violencia contra la mujer: la carga oculta de la salud. Washington: Organización panamericana de la Salud, Programa mujer, salud y desarrollo.

HEISE, L., ELLSBERG, M Y GOTTEMOELLER, M. (1999). Para acabar con la violencia contra la mujer. *Population Reports*, XXVII (4); Temas sobre salud mundial Serie L, número 11.

KELLOGG, C.E. & MORTON, N.W. (1974). *Instrumento no verbal de inteligencia. Beta II-R. Manual.* México: EL Manual Moderno, reimpresión 2000.

KERNBERG, O. & CLARKIN, J. (1995). *The inventory of personality organization*. White Plains, NY: The New York Hospital-Cornell Medical Center.

KRAEPELIN, E. (1905). *Introducción a la clínica psiquiátrica*. Trad. D. Santos Rubiano. México: Aleph S.A., 1971.

KRISTEVA, J. (1987). *Sol negro, depresión y melancolía.* Trad. M. Sánchez Urdaneta. Venezuela: Monte Ávila Editores Latinoamericanos, 1997.

LARTIGUE, T. (1999). Edipo y violencia contra la mujer. La internalización de las asimetrías y desigualdades. In *Violencia social, sexualidad y creatividad*, J. Vives (comp.), México: Asociación Psicoanalítica Mexicana/Plaza y Valdés, pp. 15-34.

LARTIGUE, T. (2001). La patología borderline durante el embarazo. Evidencias clínicas y de investigación en la ciudad de México. *Trópicos*, IX (2): 109-129.

LARTIGUE, T. & VIVES, J. (1989). El factor temporal durante el desarrollo temprano. *Cuadernos de Psicoanálisis*, XXII (3-4): 89-102.

LARTIGUE, T. & VIVES, J. (1990). Trauma psíquico y desarrollo libidinal en el Hombre de los Lobos. *Cuadernos de Psicoanálisis*, XXIII (1-2): 37-42.

LARTIGUE, T. & VIVES, J. (1992). La formación del vínculo materno-infantil. Un estudio comparativo longitudinal. *Revista Mexicana de Psicología*, 9 (2): 127-142.

LARTIGUE, T. & VIVES, J. (1994). Consideraciones psicodinámicas sobre el aborto espontáneo. In *Feminidad y Masculinidad,* eds. S. Peña y M.

Lemlij. XX Congreso Latinoamericano de Psicoanálisis, Lima: FEPAL, Vol. 3: 419-29.

LARTIGUE, T., VIVES, J., DE LA CERDA, D., CÓRDOVA, A., LÓPEZ, D.,VÁZQUEZ, M., BUKRINSKY, R., AVILA, H. & FEINHOLZ, D. (2000a). Risk factors for borderline pathology in pregnant women. Effects on the newborn and affective interaction mother-infant. Proyecto de investigación realizado con el apoyo económico del Research Advisory Board of the International Psychonalytical Association, Londres, Inglaterra

LARTIGUE, T., VIVES, J., AVILA, H., CASANOVA, G. FEINHOLZ, D., NAVA, A., SÁNCHEZ, B., NARCIO, L., FIGUEROA, L., ORTIZ, J., ARANDA, C. & VÁZQUEZ, G. (2000b). ETS-VIH/SIDA y trastornos de personalidad en mujeres embarazadas y sus parejas. Detección y prevención de prácticas de alto riesgo. Proyecto de investigación realizado con el apoyo económico de la Secretaría de Salud, el CONACYT, INPer y APM.

LEMCHE, E., GROTE, K., ORTHMANN, C., ARI, A., LENNERTZ, I., HAEFKER, J. & KLANN-DELIUS, G. (1999). Early parent-child interactions, parental representations, and emotion-regulatory patterns as measured through evoked play narratives: Results from an exploratory study in 16 preschool children, Paper presented at the 41th IPC, Santiago de Chile, Pre-Congress Research Meeting IPA.

LEWIS, M. & FEIRING, C. (1989). Infant, mother and mother-infant interaction behavior and subsequent attachment. *Child Development*, 60: 831-837.

LOPEZ, R., LARTIGUE, T., GONZÁLEZ, G. & DE LA CERDA, D. (1997). Descripción de una intervención psicodinámica con embarazo de alto riesgo y experiencia de pérdida Perinatal. *Revista Mexicana de Psicología*, 14 (1): 65-74.

LUTHAR, S., DOERNBERGER, C. & ZIGLER, E (1993). Resilience is not a unidimensional construct: Insights from a prospective study of inner-city adolescents. In *Developmental Psychopathology: Perspectives on Adjusment, Risk and Disorder*, Luthar, Burack, Cicchetti y Weisz (Eds.),Cambridge: Univ. Press.

NASIO, J.D (1996). *El libro del dolor y del amor.* Trad. V. Ackerman, Barcelona: Gedisa, 1998.

ORTEGA, L., LARTIGUE, T. & FIGUEROA, M. (2001). Prevalencia de depresión, a través de la Escala de Depresión Perinatal de Edinburgh

(EPDS) en una muestra de mujeres mexicanas embarazadas. *Perinatología y Reproducción Humana*, 15(1):15-24

PINES, D. (1972). Pregnancy and motherhood: interaction between fantasy and reality. *British Journal of Medical Psychology*, 45: 333-43.

RIQUER, F., SAUCEDO, I. & BEDOLLA, P. (1996). Agresión y violencia contra el género femenino: un asunto de salud pública. In *Mujer: sexualidad y salud reproductiva en México*, A. Langer y K. Tolbert (eds.), México: The Population Council/EDAMEX, pp. 247-287.

SECRETARÍA DE GOBERNACIÓN (1996). Alianza a favor de la Mujer del Distrito Federal 1996-2000, México.

SCHUTT, B.A. (1995). Un fantasma de nuestro tiempo. Consideraciones acerca del Sida en torno a un caso clínico. *Revista de Psicoanálisis*, 21: 135-155.

TRONICK, E., ALS, H. & BRAZELTON, T (1980). Monadic phases: a structural descriptive analysis of infant mother face-to-face interaction. *Merril Palmer Quarterly of Behavior and Development*, 26: 3-24.

URRUTIA, E. (1992). Presentación del foro de discusión sobre la mujer y el SIDA. In *Mujer y SIDA. Programa interdisciplinario de Estudios de la Mujer*, México: El Colegio de México, 1994 primera reimp., pp.7-10.

VIVES, J. (1988). Familia, conflicto e identidad psicosexual. *Cuadernos de Psicoanálisis*, XXI (1-2): 75-85.

VIVES, J. & LARTIGUE, T. (1991). Factores psicológicos del periodo perinatal. Bases teóricas. In *Salud Comunitaria: Una visión panamericana*, T. Lartigue (comp.), México: Universidad Iberoamericana, pp.135-49.

VIVES, J. & LARTIGUE, T. (Coords.) (1994). *Apego y vínculo materno-infantil*. Guadalajara: Universidad de Guadalajara/Asociación Psicoanalítica Jalisciense.

17

The Death Drive and AIDS[1]

Juan Vives and Teresa Lartigue

If we are certain of something in life, it is of the fact that we are programmed to die. Individual death derives from a programme inscribed in our genetic pool, which makes it inescapable. Does this matter have any form of representation in our psychism, and in case it does, how can we take notice of its presence, the presence of this mute but effective force that lives within us? In the same way, how does it manifest itself? Since Freud postulated in 1920, the existence of a death instinct, there has been much controversy about the pertinence or not of this concept, as well as of it's utility. One of the major difficulties has been the confusion, dating back to Freudian writings, between two different concepts: on one side, the presence of aggressive and destructive drives or instincts, to the service of the so called Ego drives; and on the other side, the existence of this sinister force, being this the way in which it's registered by the psychism, unconsciously, the presence of this programme to die –what Freud baptised, in a rather unfortunate way, as death drive. It is clear that Freud's initial confusion, when in Beyond the Pleasure Principle he defined the death drive as a synonym of the ego drives, has much to do with this lack of distinction between the aggressive drives that, as a matter of fact, are part of the Ego drives at the service of the individual's self-conservation. Later on, in The Ego and the Id (Freud, 1923) by making up for his "mistake", Freud places the aggressive forces as fused and confused with the death programme. His insistence on backing

1 Research study sponsored by the Health Secretariat, the National Council of Science and Technology, the Research Committee of the International Psychoanalytical Association, The National Institute of Perinatology and the Mexican Psychoanalytical Association. Project number MO252-9911 CONACYT; 212250-50021 INPer; 01-10 y 01-11 APM. Lic. Itzel González Pacheco was in charge of performing the clinical histories of Pilar and Adriana, and Martha Pérez Calderón, MSc was in charge of Lorenza's, they were co-researchers, scholarship workers from CONACYT hired for this research project. Translation: Martha Pérez Calderón

up his concept on a biological foundation is based on one of the biggest intuitions of Freud's genius, who adverted the genetic intertwining that proved from being creatures for death –as Heidegger would say.

However, beyond all academic discussion, we know from clinical experience, of the existence of cases in which repetition is not at the service of elaboration, but that this is constituted by a sort of compulsive reiteration of suffering or pain with no other benefit than that of subjecting the individual, over and over again, to an experience of displeasure – beyond the dynamic dictates of the pleasure principle- and without the benefit of any type of modification. In the same way, the cases in which aggression goes "beyond the necessary" –as we have proved, mainly in the cases where the practice of brutality and torture exceed, in much, the interests of a confession or the need to obtain strategic information – as well as in certain unbelievable forms of masochistic perversion (as the one pointed out by M. de M'uzan, 1991); the problem of certain melancholic states that culminate in suicide; the paradoxical negative therapeutic reaction; certain modalities of addiction, in which the individual culminates in a systematic self-destruction; and the problem of certain modalities of guilt, with their consequential need for punishment, that can dramatically manifest itself in quite a suspicious tendency towards suffering all kinds of accidents or, in certain cases, in clinical syndromes characterised by an addiction towards surgical procedures, etc.

One of the most shocking problems that we have encountered whilst studying individuals that subject themselves to the practice of high risk sexuality, has to do with the severe flaws observed in some people that do not take care of themselves, or do not take any precautions in regard to important and dangerous diseases such as AIDS or the Human Papilom Virus.

Our thesis is that an important part of the causal motives that help us explain these cases, has to do with this type of symptomatic manifestations – that derive from the action of the internal self-destructive force that operates against the individual itself - that makes him put himself at a high risk in regard to his health-behaviour, that even puts his own life at risk. With the intent to exemplify the latter thesis, we will proceed to present three clinical vignettes where the severity of this self-destructive energy is impressive, manifested through the neglect and negligence of the individuals that have sexual relations with their partners, without any type of protection, knowing that they are infected with HIV. The fact of, apparently, having an adequate knowledge about the possibilities of infection in the other member, not infected, of the couple, and therefore, knowing the risk of acquiring and/or transmitting the correspondent viral infection does not seem to be a motivation to act in a way that would guarantee the preservation of the healthy member's health.

Vignette 1 Pilar

It's about a 29-year-old woman, belonging to very low-income socio-economical class, and precarious schooling, since she barley finish elementary school. She had her first period when she was thirteen years old and got married at age sixteen, getting pregnant immediately after that. Pilar and Ricardo had two children; at the time they are twelve and nine, respectively. Later on, four years ago, and as a consequence of her husband's death due to AIDS, she found out that she had also contracted the virus, from him. Shortly after that, she got involved and started living with another man, José, and even though they both knew about her illness, they decided not to take any type of precaution or care regarding their sexual relations. Nowadays, they have a one-year-old child, who's not infected with HIV. During the interview Pilar reported that José is a submissive man, has restrictively affirmed that he doesn't care about contracting HIV; neither is he interested in undertaking the medical exams to know whether or not he is infected, this is why he remains ignorant regarding his health status. It is clear for us that behaviour as the one just described can be conceptualised as a clear suicidal equivalent, given the self-destructive component contained in it.

As a matter of fact, it is not coincidental that this man has recently had a severe accident in the workplace, that left him incapacitated to do his job for a long period of time, which lead his wife to be in charge of the family income –she works as a salesperson in a flea market.

At the present time, besides having AIDS, the patient also suffers from active Herpes Zoster, and also got infected with the Human Papilom Virus, despite this she has been particularly negligent in her medical treatment, as well as in keeping her appointments. She only seeks medical attention when the pain is intolerable –for example, she asked to be seen *in extremis* when she couldn't even sit down due to the intense pain provoked by the condilom. Previously, during her last pregnancy, she had been quite inconstant and unreliable on her prenatal care appointments, which is why she lost the right to continue attending the specialised Institute where she was taken care of.

It's a woman that appears to be older than her chronological age, that dresses with dark colours, that has neglected her body, she has a rather concrete way of thinking, and has paranoid traits, she is usually defensive. Despite the fact that she is very angry for having been infected with HIV, and in her discourse, she wishes to be helped, however, she doesn't attend her appointments, and has abandoned medical treatment as well as the research project, on two occasions –this is why there's a lot of data missing that might have helped us get a better understanding of the case. We think that this is a woman with numerous lacks in her development that are manifested in an incapacity to take care of herself and allow the care from others. The melancholic and masochistic traits of her personality can, in a given moment, express themselves in the way of a passive aggression, both in her relationship with José, her current partner –since she doesn't participate in an active way in the care of him, on the contrary, she's a passive collaborator of his negligence- as well as in her relationship to the institution that provides her with the possibility of medical care for both her and her youngest child.

The way in which she has conspired with her partner in the total lack of protection and care that could prevent him from getting infected with HIV (in which an identification with the aggressor can be elucidated- her first partner, whom infected her), as well as the fact of being infected with the Human Papilom Virus and from Herpes Zoster (by her previous husband), are indicative of a particularly aggressive bond, of a sado-masochistic type. This is a relationship in which the unconscious guilt feelings, lodged both in Pilar as well as in José, the need for consequential punishment that can be seen in both of them, and the crossed ways of gratification that are provided to their respective superego entities –very primitive and sadistically punitive- are joint in the fashion of lovers that establish a suicide pact.

The latter could seem as a strong or temerarious statement, however, when a couple rejects relatively simple ways of protection that are at their grasp, when they are immerse in a dynamic of inoculation of dangerous diseases, with an apparent indifference on both parts, and with a sort of tacit death pact, we have the right to suspect that we are before a self-destructive equivalent of great magnitude that goes beyond the individual's pleasure and self-conservation needs. Rather, it is about the repetition of neglect, of the lack and the suffering; however it's a compulsive repetition that doesn't result in a possibility for elaboration, comprehension, and integration of the lack, but rather, in a circular dynamic of repetition of the pain, that will end up in death. We think that this is a case that requires a theoretical construction, such as the death drive, in order to be able to explain a dynamic as the one just reported.

Vignette 2 Lorenza

She is a 28-year-old woman, the seventh of ten siblings, she comes from a very low socio-economical background, regarding her schooling, she only studied up until the fourth grade of elementary school. Her parent's marriage was particularly dysfunctional, due to the fact that her father's family came from a perceptibly superior economic level, in comparison to that of her mother; this is why she couldn't establish a proper relationship with them. The couple frequently engaged in discussions and fights in which the mother would hit the father. One of the main sources of conflict had to do with the fact that her mother used to leave the home for several days at a time, in order to attend dances in neighbouring towns, taking her two eldest daughters with her, this situation would present its self every two weeks. During these absences, the father would take care of the children, and when the mother came back, they had severe discussions in which she would hit him, he never answered back to her aggressions. On one occasion, when the patient was nine years old, her father decided to leave his wife and "steal" the four youngest children. The patient recalls missing her mother and asking her father to go back to her. The mother found them fifteen days later, and they managed to agree on some changes, like moving to Mexico City, and that the mother would take more care of their children. Even though the patient describes her relationship to her mother as good, it was tainted with aggression, and she was battered by her; in her own words, "my mom would not talk, she would hit before talking". Her parents split up when she was nineteen, and her mother died three years later due to a gastric carcinoma.

A very important aspect of her childhood antecedents has to do with the fact that, when she was eight years old, her eldest sister left her five month old daughter in her care, so she could go with her mother to one of the dances. Having a greater desire to play, than to take care of her little niece, the patient neglected her and the baby fell down on the floor, after which she started bleeding and getting ill. Later on, she started to vomit, had diarrhea and fever, and when the father arrived home that night, they took her to the hospital. When her sister got home, the next day, the baby had died; her sister went crazy with sorrow and guilt. As a matter of fact, she never blamed the patient for what happened, and always assumed full responsibility for what had happened, but the patient has ever since, felt guilty for her death.

Another fundamental antecedent has to do with being a victim of sexual abuse at the hand of her father, which started when he separated from his wife, and lasted from when the patient was nine until the age of thirteen, abuse that finally ended with a pregnancy. The patient could never tell what was happening with her father, since she had threatened to kill her or her mother if she said anything about it. Nobody at home noticed her pregnancy, not ever herself. It was only when she reached the eight month of gestation, that a doctor told her that she was pregnant. At that moment, the patient could not comprehend the cause of her pregnancy, since she "had never been involved with a man" and she had never had sex with Manuel, her boyfriend. She couldn't understand that the pregnancy was a consequence of her father's sexual abuse. According to her narrative, she did not know precisely what her father did to her, but at the same time, she felt that what he did was like being in hell, and saw him as a monster. When her parents asked her about the cause of her pregnancy, and without being able to tell on her father, she had to lie, and said that the father of her baby was Manuel, her boyfriend –a young man of her same age, with whom she had never had sex: they had just kissed a couple of times in the course of a three month relationship. Her parents made it compulsory for them to get married.

After giving birth to a baby boy, the adolescent couple encountered great difficulties, since he would get drunk and high on a daily basis (with marihuana, cocaine and inhalers); also because he would beat her up quite often- even when she was pregnant. It is interesting to note, that when one of her brothers tried to defend her form the punches that Manuel would administer her, the patient defended him –since "I loved him too much"- and rejected her brother's help. At the same time, Lorenza only knew what a sexual relation meant, when she was able to have sex with Manuel, after six months of living together. This happened due to the fact that in the beginning, the patient would reject her partner as soon as he would start touching and caressing her, since she thought that her father's abuse was about to repeat itself – she couldn't get that image out of her head when this happened. After this time of trouble, she finally managed to engage in sexual intercourse.

When the baby was seven months old, he died, due to dehydration caused by a severe diarrhea. Even though they didn't plan to, she got pregnant again (when she was fifteen years old) and she gave birth to a baby girl. However, her marriage crumbled down during this pregnancy – due to, as we have noted, his drug addiction and the beatings, that happened while he was high, he would maintain an almost suffocating control over her due to his jealousy, besides regularly cheating on her with other women. During the course of this pregnancy, the patient knew for the fist time, what it felt to be pregnant, all the sensations and experiences that are aroused in a pregnant woman, even though she was still haunted by the fear of her daughter dying, since she had the fantasy that "all children of that age died" (six or seven months old). When she took her daughter to meet her partner, he threatened to trough her off the top of a bridge (her daughter was a month and a half old) unless, she would promise not to look for him anymore, since he already had a new partner.

After a year long mourning process, due to her divorce, at age seventeen, Lorenza got together with a new partner, Andrés, a divorcee that doubled her age, with whom she had two more daughters (at age eighteen and twenty one, respectively). This relationship lasted ten years, and was referred to by Lorenza as "pretty good": he didn't get high or drunk, however, the relationship had a crisis when their eldest daughter caught him having sex with his ex-wife, further, she received some photographs featuring the two of them in bed. When this confrontation took place, she was pregnant with their third baby girl, and he admitted that he had been having sexual relations with his ex-wife for the past five years, besides the fact that he used to spend every Christmas and New Years Eve with his ex-wife and his four children from that marriage. Moreover, Andrés, used to mistreat his daughters, the one's he'd had with Lorenza, by hitting them with a belt or a wire; he also hit her on occasions.

When Andrés got ill and was diagnosed with tuberculosis, they found out in the hospital that he was HIV positive, neither of them knew about this previously. She took the appropriate lab tests that turned out to also be positive for HIV. Lorenza feel into a severe depressive state, with suicidal ideation –she even went as far as to arrange a suicidal pact with her three daughters (at the time eight, five and two years old) they were to kill themselves by leaving the gas open, finally she backed out of it. She was haunted by the fantasy that she was going to die immediately, and that her daughters were going to be left alone, without any support. She separated from Andés three years ago, and later on, he died, this happened a year and a half ago. Lorenza felt very guilty and had the feeling that if she had not left him, that if she had taken good care of him, he would still be alive. He didn't take care of himself, he didn't take his medication and she was in charge of doing this. This is why, even her daughters have reproached her for abandoning him at chance.

A year after her separation from Andrés, and after having overcome her depression due to the knowledge that she's HIV positive, she met her current partner, Luis: the father of her last son. He is a taxi driver that did not care about her HIV status, and insisted on being with her. At the beginning of their relationship, he would use a condom during sex, but after a year he got tired of it and decided not to use it anymore. When Lorenza told him that he was in danger and that had the risk of getting infected with the virus, he replied: "I have to die of something… we are all going to die, we are not eternal… we are both going to fight". Even though she had not planned to have a son, and the doctors had warned her that she shouldn't have children, given her HIV status, and the risk that this represented, in a "moment of neglect" –after having the medical need to remove her intrauterine device - Lorenza got pregnant.

The relationship with Luis is not going well, since he has become somewhat violent wit her and her daughters. He hits them for trivial things, kicks furniture until it breaks, he even destroys her daughters' toys. In addition to this, the youngest daughter has accused him, with her mother, of touching her in a sexual manner when they were in his care, while their mom was in the hospital. Their son was born by a caesarean operation, and is not infected with HIV.

It is not necessary to insist that in Lorenza's case we are facing the presence of a multiplicity of adverse factors that resulted in a tragic life, filled with pain and suffering. Besides having the misfortune of being emotionally abandoned by a mother that most probably worked as a prostitute (and that encouraged her two oldest daughters to follow her same path), she had to assume maternal duties early on, duties that she could never incorporate from her own mother, which is why she never had the resources nor the capacity to take care of her niece, that died due to her early age, and as it is to be expected, due to her negligence. This left her marked with guilt, a guilt that we could call unable to be elaborated, since death is the only thing that leaves us with no possibilities of reparation. Obviously, she had to pay for this death, with her firstborn –whom in addition was a child of incest- parting from the imperatives of the most primitive Superego, that of the Talion principle: an eye for an eye, and a child for a child. Although the father is passive in his relationship to his wife, from whom he tolerates everything, even physical mistreatment, he retaliates with his daughter, whom he turns into the subject of sexual abuse from the age of nine until the age of thirteen, when he gets her pregnant. Now, the weight of guilt is multiplied since, added to the weight of an incestuous sexuality is the new burden of a pregnancy –which he always needed to deny- result of such incest. It is not fortuitous that Lorenza had the fixed idea that her babies would be destined to die at the age of six or seven months.

Keeping in mind this family constellation and the vicissitudes of such a rough passage through the Oedipus complex, it is not surprising that Lorenza had the object choices that we have seen. Her first partner is an adolescent drug addict and an alcoholic that mistreats her and cheats on her with other women. Neither is it fortuitous that her pregnancies are combined with an acute crisis with her partners, since, just as with her sexuality, these are – in her unconscious phantasy, enhanced by a traumatic reality derived from paternal seduction- the fruit of sin and incest. That is why it does not seem strange that once her daughter was born, she went in search of Manuel, who threatened to kill her baby. The dimension of the filicide aggression that can rest in any of the couple's members is transparent. In this occasion, Lorenza was able to project the aggressive dictates impelled by the repetition compulsion, into the baby's father, as a resource that would prevent her form acting out herself, the sinister precept, which allowed her to act and take possession of the libidinal and protective part of her split psychism.

In her relationship with Andrés, her second partner, we can advert the economy and multidetermination of the symptoms anchored in her treacherous passage through the Oedipus complex, since at the same time that she displaced his ex-wife, in her fantasy, that represented her own father; in the long run, she had to pay a "well-deserved" punishment for being displaced by her own mother (the ex-wife) who returned as a vengeful figure that punishes her, symbolically speaking, for having had sexual intercourse with her own father. Once again, the crisis with Andrés happens exactly when she is pregnant with her third daughter, which is why the couple separates, not without first leaving her with an inheritance, the HIV positive diagnosis. Lorenza's depression manifests itself in a way which no longer astonishes us: suicidal ideation and a pact where she would kill herself along with her three daughters –pact form which she was able to rescue herself and her daughters at the last minute. When Andrés died she felt, once again, responsible for his death, as if it were inevitable to be a murderer.

With her third partner, she manages –at least for the time being- to place the thanatic components on Luis, who is now the acting part of these destructive impulses, enacted in the form of a negligent and suicidal neglect. Once more, the couple develops a crisis when she is pregnant with her fourth child, the battering appears, the aggression towards her daughters, and then the circle closes with a no way out situation when the repetition of the paternal seduction and the topic of sexual abuse appears, now enacted by her partner, with her daughters.

Lorenza is the living example of the repetition compulsion as a need imposed by a demand coming from the depths of the unconscious, without her having the ego resources to face it; it would seem like she is destined to suffering and pain; to live with horror, over and over again, the nightmare of having been responsible for the death of her niece, and to live with the unavoidable need for suitable punishment.

Vignette 3 Adriana

She's a nineteen-year-old woman, the seventh of eight siblings, she graduated form high school. She's medium built and slightly overweight, her apparent age seems to some extent older than her chorological one, however she has a somewhat childish way of talking and behaving. In the same way, there is some neglect in her physical appearance. She is a rather quite, docile, not very expressive non-receptive person, with little initiative.

When the patient was four years old, her father abandoned them, and from that moment on, he stopped assuming his economical responsibilities, which is why her mother had to work all day. From that time onwards, Adriana grew up under the care and shelter of her oldest sisters, more than that of her own mother; however since she was the youngest, she tended to be somewhat spoiled by her mother. When her adolescence began –and at the point in which her mother stopped working- their relationship became very close.

At sixteen she had her first boyfriend, however the relationship did not last long, since her mother wouldn't allow her to date boys, and her brothers were very jealous of her. Later on, in high school, she had her second boyfriend, with whom she had a two year relationship; same relationship that ended when she met Eduardo, four years her eldest and her current husband, she met him at age eighteen. He's a young man diagnosed with haemophilia and that contracted HIV at age twelve, following a blood transfusion. At age fourteen he found out about his HIV status and has been controlling his condition as well as his illnesses in an adequate manner. Six months into their courtship, Eduardo let Adriana know about his HIV status, but she didn't care; as a matter of fact, she decided to marry him after a one year long relationship. However, she has never told her mother nor her brothers about her husband's HIV positive status, because she thinks that they would accuse her of being "a fool", they would reclaim at her for no having measured the severity of the situation and they would advice her to abandon him. Although at the beginning of the relationship they encountered some difficulties, after some time they have managed to adapt in a quite gratifying manner for both. Regarding to their sex life, the couple always used a condom with the goal of protecting themselves; however, on day, the condom broke and they got pregnant, without consciously planning to. She was never afraid of getting infected, until the condom ruptured. Subsequent analyses turned out negative, meaning that she is not infected. She had a miscarriage threat at week fifteen of the pregnancy, that happened again at week twenty, however, there has been a satisfactory development of her pregnancy.

Adriana's case, despite being very different in comparison to the other two women presented beforehand, has something in common with them: the fact of joining her life with a man that has a hereditary disease and that is HIV positive. In fact, our suspicion increases due to the fact that to join Eduardo, she had to leave a previous boyfriend with whom she already had a two-year relationship. Why the need to assume the handicap that the previous conditions imply? What infantile and life history determinants lead Adriana to a choice with these characteristics? A first approximation related to her father's abandonment and the –partial- loss of her mother, that had to start working immediately after that, could lead us to a clue. Her father abandoning her in the middle of the Oedipal phase, and having to go on to be taken care of by her older sisters, could have damaged her self image in quite an important way, and hence her self-esteem. However, regaining her mother in adolescence, and the fact that she always had her love, mitigated, at least on some level, the trauma that she lived at age four. That is why there is a noticeable neglect in her physical appearance and at the same time a somewhat childish tone in her way of speaking and behaving.

What is the symbolic meaning that a hereditary disease such as haemophilia has for her? We could suspect that there can be something in here about having the opportunity through this illness, to projectively put in her husband some of her internal world –like when she projected on her family the rejection of her boyfriend's haemophilia and his HIV positive status. What's the meaning of haemophilia? The patient thoroughly informed herself about the disease and knows that one of the possibilities is to bleed to death, given the congenital deficiency of one of the factors that intervenes in blood coagulation; and it is precisely, the image that Freud gave us, in one of his letters to Flies (Manuscript G), to explain to his friend the dynamic changes consecutive to object loss and melancholia: libidinal hemorrhage.

On the other hand, what is the meaning of joining her life to an HIV positive person? Given the fact that this is a person that immediately informed herself about everything there is to know about AIDS and it's complications, she knew that there was a risk of contracting it through sexual contact, or by being exposed to Eduardo's blood –let's bare in mind that this is a person who is in constant danger of bleeding profusely. In this sense, we can realise that the combination haemophilia-HIV is a particularly risky one. Besides, Adriana knew perfectly well that her relationship to Eduardo condemned her to the impossibility of having children... unless, an accident were to happen, the significance of which, in terms of physical health, is that of playing Russian roulette, since in order for it to happen, she had to take the risk of getting infected with the virus. The latter brings us closer to the understanding of action, a lot more hidden and through less evident paths than in the two previous patients, but not for that, less effective and torturing, of the self-destructive drives.

As we can see in these three cases, both the attitudes of negligence as well as the rationalizations surrounding the motives that make an individual not consider important to take adequate precautions with the aim of protecting his life, reveal a special significance. These severe failures in care, this type of symptomatic behaviour, give the impression to correspond with what we could classify as suicidal equivalents. It is not absurd to think that we are before a behaviour that is not explainable by the dictates of the pleasure principle. This is about behaviours that surpass this type of conclusion, and that make us think of the existence of an internal force that propels the individual towards suffering and his own destruction, that is, towards his own death.

Discussion

The three vignettes selected to be discussed, have been characterised by the fact that these three women attached themselves to a partner that was infected with HIV, two of them Lorenza and Pilar, unknowingly –at least at a conscious level, and Adriana, that after been told by Eduardo during their six month relationship, of his double disease: haemophilia and HIV decided, in spite of it all, to marry him. The moment when he notified her about it was a crucial one, since she could have decided to interrupt their relationship, and after the elaboration of the consecutive mourning process, try to establish a new loving bond with another man that was healthy, all the more since she was only eighteen.

Pilar's and Lorenza's vignettes coincide in that they are two women that after the death of their partner due to AIDS, chose a new one, their relationship was characterised by the use of the condom –apparently the only mean that could protect them from contracting HIV- only in the first months of their relationship; despite their clear and concise communication regarding their HIV status. This situation could be understood as a quest, conscious or unconscious? to find their own death through a specially painful, and unfortunately, stigmatised path, as it is still HIV/AIDS, and to make it worse, with the added risk of an unplanned pregnancy, of engendering a child that may or may not be born in good medical condition, leaving aside the fact that he/she would be orphaned before concluding the adolescent period[2].

In Adriana's case, despite the use of the condom, "it breaks", what results in an unplanned pregnancy, and in the rupture of the mechanism of denial. For the first time, she becomes conscious of the risk of infection that she is taking, in spite of what Juan Vives accurately signals out in his work, a predated double risk condition, that is, the transmission of the illness by two different ways: through blood and sexually, in a sort of Russian roulette[3]

---

2 Both couples did not agree to be interviewed during the time in which the study took place, this would have allowed us to enunciate specific hypothesis regarding the psychodynamics, the way in which the death drive operates in this type of acting out.

3 It is important to note that this woman, accepted to be interviewed in a formal plain: she signed the informed consent form to participate in a research study concerning sexually

What were the symptoms of emotional discomfort reported by these women? Lorenza and Pilar expressed that they were feeling guilt, anguish, fear, unhappiness, sadness and depression, along with feeling scared, having problems to sleep and crying accesses; Lorenza with more intensity than Pilar[4]. The latter also reports that she's unsatisfied with her current life, she has feelings of futility, and a decrease in her decision making and problem solving capacities[5]. Clinical depression[6] is confirmed in both cases. On the other hand, Adriana reports no symptoms (on the EPDS and the GHQ), the same happens with her husband, Eduardo; both of them consider that they have been able to manage things pretty well; in the clinical interviews (SCID-I y SCID- II) no indicators appear for a mental disorder in Adriana[7].

Lorenza and Pilar both present a borderline personality disorder (SCID-II)[8]; the latter also presents narcissistic, paranoid and schizotypical traits; therefore, it can be inferred that both of them presented a depressive state that predated the HIV infection, within a borderline personality organization[9]. In both cases, the depression was intensified as a consequence of the HIV diagnosis (Ciesa & Roberts, 2001); in Lorenza, suicidal and filicidal tendencies were activated, and in Pilar, self-destructive tendencies

transmitted infections, the same as her husband. However, the co-researcher in charge of doing her psychological study points out the following: "we can observe a rigid and defensive person, it's difficult for her to deepen in important topics, or she minimizes the problems", that is why we regret not having such a thorough history as in the case of Lorenza, through which we could explain in greater depth her decision to join –an apparently good person, however offering such a high risk for her infection and death.

4 In the Edinburgh Perinatal Depression Scale, EPDS (Cox, Holden and Sagovsky, 1987) Lorenza had a score of 23 and Pilar of 13; Lorenza in comparison to Pilar, did answered in question 10 of the EPDS that she had thought about hurting herself; it is worthwhile noting that both in the Mexico sample in the INPer as well as in the UK one, very few women answer affirmatively to this question.

5 In the General Health Questionnaire GHQ of Goldberg (1972) Pilar got a score of seven; however Loreza's score is zero, which represents a lack of specificity of this test in chronic depression cases.

6 Through the Structured Interview for Axis I of the DSM-IV; SCID-I (First et al., 1997a).

7 Adriana agreed to participate in the second phase of the study, during the first year of postpartum; two days after giving birth, she remained without any symptoms of emotional discomfort, as it turned out on the GHQ and the EPDS.

8 First *et al.* (1997b).

9 In the Inventory of Personality Organisation IPO of Kernberg & Clarkin (1995), they got the following percentages in the scales of primitive defences: 27.14; 65.71; 28.57 identity diffusion: 21.18; 49.41; 29.41 and reality testing: 20.00; 58.46 and 24.62; Lorenza, Pilar and Adriana respectively.

manifested in her physical neglect and on the rejection of medical and psychological care.

Seven of the eight clinical manifestations of the death drive are present in the cases of Lorenza and Pilar: a) melancholic syndrome; b) repetition compulsion; c) aggression towards herself and her partner, d) extreme masochism; e) unconscious guilt feelings and need for punishment; f) high risk sexual practices and h) negative therapeutic reaction or non adhesion to treatments[10]; apparently, the only one missing is the absence of addictions. On the other hand, in Adriana, high risk sexual practices is the only one present in an explicit way[11].

Lorenza and Pilar exhibit a depressive syndrome, which main characteristics correspond to those of Bleichmar (1976,1997) apathy and inhibition (plus low self-esteem), where the self representation is consistent with that of an individual that has no power (helpless/powerless) to accomplish a wish, that is perceived as unfulfillable and to which he/she is intensely fixated. This undoable desire could have to do with narcissistic aspirations (to have good health), as well as preoccupation for the well-being of the object (their children), not in the same way, for the partner, with whom there seems to be an unconscious suicide pact. The precondition to experiment depression, can be clearly observed in the case of Lorenza –which is the one that will be referred to since we have more information on it- is the presence of an impairment in the development of the object representation, mainly due to a narcissistic injury (the early abandonment, negligence and neglect on behave of her mother) which created in her, a particular vulnerability towards the loss of the object, not having been able to reach object constancy and adequate levels in the development of object representations; thesis put forward by Blatt (1974, 1998) with which we completely coincide.

Of the different routes described by Bleichmar (1997) that can lead to clinical depression (with the correspondent activation of defensive processes, complications, and secondary gains) in Lorenza a traumatic external reality can be found, where in addition to the maternal abandonment and physical

10 It is important to point out that Pillar was invited to participate on two occasions, the first one while she as pregnant and the second one during postpartum, when her child was eighteen months old, she didn't complete the study on both occasions. Lorenza would also miss her appointments, she was reluctant to continue, however she concluded the diagnostic process.
11 It is worthwhile noting that she agrees to participate in the second phase of the study, in the follow-up of her and her baby during the first year of postpartum.

abuse, she was left at the hands of a father that did not reach the Oedipal level, which main accomplishment has to do with the internalisation of the Law and the prohibition of incest, therefore she was a victim of sexual abuse by her father for a long period of time, which produced serious deficits in her ego resources and in her capacity to sublimate. In the same way, she was a witness of marital violence since she was little, and was forced to perform maternal functions[12] during latency, without being able to complete her physical, cognitive, emotional and social development, the death of her niece motivated intense feelings of guilt, as well as persecution anxieties. Even though her sister did not blame her for this event, the hypothesis can be put forward that there could exist a fear of retaliation by the hand of this sister; finally, a direct aggression to the self can be appreciated, where the masochism that characterised her first object choices is a reversal of the external sadism; with her third partner she established a sadist-masochistic bond.

As it can be appreciated form this tight synthesis, some factors that intervene in the genesis and maintenance of a clinical depression, additionally constitute clinical manifestations of the death drive, and they can also be found in the genesis of a borderline personality organisation, mainly in aggression and domestic violence through out the different stages of the life cycle (Lartigue, 2001). It would be important to research the role of pain, of psychic suffering, as well as of living with fear, with panic and terror, and the way in which all of these unpleasant feelings "make the drives go mad" both libidinal and aggressive, and promote the predominance or magnification or increase of the death drive over the life drive. It is also necessary to have explicative models and metapsychological concepts that can account for the different psychopathological syndromes in an articulated and specific manner.

What we have found, up until now, as a common denominator amongst the twenty-five cases of pregnant and postpartum women infected with HIV[13], regards violence against women (Hesse *et al.*, 1995, 1999) as well as severe deficits in the exercise of parenthood (Lartigue, 2006).

My hypothesis is as follows: in this particular group, the first objects of love, identification and attachment –the biological parents or substitute

---

12 Quite a frequent phenomenon in our country

13 As a matter of fact the sample of this group of infection is constituted by twenty seven women, but in three of them, as it is in the case of Pilar, we do not have enough data regarding their infancy and adolescence; three more cases were included in the sample as it is in the case of Adriana, where the husband is the HIV positive one.

figures- were not able to establish good enough bonds based on object love and recognition (possibly due to a complex array of factors; socio-economical, cultural and concerning trans-generational transmission) so that their daughters could internalise a representational system of care and appreciation directed towards themselves; nor could they stimulate the necessary thought processes, of symbolisation and mentalising capacities that could allow them to successfully deal with adversity. On the contrary, those ties were characterised by violence, by sadism, that in some cases almost reached filicide; or rather, by the abrupt losses of the mother and/ or the father during childhood or adolescence, as well as the loss of some particularly significant sibling.

The mechanisms of identification with the aggressor and the sum of the accumulated traumas can be clearly seen in these patients, along with the negation of the feelings associated to such traumatic experiences, which is why during adolescence they actively do to themselves what they suffered passively. Three different trajectories of life can be differentiated. In the first one, some patients sought out refugee in drugs and alcohol, acting out thanatic impulses[14]. The second line corresponds to the patients that started a relationship with men that characterised themselves by having the same type of addictive and/or an antisocial or borderline personality disorder; this is the trajectory that Lorenza followed. The third one has to do with the structuring of a depressive-masochist personality disorder along with its consequent ego impoverishment and loss of the interest in living. The deadly repetition compulsion can now be seen in some of the new families, manifesting itself in violence that is being practiced on the next generation.

The external factors of the worldwide epidemic of AIDS regard poverty, illiteracy or low schooling levels, and segregation or social isolation, added to the fact of living in a developing country. To conclude, it is important to note that according to UNAIDS (2012) there are 34.0 (31.4-35.9) million people in the world living with HIV; in 2011, 1.7 (1.5-1.9) million people died, leaving .. million children without one or both parents. In the presence of this severe epidemic, it is surprising to see the scarcity of psychoanalytical contributions[15], that could offer some type of theoretical articulation between

---

14 It is worthwhile noting that in seven cases, the father had a serious problem of alcoholism, in two it was the mother, and in one more the mother, grandparents and uncles.

15 In comparison to the abundance of non-psychoanalytical ones. The exceptions being the papers of: Mitchell (1981); Moss (1992); Hildebrand (1992); Grosz (1993); Blechner (1993a, 1993b, 1997, 1998); Frommer (1994); Schutt (1995); Aranson (1996).

a mortal disease such as AIDS, some kind of symptomatic negligence, and the force of the self-destructive drives.

References

ARANSON, S. (1996). The bereavement process in children of parents with aids. *Psychoanal. St. Child*, 51: 422-435.

BLATT, S. (1974). Levels of object representation in analytic and introjective depression. *Psychoanal. St. Child.*, 29: 107-157.

BLATT, S. (1979) Depressive Experiences Questionnaire. Unpublished research manual, Yale University.

BLATT, S. (1998). Contributions of psychoanalysis to the understanding and treatment of depression. *JAPA* 46(3): 723-752.

BLECHNER, M. (1993a). Psychoanalysis an HIV disease. *Contemp. Psychoanal.*, 29: 61-80.

BLECHNER, M. (1993b). Homophobia in psychoanalytic writing and practice. *Psychoanal. Dialogues,* 3: 627-637.

BLECHNER, M. (1997). Psychological aspects of the AIDS epidemic. *Contemp. Psychoanal.*, 33: 89-107.

BLECHNER, M. (1998). Sexuality in the age of AIDS (Letters to the editor). *Int. J. Psycho-Anal.*, 79: 1007-1008.

BLEICHMAR, H. (1976). *La depresión: un estudio psicoanalítico*. Buenos Aires: Nueva Visión. 2ª ed. 1978.

BLEICHMAR, H. (1996). Some subtypes of depression and their implications for psychoanalytic treatment. *Int. J. Psycho-Anal.*, 77: 935-961.

BLEICHMAR, H. (1997). *Avances en psicoterapia psicoterapia psicoanalítica. Hacia una técnica de intervenciones específicas.* Barcelona: Paidós.

CIESA, J.A. & ROBERTS, J. E. (2001). Meta-analysis of the relationship between HIV infection and risk for depressive disorders. *Am J Psychiatry*, 158 (5): 725-730.

COX, L., HOLDEN, JM & SAGOVSKY, R. (1987) Detection of postnatal depression: Development of the Edinburgh Postnatal Depression Scale. *British Journal of Psychiatry*, 150, 782-786

FIRST, M., SPITZER, R., GIBBON, M., WILLIAMS, JBW. & BENJAMIN L.S. (1997a) *Guía del usuario para la entrevista clínica estructurada para los trastornos del Eje I del DSM-IV. Versión clínica SCID-I.* Barcelona: Masson, 1999.

FIRST, M., GIBBON, M., SPITZER, R., WILLIAMS, JBW & BENJAMIN
L.S, (1997b). *Guía del usuario para l entrevista clínica estructurada
para los trastornos de personalidad del Eje II del DSM-IV. Versión
clínica SCID-II.* Barcelona: Masson, 1999

FREUD, S. (1895). Draft G. Melancholia, in Masson, J.M. (ed.). *The
Complete Letters of Sigmund Freud to Wilhelm Fliess 1887-1904.*
Cambridge: Harvard Univ. Press, pp. 98-105.

FREUD, S. (1920). Beyond the Pleasure Principle. *The Complete Works
of Sigmund Freud.* London: Hogarth Press, S. E., Vol. XVIII, pp. 1-64.

FREUD, S. (1923). The Ego and the Id. *The Complete Works of Sigmund
Freud.* London: Hogarth Press, S. E., Vol. XIX, pp. 1-66.

FROMMER, M.S. (1994). Homosexuality and psychoanalysis. *Psychoanal.
Dialogues,* 4: 215-233.

GOLDBERG, D.P. (1972). *The detection of psychiatric illness by
questionnaire.* London: Oxford University Press.

GROSZ, S. (1993). A phantasy of infection. *Int. J. Psycho-Anal.,* 74: 965-
974.

HEISE, L. MOORE, K. & TOUBIA, N. (1995). *Sexual coercion and
women's reproductive health: A focus on research.* New York: Population
Council.

HEISE, L., ELLSBERG, M Y GOTTEMOELLER, M. (1999). Para acabar
con la violencia contra la mujer. *Population Reports,* XXVII (4); Temas
sobre salud mundial Serie L, número 11.

HILDEBRAND, H.P. (1992). A patient dying with AIDS. *Int. J. Psycho-
Anal.,* 73: 457-469.

KERNBERG, O. & CLARKIN, J. (1995). The inventory of personality
organization. White Plains, NY: The New York Hospital-Cornell
Medical Center.

LARTIGUE, T (2001). La patología borderline durante el embarazo.
Evidencias clínicas y de investigación en la ciudad de México. *Trópicos,*
IX (2): 109-129.

LARTIGUE, T. (2006). Parenthood and HIV/AIDS. An investigation of the
INPer based on psychoanalytic and gender theory. In *Motherhood in the
21st Century,* M. Alizade (comp), London: Karnak Books.

LARTIGUE, T., VIVES, J., DE LA CERDA, D., CÓRDOVA, A., LÓPEZ,
D.,VÁZQUEZ, M., BUKRINSKY, R., AVILA, H. & FEINHOLZ, D.
(2000a). Risk factors for borderline pathology in pregnant women.
Effects on the newborn and affective interaction mother-infant. Proyecto

de investigación realizado con el apoyo económico del Research Advisory Board of the International Psychoanalytical Association, Londres, Inglaterra.

LARTIGUE, T., VIVES, J., AVILA, H., CASANOVA, G. FEINHOLZ, D., NAVA, A., SÁNCHEZ, B., NARCIO, L., FIGUEROA, L., ORTIZ, J., ARANDA, C., FIGUEROA, L., FIGUEROA, R. Y VÁZQUEZ, G. (2000b). ETS-VIH/SIDA y trastornos de personalidad en mujeres embarazadas y sus parejas. Detección y prevención de prácticas de alto riesgo (more information Revista *Perinatología y Reproducción Humana* June 2004, 18 (2).

MITCHELL, S. (1981). The psychoanalytic treatment of homosexuality: some technical considerations. *Int. Rev. Psychoanal.* 8: 63-80.

MOSS, D. (1992). Introductory thoughts: hating in the first person plural: the example of homophobia. *Amer. Imago,* 49:277-291.

M'UZAN, M. (1991). Un caso de masoquismo perverso. Esbozo de una teoría. *Imago. Rev. De Psicoanálisis, Psiquiatría y Psicología,* 14: 13-32.

SCHUTT, B.A. (1995). Un fantasma de nuestro tiempo. Consideraciones acerca del Sida en torno a un caso clínico. *Revista de Psicoanálisis,* 21: 135-155.

UNAIDS (2012). Global Report. Epidemiology, www.unaids.org

18

An Intersubjetive Tool for Exploring Depression in Pregnant Women

Patricia Dávila Zárate

Background

This work is part of a global investigation, entitled "Maternal Depression: Its Effect on Mother-Child Interactions in the First Year of Life", by a large group of collaborators led by principal investigator Dr. Lartigue (2007) which was held at the National Institute of Perinatology "Isidrio Espinoza" (INPer) between 2004 and 2006.

The investigation group was comprised of women between the ages of eighteen and forty-three years old, who were attending the INPer for antenatal care. These women gave their prior written consent, were enrolled in courses around the twenty-eighth week of gestation (within a margin of two weeks) and were able to read and write. The overall final sample comprised of 158 women. After self-scoring tests and diagnostic interviews were conducted, the sample group was divided into three groups: the control group (no evidence of mental disorders on axes I and II of DSM-IV-R) consisted of fifty-three women; case group A (pregnant women with a mood disorder [on axis I of DSM-IV-R], a major depressive episode, major depressive disorder, dysthymic disorder, depressive disorder, depressive disorder not otherwise specified or a depressive disorder caused by organic disease without personality disorders on axis II of DSM-IV-R) constituted 53 women; and case group B (pregnant women with the same diagnoses on axis I of DSM-IV-R and also with personality disorders recognised by axis II of DSM-IV-R) numbered 52 women. Structured interviews were conducted to determine the diagnoses of axes I and II of DSM-IV-R (First *et al.*, 1997). The control group was also given a psychodynamic clinical interview (Parres, 1964 and Diaz Portillo, 1997 in Lartigue *et al.*, 2007).

All the pregnant and postnatal women in case groups A and B were given the Guide to Psychodynamic Interviews for those in Depressive States (GPIDS) produced by Lartigue (2005) and based upon the Modular

Transformational Model (MTM) of Bleichmar (1997) which is a semi structured interview with ten questions covering the seven ways of entering depressive states according to the MTM.

Introduction

How do we know who we are, what we feel and think, where we are going? The first experiences for us as children are provided by parents and caregivers who are, from the outset, the most important parts of our lives because our physical, psychological and emotional survival depends on them. Parents and caregivers deliver security, care, cuddles and limits, and later give strength and direction, and knowledge of differentiation, narcissism and identity. Thus, early experiences make a significant mark on the psyche of a person throughout their lives. In general, on the one hand there is an enabling "positive" environment, with adult figures present, which provides a sufficiently good environment. However, on the other hand, there can be a second "negative" environment which is hostile and insecure with no parental figures and/or carers and between the two environments is the midpoint for the population. This negative environment includes various circumstances which, when they arise in combination with other elements, trigger mental illnesses including depressive disorders. Depression has been a research topic for a long time, and is a contemporary disease of our globalised twenty-first century world. It affects children, adolescents, adults, the elderly, and men and women everywhere in the world. It is a mental illness that affects nearly 73 million adult women worldwide (WHO, 2009).

Some pregnant women who are enrolled at the INPer live within the negative environment described and, as well as revealing the above characteristics, are also economically disadvantaged and have high-risk pregnancies. With the articulation of various risk factors throughout their lives, many women experience depression: some of them did not know this before becoming pregnant, some had shown evidence of several depressive symptoms, and some knew but did not express this verbally or felt they were unable to speak about it.

This investigation is the first attempt to complete the puzzle of depressive states from "the fusion of two horizons" (Gadamer, 1997 in Silva, 2005) and to understand women through their own narrative. It is about finding the meanings that pregnant women assign to their depression: how they interpret their depressive disorders and the way this information can be interpreted or assigned a meaning in relation to their emotional states in order to provide a third way of viewing depression in pregnant women. Thus, taking into account the complex thoughts of women we found, in the articulation of their emotions, perceptions and experiences – in other words, through the subjectivity of women – an understanding of their psychic lives or different psychic lives to the first (Dilthey, 1900 in Martínez, 1996) which produce processes that are linked in serial and parallel networks. These processes, through transformations, create emergent properties: i.e. the combination of emotions, experiences and perceptions create new configurations which did not exist before in that there is feedback on the parts (influenced by previous processes) which control recursive phenomena, so called because they repeat upon themselves (Bleichmar, 1997).

The data obtained so far about maternal depression, and our lack of understanding of this specific population, is woven together to generate the questions: What are the categories of depressive states suffered by pregnant women? How did they reach these depressive states and how do they relate to the way they describe and understand what they are living, thinking and feeling? What are the links between these components in the lives of people who suffer from depression? That is, we identified the need for a "voice" to express their ailment, so as for them to be able to articulate their need for care provision or specific intervention while they are pregnant in order to reduce the risk of postnatal depression and the impact on future generations suffering from the same problems.

The focus of this research was the Modular Transformational Model (MTM) by Bleichmar (1997) which proposed a *transformational modular psychopathology* (my emphasis) in which the study of the successive steps of the flow of psychic functioning and of the structures that form this become the axes for diagnosis. The focus of the model is to establish components or categories that characterise the psychopathological structures and to analyse the multiple ways in which these components are formed, articulated and transformed throughout the process of expression. This model proposes the definition of depressive states in a single unit composed of four categories (unfulfillment wish, helplessness/hopelessness, unpleasant affects and *psychomotor retardation*) and seven routes of entry into depression (aggressiveness, guilt, narcissistic disorders, persecutory anxieties, role identification, ego deficits, and traumatic external realities) which can form the core of depression. It also gives importance to the activation of motivational systems (attachment, narcissism, sensual/sexual feelings and group/self-conservation) and how they relate to the routes of entry into depression and its central core. The model was chosen for its hermeneutic approach in combination with a content-analysis technique. The hermeneutic discipline provided a systemic approach to achieving a valid understanding and interpretation of a text which, in turn, revealed the sense of meaning that the interpreter adds to a text (within his/her reflexive world). This method led to the search for the understanding of others as well as him/herself and was taken from the accounts of women who could offer an explanatory hypothesis to account for the continuance and maintenance of depression in pregnant women.

The methodology, which includes meticulous content analysis, gave formats to individual categories of narratives and revealed the categories of: a core of depression (CD), routes of entry into depression (RE), motivational systems (MS) and the emergence of new categories (NC) in the methodological evaluation and respective breakdown of subcategories. The information revealed the principal hermeneutic spiral through the dialectic between the reader's/interviewer's world and the world of the text. It identified attitudes, on both sides, during the interview which were articulated in order to create intersubjetive meaning, which contains some specific attitudes of depressed pregnant women and the attitudes of the interviewer towards them, as well as the articulation of the core of depression, routes of entry into depression, new categories and motivational systems. Also, horizontal analysis was performed on all individual category formats and this resulted in the development of conceptual maps of the general narrative of depressed pregnant women; from deconstruction and synthesis of these we obtained diagnostic models.

Population and Sample

The pregnant women who were studied in this sample were taken from case group A, and had a mood disorder on axis I of DSM-IV-R, a major depressive episode, major depressive disorder, dysthymic disorder, depressive disorder or depressive disorder not otherwise caused by an organic disease and without personality disorders found on axis II of DSM-IV-R (n=53). The main criterion for inclusion was that the interviewer had conducted the interviews (n=33); the criterion that was used to compare depressed women who were pregnant was the application of the GPIDS (n=25). As a result, women who were interviewed in the postnatal period were excluded (n=8). Exclusion criteria, in order to homogenise the sample, were that women must be equal to or less than twenty years old (n=5) and equal to or older than forty years of age (n=2). Other elimination criteria were that some of the *cassette*s used to record the interviews suffered from recording problems and, as a result, did not allow for a verbatim transcription of the audio in a reliable manner (n=3), that for some interviews there was no direct access to the *cassette* or the transcript (n=3), or that there was access only to the printed interview without the cassette (n=1). One woman was included within the exclusion and elimination criteria: over forty years of age, and the cassette was audible. The final sample was composed of ten clinical cases.

Procedure

Hermeneutic Capture

The first step was to conduct the interview that was audio recorded onto a cassette. The hermeneutic procedure started with the transcript because the interviewer was a participant (in listening to each cassette in order to generate the text), contributing prior knowledge and various automatic responses. These reflections were recorded with different colour coding from the original source, after the questions of the interviewer or the answer of the patient: the reflections were either theoretical or automatic responses and were related to the attitude of the respondent or the interviewer. When related to the patient they reflected the tone of voice, reaction time to the questions, the types of response given and in the interviewer we noted the theoretical reflection and automatic responses. Necessary corrections were made to the *verbatim* transcript. After correcting the interview and adding spontaneous reflections they were printed. This first step resulted in a hermeneutic element. On the whole it became the first hermeneutic spiral.

Hermeneutic Categorisation Process: From the hermeneutic unit, there was a formal "first categorisation process" in which the focus was the core of depression and the routes of entry into depression through the Modular Transformational Model which consisted of the act of reading, identifying and classifying the elements of the core of depression (CD) throughout the interview with the pregnant woman. This process included the colour coding of the four categories which make up the CD. The same procedure was followed for the new routes of entry into depression (RE) each with its respective colour code, throughout the written interview, and also for the new categories (NC), which emerged from both the process of data capture and followed the same procedure.

Once the categories within the narratives of the women had been identified and classified, the contents were put into a format which provided the definition of each category. In this second stage the contents were reclassified and reorganised by theme and content, separated and divided, i.e. they were deconstructed. For example, the CD had been underlined with a single colour and to reorganise it, it was separated into the five categories of which it is comprised. Each, in turn, was divided into subcategories; we used the same procedure for the other categories. We also performed analysis of the last category, motivational systems, which, from the content-analysis technique, gave the latent meaning. We were able to make inferences about which systems were identified in the women, and these were also categorised.

In the hermeneutic inquiry we continued to give literal meaning to the text to interpret, reflect and question what the women wanted to say about their depression and how this was interpreted by the interviewer. In this way we developed a second hermeneutical spiral which contained the refiguring, not only of the text but also of the appropriation of the text, and the deconstruction and rebuilding of the text. It "defined" the narrative between the dialectic of the "world of the text" and the "world of the reader". There was then a need to confirm and find more information so we returned to the hermeneutic element and/or the audiotape to add more validity to the procedure.

On the other hand, the hermeneutic element allowed for the development of a short clinical vignette composed of the patient's identity card, current relationship status, family history, personal history and attitude during the interview. Finally, to ensure that each reading was commented upon free of the associations that emerged in the theoretical and automatic responses in the hermeneutic element, we confirmed or dismissed the capture of automatic responses (heard) together and in this second period redefined them as reflective responses.

Hermeneutic Clinical Analysis: Category formats were used as a "thread" to interweave the two components: the clinical vignette and the reflective response, which resulted in the hermeneutic clinical analysis. What was then needed was to confirm or find more information, within the hermeneutic unit formats or categories which would give more validity to the procedure. To give meaning to the interview transcripts, and to reflect on the interviewees' thoughts and those of the interviewer, I referred to several authors of psychoanalytic or psycho-systemic theory as well as the context and history of the patient and interviewer. These were documented. I then turned to the question of recompression and recalculation in terms of appropriation and exegesis in a third hermeneutic spiral (figure 3).

Finally, in order to close the hermeneutic circle, I made reference to hermeneutic reflection in terms of self-understanding and self-reflection of the patients' circumstances (Prado, 1992). In this I "concluded" with the hermeneutic clinical analysis case by case, as seen in chapter 4's "analysis of results". The hermeneutical method described previously was used consistently from the point of view of the witness-narrator.

Horizontal Integration: Afterwards, the hermeneutic category formats were pooled together and organised and we integrated all categories of the MTM, i.e. the categories and subcategories of depressed pregnant women, in a single format of integrated categories. This integrated format allowed me to draw up text maps of all the women from whom I acquired concept maps. These yielded two types of results: a) The definitions of depression (CD, P and NC) were plotted in a visual tool (*Mindmanager X5*) which allowed for greater organisation and communication of the ideas that I wanted to convey. B) Through the deconstruction and synthesis of the concept maps plotted I generated diagnostic models for CD, P, NC and MS.

Results

Because the results were rich and varied, and sometimes overwhelming, it was important to create subcategories in order to understand that women's depression is based on the details within the information, the specifics that are found in this part of their environment. The results were grouped into four general categories that are the result of each hermeneutic step: clinical vignette, category formats (concept maps), diagnosis and hermeneutic clinical analysis models, each containing categories and subcategories. I created thirty-three concept maps. In this paper I show only four concept maps to illustrate the process of the hermeneutic process. The first is the narrative of the depressed pregnant women (appendix 1). The second is the sub-category of unfulfillment wish in the CD which allows for the depiction of the deconstruction performed at each step of the Modular Transformational Model (CD and P) and the new categories that emerged during the research process (appendix 2). The third map is of the intersubjective resonance that includes the hermeneutic elements of the participants (appendix 3). The last map is of the overall diagnostic scheme of the pregnant depressed Mexican women who came to the INPer for medical care (appendix 4).

Clinical Vignette

The clinical vignette produced information which allowed patients to contextualise their own prejudices, and family and cultural traditions. It consisted of information gleaned from each woman's identity card, current relationship status, personal history and attitude during the interview. The latter is a sub-category in a process and, in a subsequent process, is a category in itself.

1) Socio-demographic variables forming part of the identity card of the patients found that the average *age* of the women was 32.8 years. The standard deviation was 4.686; the minimum *age* was 22 and the maximum 38. The *education* of the women was distributed as follows: four women had a basic education, four women had a high school education and two had an undergraduate degree. *Marital status* was characterised by seven women in a relationship and three not in a relationship: four were married, three were in an open relationship, two were single and one was widowed. In terms of *occupation* it was found that eight were homemakers, one worked in a business and one was a professional. As a result, 80% of the women had an unpaid occupation. Finally, in terms of socio-economic status, six belonged to the lower class and four to the lower-middle class (as defined by the classification of the INPer).

2) Patients' current situations included definitions of their depression, reasons why they thought they were currently depressed, which were accompanied, in all the categories of unfulfillment wish, with unpleasant feelings. The topics were focussed on four key issues: a troubled relationship with a partner, problems with the close family and/or the nuclear family, medical conditions, and the current pregnancy. It also included a summary of the identity card.

3) Family and personal history. The latter was divided into three parts: childhood, adolescence and adulthood, as understood by family and cultural traditions.

4) Attitude during the interview was characterised only by the categories of the women and the categories of the interviewer. The categories of the interactions between them were characterised by intersubjectivity and were later classified as part of the hermeneutic clinical analysis.

Category Formats

Using graphs, 26 concept maps were obtained which included the narrative defining the depression of pregnant women: the core of depression (CD), routes of entry (RE) and new categories (ND). Due to the vast and manifest content provided by the patients, these maps were made individually, and sometimes divided by subcategories. They each included: 1.The definition of the depression of each of the ten women. 2. The core of depression (CD) which comprises five different categories, each with corresponding subcategories: unfulfillment wish, helplessness, hopelessness, unpleasant feelings and psychomotor retardation/hyper-arousal. 3. The Routes of entry (RE) into depression which includes nine categories with their respective subcategories: traumatic external reality, identification with parental figures, narcissistic disorders, medical diseases, guilt, persecutory anxiety, aggressive, negative gender stereotypes and ego deficits. 4. New categories (ND) are four categories with their subcategories: object, ego resources, mechanisms/management and close/extended family.

Within ego resources we classify ego strength, motivation to change and awareness of disease. The object can be rescuer, container or protector and usually includes children, family, extended family or the current pregnancy (which they refered to as "baby"). The mechanisms/management of depression were classified according to the type of management that formed the overloading/displacement in relation to other people, the assigning of roles to displace their children, to create defence and armour, and to protect them from suffering the same problems. Finally, the close family/ extended family represent extensive support networks but also have parental roles.

Diagnostic Models

During the process of the deconstruction/synthesis of the concept maps (category formats) diagnostic models were developed which omitted the narratives of the women but were explained in and of themselves through the subcategories. There are four: core of depression (CD) with five subcategories (unfulfillment wish, helplessness, hopelessness, unpleasant feelings and psychomotor retardation/hyper-arousal), the routes of entry (RE1) and (RE2) and motivational systems with four subcategories (system attachment, narcissism, sensual/sexual feelings and hetero/self-preservation).

1) With respect to the core of depression, the five criteria were present in ten women – unfulfillment wish, helplessness, hopelessness, unpleasant feelings

and psychomotor retardation – in two of the women the last criterion was hyper-arousal. This allowed me to confirm that within *unfulfillment wish* are four subcategories: the partner, the maternal figure, the paternal figure and the current pregnancy.

The dyad of *helplessness/hopelessness* was separated to define the mood of the patients. Although they are both interrelated, the mood of the patient appeared to differentiate between the narratives. Thus, both contain aspects related to the current pregnancy, current partner, the maternal role, the close family and abortion. The difference was also found in the subcategories of these five groups.

Unpleasant feelings was the largest of the five: all the women identified feelings of sadness, anger, despair, distress and crying as well as other symptoms related to their various stages in life. Lastly, psychomotor retardation was present in three subcategories: current pregnancy, partners and close family.

2) As for the routes of entry, four categories of (RE1) were present in the ten clinical cases. The way they were articulated started in traumatic external realities – different types of loss, both real and imaginary – that were directly related to the identification of parental figures, which modified the narcissistic disorders and ended with medical illnesses which required entry into the INPer. The latter was part of a traumatic external reality created by the loss of health.

Medical conditions are considered a category in themselves, but are also a subcategory –when a part of external reality is traumatic because of a loss of health before pregnancy– if identified as the main route of entry into depression for the current pregnancy. The latter categorisation led me to consider – without stating – that, after pregnancy, symptoms of depressive states may decrease or disappear in some women . While in other clinical cases they have been part of life for the patient even before pregnancy so this is only one factor in the articulation of their depression.

The other five routes of entry (RE2): persecutory anxiety, guilt, aggression, negative gender stereotypes and ego deficits, were present in some of the women. This makes each patient unique and their form of depression unrepeatable in other women. The Modular Transformational Modal of depressed pregnant women who suffer from severe socio-economic disadvantage is based on four routes of entry which are articulated with five others of a different type. Together they create depressive states, the introversion and repetition of depression which maintains the current state of depression and increases its likelihood to be maintained or return in the future.

3) With regard to the motivational systems, all four systems were present in the women. The type of attachment that prevailed was of insecurity/ anxiousness, in its two variants, anxiousness (n=6) and devaluation (n=4). The concern was inferred from the type of exaggerated or inappropriate response that was given by the patients about their mothers or the surrogate figures as well as the type of response they have towards their child or children. The women suffering from devaluation reported that their mothers or surrogate figures showed little interest in them, usually through abandonment, absence and/or the low self-esteem of the mother.

The narcissistic system confirmed that all depressed pregnant women have low self-esteem with its respective variants which, in relation to the *self*, can be seen as decreased self-esteem which is loosely cohesive and has negative and/or grandiose representations. In all of them the loss of ego was also identified in different ways: the most prevalent was disappointment in the partner or parental figures.

The sensual/sexual feelings system was clustered into four categories: sexual abuse in childhood/adolescence, the maternal figure displayed sensual pleasure, the maternal figure displayed no sensual pleasure and the figure displayed no substitute of sensual pleasure, each with its respective forms.

Finally, the hetero/self-preservation system in which more subtle differences were found: three women were characterised as having a hetero-preservation figure, and two women without hetero-preservation figures with their respective derivatives. These derivatives were grouped into five subcategories: a)Basic hetero/self-preservation and no psychic hetero/self-preservation; b)Basic hetero/self-preservation and no psychic self-preservation; c) Basic hetero/self-preservation and no psychic hetero-preservation; d) No basic hetero-preservation, basic hetero/self-preservation and no psychic hetero/self-preservation; e) No basic hetero-preservation, basic self-preservation and no basic or psychic hetero-preservation.

Hermeneutic Clinical Analysis

The hermeneutic clinical analysis yielded mixed results which are the third element of the hermeneutic spiral. Among them were the differential scheme, the attitude of the depressed pregnant women, intersubjective resonance and articulation of routes of entry into depression, the motivational systems and the core of depression of the specific person.

1) The differential scheme consisted of five categories: purpose, support networks, ego resources, mechanisms/management and close/extended family. It was the result of differences that were found in the accounts of the depressed patients, for example the identification of the type of object – rescuer, protective container – or the networks of support they had in their lives that provided some degree of ego-centred force/motivation to change. On the other hand, this provides new elements that can work in the here and now: the management and mechanisms that the women use in their depression or the roles assigned by their close or extended family or with those with whom they have lived for a long period. While these were not found in all women this could be a differential for the deconstruction of depressions present in pregnant women with severe socio-economic disadvantage because within them there is a way of rescuing them or helping them to manage the resource systems in their lives.

2) The attitude of depressed pregnant women with severe socio-economic disadvantages who come to the INPer are characterised by complex categories and sub-categories that are governed by the laws of a singular and rigid vision of a "dip" in a dual and *subjective time-frame* which constitutes both the time before and after a specific event changed the woman's life. Within the depressive system of the depressed pregnant woman the phenomenon was shown to be recursive. The patients described their symptoms as sadness, anger, despair, distress and crying, sometimes combined with the feeling that they are not quite themselves and not the protagonists of their depression: often their *accounts* were in the third person or gave the impression that their feelings were alien to them. On other occasions they seemed so disconnected that their voices were monotonous, boring, dull, slow and lifeless.

3) The intersubjetive resonance was composed of the *automatic resonance*, achieved while listening to the interview, and the reflexive resonance of the Hermeneutic Clinical Analysis (HCA). Of the components found in the automatic resonance four were identified: the attitude of the interviewee during the interview, their tone of voice, the attitude of the interviewer and the interaction between the interviewer and interviewee. When this was formulated, three of the components combine to activate the fourth: the tone of voice and attitude during the interview activate the

attitude of the interviewer or the interviewee's attitude arouses a reaction in the interviewer which, in turn, returns to the isomorphic system, which is not detected during the interview. These dyadic interactions, which took place during the interview, were characterised by saturation/repetition, rebound/disinterest and passive/active. The *reflexive resonance* identified the unique/rigid vision of the accounts: that it can be depressed, fanciful (like a fairy tale), disorganised, ambivalent, abused, polarised or in denial. In their accounts, the women sent messages that discussed wanting to be saved or protected, that they were victims or that nothing had happened. The same resonance – action, thought, emotion, the account of the patient or the operating referential scheme, that showed that the process of thought, feeling and background were generated by the account – written or spoken – given by the patient. An important part of this latter process was that the identified resonances varied according to each life story. While a woman may provide abundant theoretical resonances, other woman can produce few resonances. These lead to a level of various hypotheses, and another level of emotions and interactions. These will vary depending on the attitude and autoanalysis of each interviewer, which could be seen as a "blind spot" for conducting and analysing interviews.

The diagnosis refers to psychoanalytic authors such as Sigmund Freud and/or Melanie Klein. Only two patients demonstrated the symbiotic phase of Margaret Mahler. Regression and/or attachment to the paranoid/ schizophrenic or anal/sadistic stages or from object libido to narcissistic libido were constant in most cases. The ambivalence toward the object and the split structural/defence mechanism are the most commonly detected phases in pregnant women which, with their respective variants, were diagnosed by the two authors above.

4) Within these articulations were the core components of depression, the routes of entry into depression, motivational systems and new categories, categories and subcategories that are combined with each other, sometimes as a component hierarchy for other components. The medical condition of entry is via its own subcategory of traumatic external reality (a pathway may trigger other pathways) which may relate to identification with parental figures, persecutory anxieties, guilt or narcissistic disorders – which are articulated within the core of depression. The loss of the ideal that is generated by unfulfillment wish is connected to the other categories of CD and routes of entry into depression, which transform themselves and others (see chapter on analysis of results).

Finally, the MTM model that became the guiding principle for this research added new categories and tools that revealed the inter-specific characteristics of depressed pregnant Mexican women with severe socio-economic disadvantages who came to the INPer for medical care.

Discussion & Conclusions

This research went a long way; the text and the reader were always involved and articulated themselves. Within this combination was a hermeneutic legacy that may be useful for a future dialectic between a speaker and a listener as we already know that there is a specific message that can be deciphered in depressed pregnant women with severe socio-economic disadvantages. The women who took part in the research were not *any* women who came for prenatal care but rather women who, for many years, have been exposed to and have gained many experiences – the vast majority of them not resolved – who have financial problems and a high-risk pregnancy. Therefore, they are a *specific* population which needs assistance, help and support *during* their pregnancies.

The structural evolution of pregnant women attending the INPer, when they are *heard*, is subdued: their voices are monotonous, complaining, and often give the impression that they are *not* the ones giving the account but rather the narrator is a third-person character outside of the story. They cannot be heard because their voices are low, slow, quiet, in silence and self-absorbed. Other women *seem* normal, happy and lively, and give the impression that they have no problems and, while telling a sad story, release a giggle which makes them seem cold, distant, tough and resistant: they give the impression that their feelings "bounce". The act of reading can be, for the reader/listener, heavy, overpowering, overwhelming, boring and sometimes difficult to concentrate. The reflexion that arises here is that at some point in life (to a greater or lesser degree) the majority of people have seen and heard about the same form of problems. The question is: why are these women different from the rest of us? The answers are varied, each with its own details and specificities which make them unique. What they do have in common, though, are the defensive visions and mechanisms they have in their lives, and everyday situations which have been established as rigid structures; with a stagnant and viscous libido.

In conclusion, the work done in this research confirms that low-income pregnant women show, in the core of depression, four criteria which are maintained by the principal function of the traumatic external reality, identification with parental figures, narcissistic disorders and medical illness which, in combination with the five other categories cause the individuality of the depressions. The motivational systems gave a closer approximation of why depressed pregnant Mexican women have low self-esteem, characterised by a *self* which induces a reduced or negative representation or one that is inconsistent or falsely grandiose; most of the women did not feel that they had the ability to self-conserve their psyche, did not feel the love, affection or sensual pleasure they were given or, if they did feel it, it was lost with hindsight, had not been recovered and they did not want to recover it. In relation to the unfulfillment wish located in the CD, depression rebuilds itself. Through these means it is possible to answer the first two research questions of this research. The contribution is then (the third research question), the ability of the reader/speaker to use their *"automatic reflexes"* to detect a possible early core of depression – which is confirmed by the GPIDS (Lartigue, 2005) – in these women and route them into specialised care.

In this way we can obtain dialectic between the speaker and the listener, including pregnant women and health personnel (doctors, nurses, social workers, psychotherapists, psychologists, among others). Through the account, manner of speech, a consultation conversation or check-up it may be possible to see, as a result of the tone of voice, content of the account given, attitude of the pregnant woman and the resonance and attitude of the interviewer/listener, the possible depression. This can subsequently be confirmed using instruments and interviews. The most critical factor is that if depression is suspected, the suspicion must be acted upon immediately as *timing* for these women is very important. To end, one can only emphasise that the proposal of this research is only an approximation toward the understanding of depression in women with a high risk pregnancy and who are socially vulnerable that come to the INPer for their health care. The use of intersubjective tools which included the categories of the MTM was developed through hermeneutic evolution.

References

BLEICHMAR, H (1997). *Avances en psicoterapia psicoanalítica. Hacia una técnica de intervenciones específicas*, Buenos Aires: Paidós.

LARTIGUE, T. (2005). Guía para la entrevista clínica psicodinámica de los estados depresivos con base en el modelo de Hugo Bleichmar. *Aperturas Psicoanalíticas*, Diciembre. (21)

LARTIGUE, T. *ET AL.*(2007). La depresión materna. Su efecto en las interacciones madre – hijo en el primer año de vida. *Cuadernos de Psicoanálisis.* XL (1 y 2): 131- 166.

MARTÍNEZ, JL. (2002). La resonancia, mecanoescrito, México, D.F.

MARTÍNEZ, M. (1996). *Comportamiento humano: nuevos métodos de investigación.* México: Trillas, 167-188.

PARRES, R. (1964). Guía para la elaboración de la historia clínica. Material inédito, Clínica de la Asociación Psicoanalítica Mexicana.

PRADO, G. (1992) *Creación, Recepción y Efecto. Una aproximación hermenéutica a la obra literaria.* México: Diana.

SILVA, E. (2005), Paul Ricoeur y los desplazamientos de la hermenéutica, *Teología y Vida,* Vol. XLVI: 167 - 205

Apendix 1

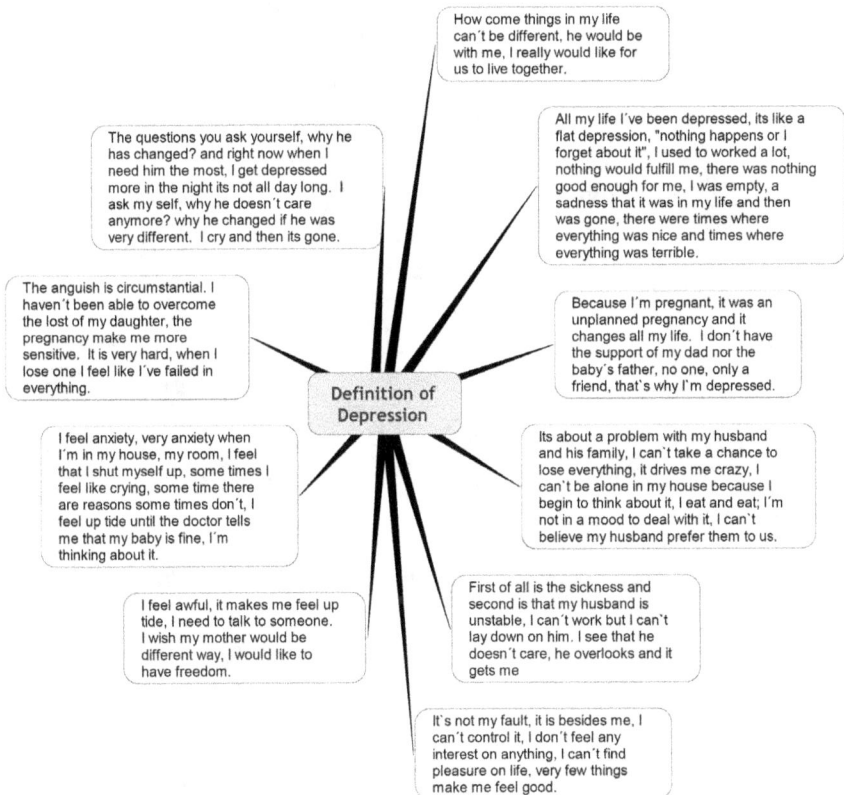

How come things in my life can´t be different, he would be with me, I really would like for us to live together.

The questions you ask yourself, why he has changed? and right now when I need him the most, I get depressed more in the night its not all day long. I ask my self, why he doesn´t care anymore? why he changed if he was very different. I cry and then its gone.

All my life I´ve been depressed, its like a flat depression, "nothing happens or I forget about it", I used to worked a lot, nothing would fulfill me, there was nothing good enough for me, I was empty, a sadness that it was in my life and then was gone, there were times where everything was nice and times where everything was terrible.

The anguish is circumstantial. I haven´t been able to overcome the lost of my daughter, the pregnancy make me more sensitive. It is very hard, when I lose one I feel like I´ve failed in everything.

Because I´m pregnant, it was an unplanned pregnancy and it changes all my life. I don´t have the support of my dad nor the baby´s father, no one, only a friend, that´s why I´m depressed.

Definition of Depression

I feel anxiety, very anxiety when I´m in my house, my room, I feel that I shut myself up, some times I feel like crying, some time there are reasons some times don´t, I feel up tide until the doctor tells me that my baby is fine, I´m thinking about it.

Its about a problem with my husband and his family, I can´t take a chance to lose everything, it drives me crazy, I can´t be alone in my house because I begin to think about it, I eat and eat; I´m not in a mood to deal with it, I can´t believe my husband prefer them to us.

I feel awful, it makes me feel up tide, I need to talk to someone. I wish my mother would be different way, I would like to have freedom.

First of all is the sickness and second is that my husband is unstable, I can´t work but I can´t lay down on him. I see that he doesn´t care, he overlooks and it gets me

It´s not my fault, it is besides me, I can´t control it, I don´t feel any interest on anything, I can´t find pleasure on life, very few things make me feel good.

Apendix 2

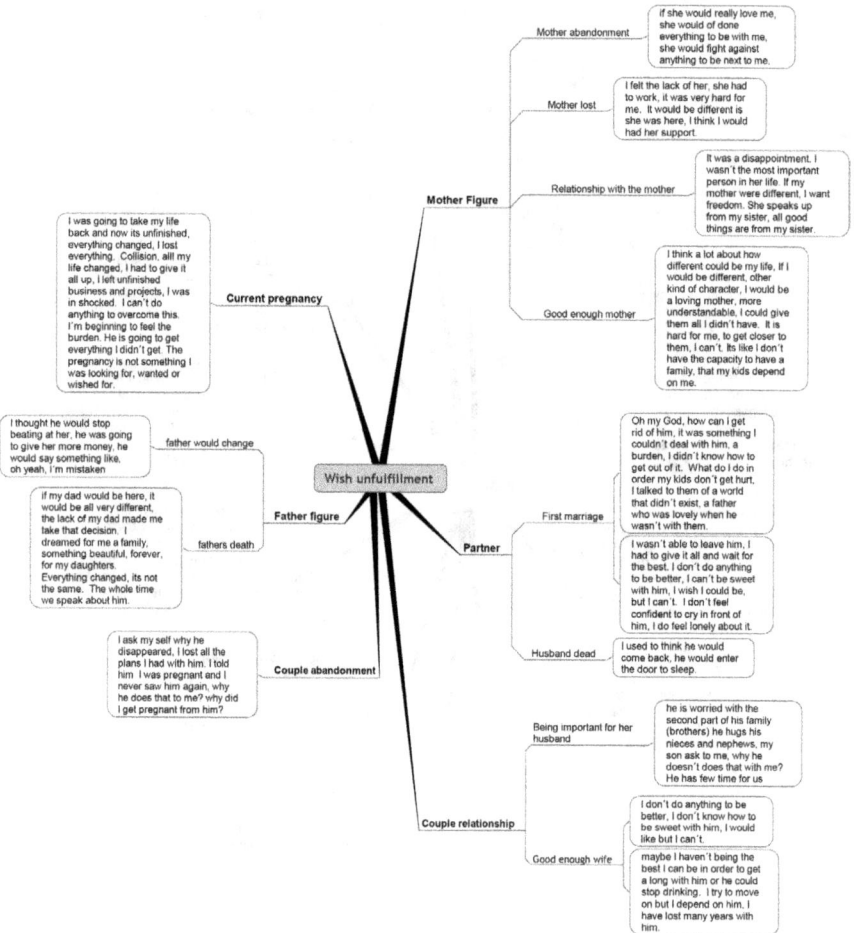

Apendix 3

Intersubjective Resonance

During interview (automatic resonance)

Attitude during the interview
- runny nose
- disgust, a tissue is offered
- slow answer or "nothing happens"
- despair, a wish to end the interview rapidly
- "reflect" in the story
- there is interest in the story, which is long, thorough and repetitive

Voice tone
- slow, monotone, paused, sadness, difficulty to connect one theme with another
- there is affect, normal, connect one theme with another

Interaction
- dyad
  - saturation/repetition
  - bounce/disinterest
  - passive/active

Resonance
- emotions: despair, anxiety, apathy, strangeness, boring, shock, disgust.
- action: distancing, rejecting, limited, stagnation, disinterest, repetitive.
- thinking: stagnation, split, dissociation, diffusion, thinking block.

Attitude of the interviewer
- it goes from one theme to another, difficulty to concentrate and to connect
- empathy, there is time to elaborate, it shows interest in the story.

During hermeneutic clinical analysis (reflexive resonance)

Visions
- fantasies (fairy tales)
  - they wish there were a prince, need to be rescue from their lives, protected or contained. There is a witch, who makes their live impossible.
- depressive
  - overwhelming/suffocating/trapped, victim/limited/despair, uncertain/ambivalent/uncertain, victim/rejected/distance, unnamable/incomprehensible/uncertain, third person/strangeness/distance.
- disorganized
  - saturation/confusion
  - resistance/diffusion
- ambivalence
  - splits/despair/bounce
- denial
- polarized
  - all or nothing, life or death, with me or against me, in or out.

Resonance
- emotions: despair, anxiety, anger, apathy, uncertainty, ambivalence, strangeness, boring, shock.
- action: distance, rejecting, limited, stagnation, disinterest, repetitive.
- thinking: stagnation, split, dissociation, diffusion, thinking block.
- referential operative scheme
  - psychoanalytical authors
  - systemic authors
  - family therapy authors
- in the story telling
  - it feels like they are not themselves who is telling the story, alien to them, its a third person, depersonalization, bouncing stage, bounces, disbief, prank, repetitive, it evokes phantasy or doubts.

Diagnostic
- regression to a schizoid paranoid phase, anal/sadistic phase, split structure.
- melancholia

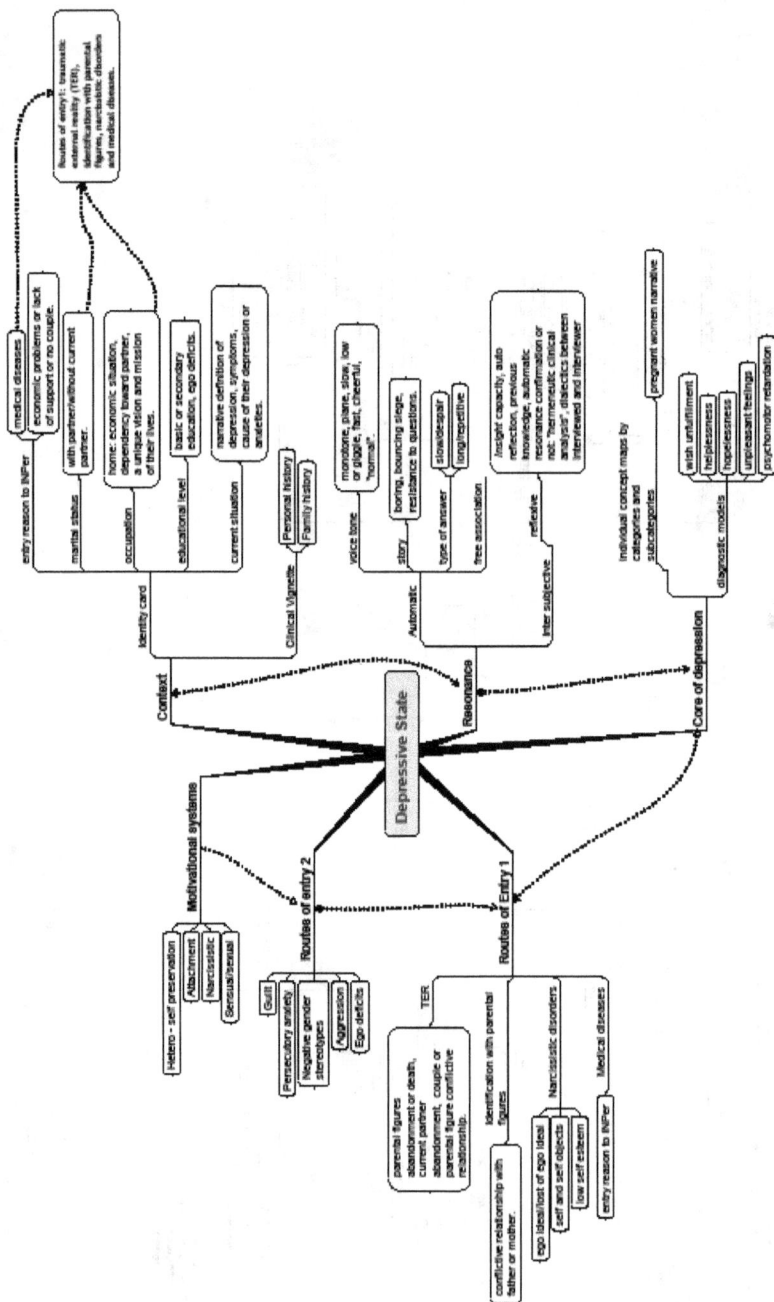

Apendix 4

Routes of entry1: traumatic external reality (TER), identification with parental figures, narcissistic disorders and medical disease.

medical disease

economic problems or lack of support or no couple.

entry reason to INPer

with partner/without current partner.

marital status

home: economic situation, dependency toward partner, a unique vision and mission of their lives.

occupation

basic or secondary education, ego deficits.

educational level

narrative definition of depression, symptoms, cause of their depression or anxieties.

current situation

Personal history
Family history

Identity card

Clinical Vignette

monotone, plane, slow, low or giggle, fast, cheerful, "normal".

voice tone

boring, bouncing step, resistance to questions.

story

slow/despair
long/repetitive

type of answer

free association

Automatic

Insight capacity, auto reflection, previous knowledge, automatic resonance confirmation or not: "hermeneutic clinical analysis": dialectics between interviewed and interviewer

reflexive

Inter subjective

Individual concept maps by categories and subcategories

pregnant women narrative

wish unfulfillment
helplessness
hopelessness
unpleasant feelings
psychomotor retardation

diagnostic models

Context

Resonance

Core of depression

Depressive State

Motivational systems

Routes of entry 2

Routes of Entry 1

Hetero - self preservation
Attachment
Narcissistic
Sensual/sexual

Guilt

Persecutory anxiety

Negative gender stereotypes
Aggression
Ego deficits

TER

parental figures abandonment or death, current partner abandonment, couple or parental figure conflictive relationship.

Identification with parental figures

Narcissistic disorders

Medical diseases

conflictive relationship with father or mother.

ego ideal/lost of ego ideal
self and self objects
low self esteem

entry reason to INPer

19

Presence and Correlates of Suicide Ideation Among Mexican Postpartum Women[1]

José Cuenca

Introduction

Past research suggests that individuals with a history of suicide ideation are at an increased risk of attempting or committing suicide (Brezo *et al.*, 2007; Hawton & van Heeringen, 2009). Among postpartum women, suicide in the first postpartum year appears to be an uncommon event when compared with the number of suicides of non-postpartum women (Appleby, 1991; Gissler, Hemminki & Lönnqvist, 1996). However, postpartum women with a psychiatric disorder appear to be at an increased risk of attempting suicide (Austin, Kildea & Sullivan, 2007). This suggests an urgent need to further investigate suicide ideation among postpartum women with a psychiatric disorder in order to prevent suicidal behaviour.

Few studies have investigated suicide ideation among postpartum women. Among these studies, Pinheiro *et al.* (2008) examined two groups of postpartum women: women with depression and women randomly selected from the general population. Of the 317 women with depression, those with a previous history of attempted suicide were more likely to exhibit suicide ideation. Of the 386 women from the general population, those who screened positive on a depression test were more likely to exhibit suicide ideation.

Although relatively few studies have examined suicide ideation among postpartum women, there is indirect evidence from studies on pregnant women suggesting possible correlates of suicide ideation in postpartum women. A study conducted with 383 pregnant women attending a clinic

1 This chapter is based in part on the author's MSc dissertation. The dissertation was supervised by Dr Anne Kouvonen at the Institute of Work Health and Organisations (IWHO) of the University of Nottingham, and is part of a global investigation, entitled "Maternal Depression: Its Effect on Mother-Child Interactions in the First Year of Life" (Lartigue et al., 2007).

for psychiatric disorder found that women with either depression or an unplanned pregnancy were more likely to report suicide ideation (Newport, Levey, Pennell, Ragan & Stowe, 2007).

Taken together, past research on suicide ideation among postpartum and pregnant women suggest that depression and an unplanned pregnancy are associated with suicide ideation. Because there appears to be limited research on suicide ideation among postpartum women, particularly research using longitudinal designs, it seemed important to investigate the presence, course and correlates of suicide ideation among this population.

The present study

The main purpose of the study reported here was to examine the presence and course of suicide ideation among postpartum women. A secondary aim of the study was to examine possible correlates of suicide ideation during the postpartum. As part of a large longitudinal multi-cohort study of maternal depression, three groups of postpartum women answered the Edinburgh Postnatal Depression Scale (EPDS; Cox, Holden & Sagovsky, 1987) two weeks after childbirth, and during the 1st, 3rd, 6th, 9th and 12th month postpartum. The groups studied were formed by postpartum women with: (a) depression; (b) depression and a personality disorder; and (c) without a psychiatric disorder.

Methods

Procedure and participants

Data were gathered as part of a large longitudinal multi-cohort study of maternal depression. The research was conducted in Mexico City at the National Institute of Perinatology "Isidro Espinosa de los Reyes" (INPer), which specialises in reproductive problems and treat women and their partners who do not have access to social security. Women at 28 weeks gestation (± two weeks) who attended the INPer for antenatal care were invited to participate in a longitudinal study while waiting to see a clinician. The study was an explained in detail prior to asking for participants' informed consent to participate. Additional details on the methods of recruitment and sampling for the study can be found in Lartigue et al. (2007).

During pregnancy participants were interviewed using the Structured Clinical Interview for DSM-IV Axis I Disorders and Axis II Personality Disorders. On the day of the interview, participants answered on-site questionnaires addressing demographic information and psychological characteristics. Based on the responses to the Structured Clinical Interview, participants were considered as pertaining to three diagnostic groups: (a) depression (n = 53) (major depressive disorder, dysthymic disorder, depressive disorder not otherwise specified or depressive disorder due to a general medical condition); (a) depression and a personality disorder (n = 52) (same depressive disorders and *at least one* personality disorder); and (c) without a psychiatric disorder (n = 53). Exclusion criteria consisted of women with a current or past psychotic disorder, a neurological disease or multiple pregnancies.

Women of the three diagnostic groups were asked to attend the INPer six times during the postpartum to complete EPDS (Cox *et al.*, 1987) and other psychological measures. The six assessment points during the postpartum were at: (a) two weeks; (b) one month; (c) three months; (d) six months; (e) nine months; and (f) 12 months postpartum. At each assessment point, sample sizes in each group varied because participants missed their follow-up appointment, could not be located or stopped participating. For each group, the number of participants who completed *at least one* assessment during the postpartum was: 44 for the group with depression; 41 for the group with depression and a personality disorder; and 41 for the group without a psychiatric disorder.

Measures

Demographic information. Participants completed a demographic questionnaire that is routinely administered at intake in the INPer. The questionnaire was included to obtain background information about the participants, such as age, socio-economic status, marital status and obstetric information.

Suicide ideation. Participants completed the Spanish version of the EPDS (Cox *et al.*, 1987) that Ortega, Lartigue & Figueroa (2001) validated for the Mexican population . The EPDS is a 10-item self-report questionnaire designed to measure depressive symptoms among childbearing women. Item 10 of the EPDS (i.e., "The thought of harming myself has occurred to me") was used to assess suicide ideation. Response options for this item were "never", "hardly ever", "sometimes" and "yes, quite often". A response other than "never" was considered as an indicator of suicide ideation.

Results

The demographic characteristics of the three groups of postpartum women are presented in Table A. Overall, the groups were quite similar on the demographic characteristics examined. However, the groups differed significantly between each other in terms of socio-economic status and unplanned pregnancy. Using Pearson's $\chi 2$, follow-up pairwise comparisons were conducted to evaluate differences between the groups on these variables. A Bonferroni correction for three comparisons resulted in α = .016. In terms of unplanned pregnancy, the only pairwise difference that was significant was between the group without a psychiatric disorder and the group with depression; in that women with depression were more likely to have an unplanned pregnancy. In terms of socio-economic status, the pairwise difference between the group without a psychiatric disorder and the group with depression was marginally significant.

Table A

Demographic Characteristics of Postpartum Women

	No psychiatric disorder		Depression		Depression and personality disorder		Test statistic
	(n = 41)		(n = 44)		(n = 41)		
	M	(SD)	M	(SD)	M	(SD)	
Age in years	30.8	(6.2)	30.1	(6.9)	29.6	(6.5)	$F(2, 123) = 0.33$
	n	(%)	n	(%)	n	(%)	
Socio-economic status							$\chi^2(2) = 6.66*$
Low	7	(17.1)	18	(40.9)	16	(39.0)	
Medium	34	(82.9)	26	(59.1)	25	(61.0)	
Education							$\chi^2(4) = 5.36$
Primary school	11	(26.8)	14	(31.8)	17	(41.5)	
High school	24	(58.5)	23	(52.3)	14	(34.1)	
College	6	(14.6)	7	(15.9)	10	(24.4)	
Marital status							$\chi^2(2) = 4.55$
Single	5	(12.2)	11	(25.0)	13	(31.7)	
Married or cohabitating	36	(87.8)	33	(75.0)	28	(68.3)	
Unplanned pregnancy	24	(58.5)	38	(86.4)	31	(75.6)	$\chi^2(2) = 8.60*$
*p < .05.							

The first aim of the study was to examine the presence and course of suicide ideation during the first postpartum year. Table B shows the number and percentage of cases with suicide ideation at different postpartum periods. During the first postpartum year, the presence of suicide ideation was low among the group without a psychiatric disorder. In contrast, during the first postpartum year, the presence of suicide ideation was considerably higher among the group with depression and the group with depression and a personality disorder. In the group with depression, the presence of suicide ideation ranged from 14.3% (at three months postpartum) to 22.2% (at six months postpartum). In the group with depression and a personality disorder, the presence of suicide ideation ranged from 9.5% (at nine months postpartum) to 26.9% (at three months postpartum). Of note, in any of the postpartum periods examined did the proportion of women with suicide ideation differ significantly between the group with depression and the group with depression and a personality disorder This finding suggests that during the first postpartum year, the presence of suicide ideation was similar in the group with depression and the group with depression and a personality disorder.

Table B
Presence of Suicide Ideation During the First Year Postpartum

Postpartum period	No psychiatric disorder	Depression	Depression and personality disorder
Two weeks	n = 26	n = 23	n = 27
Suicide ideation, n (%)	0	4 (17.4)	7 (25.9)
One month	n = 18	n = 31	n = 21
Suicide ideation, n (%)	0	5 (16.1)	5 (23.8)
Three months	n = 30	n = 28	n = 26
Suicide ideation, n (%)	1 (3.3)	4 (14.3)	7 (26.9)
Six months	n = 26	n = 27	n = 26
Suicide ideation, n (%)	0	6 (22.2)	3 (11.5)
Nine months	n = 25	n = 29	n = 21
Suicide ideation, n (%)	2 (8.0)	5 (17.2)	2 (9.5)
Twelve months	n = 23	n = 20	n = 22
Suicide ideation, n (%)	1 (4.3)	4 (20.0)	4 (18.2)

Figure C presents the percentage of women with suicide ideation from each diagnostic group plotted across the six assessment points in the postpartum. During the first postpartum year, the presence of suicide ideation was consistently higher among the group with depression and the group with depression and a personality disorder. Note, however, that the presence of suicide ideation among the group without a psychiatric disorder tended to increase during the first postpartum year. A similar pattern of results emerged in the group with depression, where the presence of suicide ideation increased towards the end of the postpartum year. In the group with depression and a personality disorder the presence of suicide ideation decreased sharply at six months postpartum, but it increased towards the end of the first postpartum year.

Figure C

Percentage of Women with Suicide Ideation During the First Year Postpartum

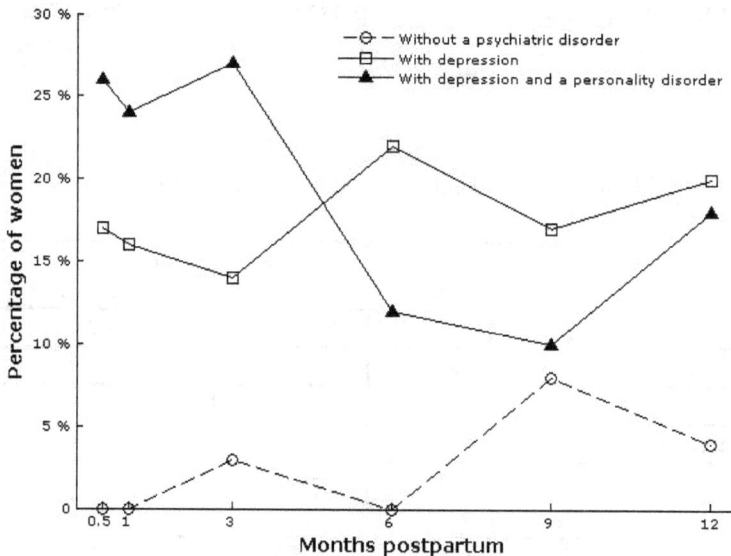

The second aim of the study was to examine correlates of suicide ideation during the first postpartum year. Since the group without a psychiatric disorder had few cases with suicide ideation during the first year postpartum, data from this group was not included in the analysis. To increase statistical power, the groups of women with depression and women with depression and a personality disorder were combined to form a single group. In addition, a case with suicide ideation was considered if any member of this newly formed group reported suicide ideation at least once during the first year postpartum. This resulted in a sample size of 84 women with depression with or without a personality disorder, of which 25 cases reported suicide ideation at least once during the postpartum.

Table D
Comparison of Postpartum Women with a Psychiatric Disorder

	Postpartum women with psychiatric disorder					
	No suicide ideation		Suicide ideation		Test statistic
	(n = 59)		(n = 25)		
	M	(SD)	M	(SD)	
Age in years	30.3	(6.9)	28.8	(6.0)	$t(82) = 0.94$
	n	(%)	n	(%)	
Socio-economic status					$\chi^2(1) = 6.40*$
Low	18	(30.5)	15	(60.0)	
Medium	41	(69.5)	10	(40.0)	
Education					$\chi^2(2) = 0.54$
Primary school	22	(37.3)	9	(36.0)	
High school	24	(40.7)	12	(48.0)	
College	13	(22.0)	4	(16.0)	
Marital status					$\chi^2(1) = 0.38$
Single	15	(25.4)	8	(32.0)	
Married or cohabitating	44	(74.6)	17	(68.0)	
Unplanned pregnancy	44	(74.6)	24	(96.0)	Fisher's exact test*
*p < .05					

As Table D shows, women who reported suicide ideation at least once during the first year postpartum were more likely to be from a low socio-economic status and to report an unplanned pregnancy. To examine whether these variables predicted suicide ideation during the first year postpartum, a logistic regression analysis was conducted with suicide ideation as outcome and socio-economic status and unplanned pregnancy as predictors. The logistic regression revealed that low socio-economic status was a significant predictor of suicide ideation during the first year postpartum (odds ratio [OR] = 3.37, 95% confidence interval [CI] = 1.23 – 9.2); but unplanned pregnancy was not (OR = 8.02, 95% CI = 0.97 – 66.41).

Discussion

This study set out to examine the presence and course of suicide ideation among postpartum women. In addition, the study investigated possible correlates of suicide ideation in the first year postpartum. Three broad results were found: (a) during the first year postpartum, suicide ideation was consistently higher among women with depression and women with depression and a personality disorder; (b) the presence of suicide ideation among women with depression and women with depression and a personality disorder was quite similar; and (c) after combining these two groups to form a single group, low socio-economic status predicted the presence suicide ideation at least once during the first year postpartum.

With regard to the first finding, the presence of suicide ideation during the first year postpartum was high among women with a psychiatric disorder; specifically, among women with depression and with depression and a personality disorder. This finding seems broadly consistent with the study reported by Pinheiro *et al.* (2008) in which postpartum women with depression were likely to report suicide ideation. In addition, the present finding seems consistent with general population studies (e.g., Nock *et al.* 2008) in which a psychiatric disorder has been found to be associated with suicide ideation.

The second result was that during the first year postpartum the presence of suicide ideation was relatively similar among women with depression and women with depression and a personality disorder. To the author's knowledge, past research has not examined the presence of suicide ideation in postpartum women with depression and a personality disorder. Yet, based on studies with non-postpartum or non-pregnant women (e.g., Hawton *et al.*, 2003), individuals with a co-morbid disorder may be expected to be at higher risk of experiencing suicide ideation than individuals with only one disorder. Future studies are needed to determine whether postpartum women with a co-morbid disorder are at an increased risk of experiencing suicide ideation in the first year postpartum.

The third result was that when women with depression and women with depression and a personality disorder were considered as a single group, low socio-economic status predicted reporting suicide ideation at least once during the first year postpartum. This finding is consistent with past research that suggests that deprivation is associated with suicidal behaviour (Martikainen, Maki & Blomgren, 2004). However, it is unclear *why* postpartum women with a psychiatric disorder and from a low socio-economic status were likely to experience suicide ideation. One possibility is that women from a low socio-economic status are exposed to stressors that contribute to suicide ideation. O'Campo *et al.* (1995) found that women in the childbearing year who lived in neighbourhoods with high unemployment levels were at risk of experiencing physical violence. The association between low socio-economic status and suicide ideation among postpartum women with a psychiatric disorder highlights the need to further investigate protective factors among a vulnerable population.

The findings of the study reported in this chapter should be interpreted in light of a number of limitations. First, combining the group of women with depression and the group of women with depression and a personality disorder increased the sample size and the number of cases who reported suicide ideation at least once during the postpartum. However, this strategy does not allow examining which characteristics render women more vulnerable to exhibit suicide ideation at specific periods of the postpartum. Second, the present study did not examine other variables, such as a history of suicide attempt, that might help to better understand suicide ideation among postpartum women. Third, although previous studies have used item-10 of the EPDS to examine suicide ideation, this item may not reflect intent to commit suicide (Lindahl *et al.*, 2005). Future studies using more comprehensive measures of suicide ideation are required to examine its presence among postpartum women. Finally, the findings may not be generalised due to the relatively small sample sizes and the characteristics of the sample.

The main clinical implication is that the identification of women with depression and depression and a personality disorder may be a central task in the management of postpartum women who may be at risk of attempting or committing suicide. In addition, women from a low socio-economic status may require special care and attention during the postpartum; possibly by exploring possible stressors in their social and family environment. Because postpartum women without a psychiatric disorder also exhibited suicide ideation, this population may require assessment of suicide ideation to monitor its occurrence during the first year postpartum.

In conclusion, while the findings of the study are mostly based on descriptive data, the presence of suicide ideation was high among postpartum women with depression and women with depression and a personality disorder. This highlights the importance of closely monitoring and implementing intervention strategies with this population to reduce the risk of attempted or completed suicide. Among these women, those from a low socio-economic status were likely to experience suicide ideation at least once during the postpartum, further suggesting that this subgroup may require special attention and care during the first postpartum year.

References

APPLEBY, L. (1991). Suicide during pregnancy and in the first postnatal year. *British Medical Journal, 302,* 137-140.

AUSTIN, M. P., KILDEA, S., & SULLIVAN, E. (2007). Maternal mortality and psychiatric morbidity in the perinatal period: Challenges and opportunities for prevention in the Australian setting. *The Medical Journal of Australia, 186,* 364-367.

BREZO, J., PARIS, J., TREMBLAY, R., VITARO, F., HÉBERT, M., & TURECKI, G. (2007). Identifying correlates of suicide attempts in suicidal ideators: A population-based study. *Psychological Medicine, 37,* 1551-1562.

COX, J. L., HOLDEN, J. M., & SAGOVSKY, R. (1987). Detection of postnatal depression: Development of the 10-item Edinburgh Postnatal Depression Scale. *British Journal of Psychiatry, 150,* 782-786.

CUENCA, J. (2008). Suicidal ideation in the postpartum: Prevalence and risk factors among Mexican women from a low socioeconomic status (Master's thesis). University of Nottingham, Nottingham, United Kingdom.

GISSLER, M., HEMMINKI, E., & LÖNNQVIST, J. (1996). Suicides after pregnancy in Finland, 1987-94: Register linkage study. *British Medical Journal, 313,* 1431-1434.

HAWTON, K., HOUSTON, K., HAW, C., TOWNSEND, E., & HARRISS, L. (2003). Comorbidity of axis I and axis II disorders in patients who attempted suicide. *American Journal of Psychiatry, 160,* 1494-1500.

HAWTON, K., & VAN HEERINGEN, K. (2009). Suicide. Lancet, 373, 1372-1381.

LARTIGUE, T., GONZÁLEZ, I., CÓRDOVA, A., VÁZQUEZ, M., NAVA, A. A., CHÁVEZ, M. *ET AL.* (2007). La depresión maternal: Su efecto en las interacciones madre-hijo en el primer año de vida. [Maternal depression: Its effect on mother-infant interactions in the first year of life]. *Cuadernos de Psicoanálisis*, XL (1-2), 131-166.

LARTIGUE, T., CASANOVA, G, ORTIZ, J. Y ARANDA, C. (2004). Indicadores de malestar y depresión en mujeres embarazadas con ITS-VIH/SIDA. *Perinatología y Reproducción Humana*, 18 (2): 73-90.

LARTIGUE, T. Y VÁZQUEZ, G. (2009). Validación de tres instrumentos de tamizaje EPDS, GHQ y STAI-S en embarazadas. *Cuadernos de Psicoanálisis*, XLII (3-4): 135-152.

LINDAHL, V., PEARSON, J. L., & COLPE, L. (2005). Prevalence of suicidality during pregnancy and the postpartum. *Archives of Women's Mental Health, 8,* 77-87.

MARTIKAINEN, P., MÄKI, N., & BLOMGREN, J. (2004). The effects of area and individual social characteristics on suicide risk: A multilevel study of relative contribution and effect modification. *European Journal of Population, 20,* 323-350.

NEWPORT, D. J., LEVEY, L. C., PENNELL, P. B., RAGAN, K., & STOWE, Z. N. (2007). Suicidal ideation in pregnancy: Assessment and clinical implications. *Archives of Women's Mental Health, 10,* 181-187.

NOCK, M.K., BORGES, G., BROMET, E.J., CHA, C.B., KESSLER, R.C., & LEE, S. (2008). Suicide and suicidal behavior. Epidemiologic Reviews, 30, 133-154.

O'CAMPO, P., GIELEN, A. C., FADEN, R. R., XUE, X., KASS, N., & WANG, M. C. (1995). Violence by male partners against women during the childbearing year: A contextual analysis. *American Journal of Public Health, 85,* 1092-1097.

ORTEGA, L., LARTIGUE, T., & FIGUEROA, M. E. (2001). Prevalencia de depresión, a través de la Escala de Depresión Perinatal de Edinburgh (EPDS), en una muestra de mujeres mexicanas embarazadas [Prevalence of depression, using the Edinburgh Perinatal Depression Scale (EPDS), in a sample of Mexican pregnant women]. *Perinatología y Reproducción Humana, 15,* 11-20.

PINHEIRO, R. T., DA SILVA, R. A., MAGALHÃES, P. V. S., HORTA, B. L., & PINHEIRO, K. A. T. (2008). Two studies on suicidality in the postpartum. *Acta Psychiatrica Scandinavica, 118,* 160-163

20

Dissociative Phenomena during Pregnancy and the Post-partum: the Mother, the Infant and the Family

J. Martín Maldonado-Durán, Manuel Morales Monsalve,
Kenia Gómez, Ahmed Maher, Matthew Brown
and Ángela Camacho-Durán

Initial presentation: Beyond depression, anxiety and mood instability

In the process of developing a perinatal mental health consultation service for women and their partners at very high psychosocial risk in a large inner city general hospital, we were struck by the complex and very severe nature of the psychopathology observed. The clinicians were prepared to deal with commonly observed problems (Maldonado-Durán *et al.* 1998) such as pre and post-partum depression, high anxiety about the pregnancy and fear of delivery, fear of becoming a mother and feeling overwhelmed with the enormous care needs of the newborn. However, these problems in their "simple form" were encountered very rarely in the clients: the reality in the field was much more multifaceted and complicated. A majority of the women evaluated exhibited multiple, chronic and severe difficulties. Eliminar espacios en los punto y aparte por favor

A review of over 100 cases of women evaluated in this service (submitted), showed the complex nature of these situations: the women themselves gave as presenting problems, issues like "depression", "mood swings" "constant nervousness" and many said they had "bipolar disorder". However, as we evaluated in depth the nature of these problems, we were faced with much more complicated phenomena. The clientele of our service is an "inner city" population, of very low socio-economical status (a proportion of the women were homeless and lived in shelters), and who have very little or no psychosocial support. Most women live in very stressful conditions and often depend on the "welfare system" to deal with their pregnancy and the needs of the baby. They experience almost constantly a number of stressors, due to the uncertainty of access to food, housing, health care and other essentials, in addition to a chronic baggage of chronic deprivation, transgenerational poverty, and being "trapped" in cycles of disadvantage. Of the 100 women, 56% had antecedent of some form of abuse or neglect during childhood. Over a fourth informed they had experienced physical abuse. A significant number (28%) had endured sexual abuse during childhood, usually by other men living in the house, such as stepfathers or even the biological father. Some of them had suffered the abuse for years. Many felt unprotected by their mother figure, who "did not know, did not want to know"or "did not do anything about it", in order not to lose the relationship with their partner, sacrificing, so to speak, their child.

Also, a high proportion had experienced neglect (55%) and antipathy (56%) by the parenting figures. The long term effects of chronic neglect are a seldom studied phenomenon, but it may have as negative effects as chronic abuse. In our sample, women reported indifference on the part of the caregivers, they did not keep track of the child, did not know their whereabouts and also did not tend to the child when sick and did not care about how they did in school. This seemed to have a profound impact on the self esteem of the woman, who often felt unimportant, worthless, or as a nuisance. Many of the women had undergone several forms of maltreatment and neglect concurrently.We focus here on the phenomena related to dissociation in the women who were evaluated and treated. Maternity brings particular challenges for any woman, but in conditions of history of chronic severe trauma, neglect and unresolved losses there are particular difficulties that may impact the transition to motherhood.

The mother-to-be and the new mother
Discontinuities in the mental life

As we attempted to characterize the effects of the trauma reported by many of the women, the issues related to anxiety and dissociation became evident. Many women reported feeling "always scared" or constantly afraid that something bad was going to happen. The sympathetic system was mostly "on alert" and chronically so. In those circumstances mammalian defense strategies such as fight, flight, submission or freezing may become activated in the psyche of the patient. While transient dissociative experiences are a part of the normal psychic life, they become problematic when they assume the role of an adaptation to difficult circumstances, such as severe stress, a difficult life situation or unbearable life experiences. We conceptualice dissociation as a coping strategy, as an attempt to escape, or to withstand difficult experiences. Since childhood, the victim may attempt to "become someone else", "not to be there" or to have companions or alternative selves that are able to face the problems, as noted by Ferenczi in his writings on trauma (Gutierrez-Palaez, 2009). Janet (1904) called these alternative states "emotional personalities", which may become "specialized" parts of the apparently normal personality to deal with particular issues, or dedicated parts of the self, designed to face aggression, seduction, etc. These "emotional personalities" can become activated when something triggers memories of trauma and those are evoked to confront those painful situations, emotions, sensations, memories or to reenact aspects of the previous trauma (Van der Hart, Nijenhuis and Steele, 2006). Chronic and severe emotional trauma can also cause psychosomatic disturbances or "somatic dissociation", in which the somatic symptoms embody the traumatic memories in a procedural fashion.

Ms. S., a young woman who recently had a baby, had been speaking during a session, for about 20 minutes, of her anger at having her child removed from her care due to her use of marijuana. As we explored the reasons for her smoking, she mentioned her constant discomfort and we linked this with her memories of seduction by her father. As she started to talk about this, she "broke into a sweat" that was intense and visible to the eye. She complained that the office was 'too hot". After a few minutes she changed the topic and unwittingly her sensation of heat disappeared, she did not mention the heat anymore. Later on, this episode was explored with her, and it related to fright at emerging memories of sexual abuse during childhood.

Some women informed that they hardly every would go to the outside, or would only go out reluctantly and in constant fear that something bad might happen, being attacked, hurt or robbed. In those situations some experienced symptoms such as panic attacks, free floating anxiety and flash-backs .

In approximately a fourth of the traumatized women, there is a report of enormous difficulties concentrating and even knowing what day it is. Some report "living in a fog" or forgetting parts of the day. It can be very hard to remember things, such as appointments and other duties. The patient may feel that it is very hard to remember the past, and sometimes they are unable to recall entire periods of the day or days. Using items from the "dissociative experiences scale" of Carlson and Putnam, the experiences are readily detectable. The woman herself may describe "attention deficit" and being "totally scattered" or disorganized and needing someone to remind her of what she has to do. This led to the more systematic inquiry about dissociative experiences.

Ms. P, was able to discuss her problems related to trauma only after an episode of dissociation. She would come to sessions only episodically, after periods of weeks, and often in a panicked state, hoping a medicine would help her feel better. As the clinician tried to explore what made her feel so nervous and scared, she spoke about physical abuse by her mother, but without affect and said that all was in the past. During one of those episodes of great anxiety, she was seen and she spoke of her disappointment at her older children's problems. She expressed much emotion as she spoke of her anger at her older children. We connected her anxiety with her feeling as a failure and made an appointment for the next week. Ms. P. came the next day saying she was coming to the scheduled session. She was annoyed at the secretary who told her she had been here yesterday. As she was seen impromptu, she denied any recollection of the session of the day before and was very surprised that she had "forgotten everything".

As described by Mary Main in her account of "disorganized attachment" in the adult (Main, 1996), many of the women with these antecedents incur in multiple contradictions as they narrate their past and are unaware of such contradictions (Lyons-Ruth *et al.*, 1999). A woman may report that she had lost contact with her father years ago, and later in the interview inform that she had had a fight with her father two weeks ago. A patient reported for instance that she "had gone outside to calm down" when she threw a fit as she had burned some food while cooking when her boyfriend came to the house. In the next sentence she reported the same incident, but this time said that her boyfriend had come to talk to her in her room while she was crying. As we attempted to clarify, she just said " I was in my room, my bad". The patient is often not anchored in the historical narrative, but more in a "dramatic truth", telling a story perhaps to elicit a reaction in the other and to make a point, rather than to convey real events, in the usual sense of the word.

Other frequently reported experiences were episodes of depersonalization, like not recognizing oneself in the mirror, or feeling that one had abandoned the body, as well as derealization, and multiple psychosomatic disturbances, gastrointestinal, respiratory and chronic pain. In many instances, the patient cannot remember her appointments or attend them without reminders, and to engage the patient requires especial interventions in the part of the therapist or the treating team.

Dissociation in identity

In approximately ten cases, there was a more profound dissociative repertoire. In all of them there was the antecedent of severe neglect, chronic sexual abuse, and loss of caregivers or betrayal by the mother and father figures. At times the dissociation is not so clear cut as in "multiple personality disorder", but more a feeling that there are other states as a part of the patient's experience. A woman reported that there was a little girl inside of her. This little girl was "good" and protective, played with her and gave her advice. She is a sort of "imaginary friend" that has lived with the patient for many years and has helped her to deal with horrendous circumstances. One can think of her as a sort of "angel" in the sense described by Alicia Lieberman in "angels in the nursery" (Lieberman *et al.*,2005), only that in this case there is not real "benign person", but a made up "good person" that is the source of comfort and pleasure. The patient readily speaks about this "imaginary friend" or companion, that at times has a real name, and feels like a constant presence.

In a few cases, the full development of alternative personalities is encountered. Usually, these assume rather extreme or polarized characteristics as representing extremes of being in the world. In one case, a woman who had multiple trauma developed a persona called 'Sunshine' who spends all the money, uses drugs and "does not care about anything" , she is very generous and always happy, in contrast with her predominant state of being constantly scared and afraid of the "host" personality. In another case, a woman who is constantly depressed and dejected, feeling exploited by her adult children, during her pregnancy reported the existence of "Rainbow", a rather masculinized drug user, who constantly encourages the depressed persona to use drugs, to have sex with multiple partners, to party and abandon her baby and give her to the child protective services because she is a burden for her, not allowing her to have fun. This "persona' manifested itself after approximately one year of treatment with the depressed anchor personality that usually came to the sessions.

In another example, a pregnant obese Afro-American woman who calls herself AD, informs the psychiatrist that she hates children, that she is very angry at being pregnant, and that babies are "viscous infested creatures" that are good for nothing, full of infections and disgusting. She absolutely does not want to have a baby but she was "too late to have an abortion". In the following session, the patient comes in another state, as "America", who is the other extreme. She "talks like a white girl", is extremely sweet and very kind. She wants to have the baby as she thinks babies are adorable and this will fulfill her life. America is aware of "AD", the alter ego, and viceversa, and they struggle to manifest themselves and take over the body. America says that they "share a body" and this is why she is so obese.

Dissociation and pregnancy

Many women have very little sense of control of mostly anything in their lives, including being pregnant. In most cases, the pregnancy came as a surprise and also as a stressful and scary situation. At times, a redeeming aspect of pregnancy is that other people tend to celebrate the fact that someone is expecting a baby, i.e. there is a positive response to the pregnancy, as other people are "nicer" during this time and provide support, such as relatives, a partner, or friends, because of the cultural belief that the woman is in a delicate state and needs help. For others there is a strong ambivalence toward the pregnancy and the baby *in utero*.

In pregnancy, some women also appeared fairly emotionally distant from the baby, and the baby 'did not seem real". That is, in the course of the consultation sessions, the baby is far from the mind, and the focus of the client is on her own emotional needs, her fears, her material needs and what she is going to do. In some cases, there is continued use of substances such as alcohol and marijuana, or other drugs, as a way to "escape intolerable states of mind" and find solace even if for a brief period of time. The patient may know that "this is not good for the baby" but literally, her needs take precedence over those of the baby. She has to use the substances to be able to deal with life and the needs of the baby are not a very prominent part of their life.

Other two possibilities are the idealization of the baby or a negative view of the child to be born. In the first case, the mother hopes that the baby is a demonstration that she is good and capable of being a mother. She may idealize the situation and perceive the child as a sort of savior that will give her a *raison d'etre* and a meaning to her life. She intends to become an excellent mother and to give the baby everything that she did not get and spare him or her the suffering that she endured as a child.

In a few cases there is a negative view of the baby, as a very ambitious creature that is "eating everything" and competes with the mother for nutrients, attention and is perceived as a devouring person inside. When there is a very negative view of the baby's father, the future mother may project her feelings onto the baby, telling us for instance, "the baby will be bipolar", or "he will be mean like his daddy". With the use of ultrasound and knowing the gender of the baby, the knowledge that the baby is a girl may bring additional feelings. A woman told us " I better not have a girl " because all women are evil and "bitches", she could only tolerate a boy and felt very angry when she realized she was having a baby girl. Another mother, very traumatized and hurt by adults in her life, operated very much like a little girl. She experienced the baby kicking inside of her as the fetus having "temper tantrums" and wanted to discipline the child by hitting her abdomen with her fingers, to show the child "who is the boss".

Finally, some women with severe history of trauma have extensive somatic symptoms, as described elsewhere in the literature. Several patients had "chronic pain" in the back or their limbs, constant headaches, hurting in their abdomen, the genital area, asthma, frequent urinary infections, chest pains, multiple allergies, pruritus, chronic cough, and a feeling of not inhaling enough air. These are very baffling and taxing for the obstetrician. The woman can report being in excruciating back pain, and immediately laugh loudly about a joke, suggesting a dissociation in the experience of her own body. One needs to evoke the notion of "disembodiment" in many of states (Henningsen, 2010)

Dissociation and the maternal function, the baby

Several authors have described the perils for the infant of a severely traumatized mother (Schechter et al, 2007). For instance, the is the possibility of the transgenerational transmission of a disorganized attachment style (disorganizing for the infant) as well as states of anxiety, the possibility of maltreatment and neglect and a distorted perception of the baby or distorted interactions with him or her (Lyons Ruth *et al.*, 2005).

Ms. R. is a 28 year old woman who brings two young children, a two year old girl and a 3 year old boy, her stepchildren, for consultation because "they are always hungry", and eat "all the time". The two children are however, undernourished and have failure to thrive. They hardly play and seem quite dejected, "frozen on site", watching their stepmother with fear before they make any move. The paradox of "excessive eating" and undernourishment was investigated. When we compared the two stepchildren with Ms. R.'s biological children (from other relationships, ages 6, 3 and 1). Ms. R.'s biological children looked well nourished and energetic , they had toys and were thriving normally. The other two children looked malnourished, extremely thin and "frozen on site", not moving without their stepmother's permission. As the situation was investigated over several sessions, it was discovered that Ms. R. would interrupt the children's feeding if they showed "bad manners" and she would send them to their room for periods of hours. There were no toys in their room, which was in the basement and they slept in a very simple bunk bed. Her biological children, on the other hand, slept upstairs and had a room each, with abundant toys and children's furniture (castle, race car, etc). It seemed that Ms. R. had dissociative experiences in which she identified her stepchildren as "the bad ones" who were "just like her as a child", and would punish them repeatedly,, depriving them of food. She was not fully aware of the effects of her behavior on the young children, and she felt she loved them and was "a good mother to them". She seemed not to be aware of the extent of her own maltreatment to these children, which may have been compartmentalized form her conscious mental life.

In other cases, it seems that even when a woman has severe interpersonal problems. Anxiety and major conflicts with others, the "maternal function" may be preserved, by one aspect of her personality (or emotional personality, in Janet's terms) (Van der Hart, 2006).

There is a number of other possible reactions to the presence of the baby. First, the baby has peremptory needs and a physicality that is undeniable. The baby cries, expects to be fed, carried and cared for on a continuous basis. For any woman, the needs of the baby are to a degree in competition with the needs of the mother (for rest, freedom of movement, doing what she wants, taking care of herself). Most women successfully put their needs in the second place to meet those of the baby. This goes better of course if there are assistants to her and people who offer her support, relief and comfort. The same would seem to occur with very traumatized or dissociative women. The presence of others who may alleviate the burdens of the baby, a boyfriend, partner, husband, mother or friend may provide needed rest, assistance with meeting the needs of the baby and anchoring in reality to take the baby to pediatric appointments, obtain vaccines, remember to feed him or her, changing diapers, etc. There are some instances that merit mention as they require special assistance to the mother and the infant.

Role reversal and idealization

This phenomenon has been described by several authors (Schecher et al, 2007) a traumatized woman who is very vulnerable and scared, may resort to the baby as a source of comfort and strength, seeking protection from the baby. At times, a scared woman may hold her baby and find solace in the physical contact with the baby who makes her feel reassured. At other times, a new mother may alert the baby to her internal states at all times. When she feels scared, threatened or abandoned, she informs the baby and displays exaggerated emotions (crying, lying on the floor, screaming in pain) so that the infant particularly after one year of age, notice her emotions and may become very attentive and preoccupied with comforting his or her mother. She elicits empathic responses and conveys to the child the duty to monitor her at all times.

In a few instances, the child was invested with the perception of extraordinary powers. A mother who had lost her parents as a child, and who had grown up in the 'foster care system", saw her infant, since he was about eight months old, as a very protective child who "knew exactly who is good and who is bad'. The baby would make a smiling face if the person approaching his mother had good intentions and would "frown" and grunt if the person was evil. She also saw over the head of the baby a 'sort of light" that conveyed that he had a gift to see other people's auras, and this is how he could distinguish people's intentions. Another mother had severe fears at night and insomnia, as she felt she could be attacked and feared ever noise in the house. She would go into the infant's bed, put his hands on her face and "cuddle beside him" feeling protected. As the child grows older, he or she may be extremely sensitive and hypervigilant, and alerts the clinician that his mother has to pay the rent, the electricity was cut off, mother's latest boyfriend "might come back", etc, suggesting that the mother sees the child as a confident and a source of support.

Frightened and frightening mother

Unfortunately, the mother who has been so scared, at times has also identified with the aggressor, and in a dissociative state may be quite harsh and scary to the baby. A woman treated by us exhibited mostly good intentions and kindness to her older children. However, when her one year old infant was vying for attention, she suddenly made a very loud and deep sound with her voice and scared him, making him cry. When asked about this, she said she liked to see "his scared little face when he is about to cry". She was amused by the face, and unaware of the internal experience of the baby. Her older children also "scared each other" perhaps reenacting their own experiences as infants. The cost to the mental life in terms of a disorganized attachment style and dissociation in the child have been described by Lyons Ruth and others (Haugaard, 2004. Lyons-Ruth et al., 2006).

Negative projections toward the child

When there are dissociative phenomena in the mother, she may report puzzling events or there may be unexplained experiences in the child. The son or daughter for instance, may present a fractured bone, a burn or a hematoma, and the mother genuinely denies any awareness of what might have happened. She really does not know and feels attacked when someone insinuates that she ma have produced (or allow to be produced) these injuries. In other cases she may restrict the feeding of the a baby, withdrawing food as a punishment.

Intervention strategies

One should not assume that a woman with these antecedents and dissociative experiences cannot take care of her baby. This perhaps highlights the "adaptive value of dissociation" in the sense that some of the maternal functions and responsiveness may be preserved, even when the woman may be plagued by voices, fears, sleeping problems, multiple somatic symptoms and mood dysregulation, or by alternate states of being in the world (multiple personality).

We have been faced with several women with multiple personality who are able to care for the baby and are not neglectful, abusive or oblivious to the emotional life of the child, as one would expect they would be. We have observed several of these dyads where it would seem that the biological imperatives and altruistic tendencies of caregiving seem to predominate and the child seems attached to his or her mother, curious, interested in the world and fairly happy and responsive. This is not to say that the mother is "perfect" or healthy. The clinician is left with having to monitor the development of the baby, treating the mother as much as possible, and coaching her on how to respond and meet the needs of her child.

The traditional psychotherapeutic models, expecting the woman to come to the office and keep appointments, talk about her internal life and appear regularly, seem insufficient. Often one needs to implement a "multimodal" set of interventions that may require the intervention of a team, including a psychiatrist a case manager, as well as individual and group psychotherapies We have utilized the "mentalization based" psychotherapy model described by Bateman and Fonagy (2006) for the treatment or borderline personality disorder, in combination with psychotherapy, home-based therapy and offering practical help to the patients. The mentalization approach appears very suitable to help the patient think about her mind and the mind of the baby (*in utero* or once born), as well as about the mind of those around her, like her partner or relatives (Allen et al, 2008). This has allowed us to "open a door" to help the patient understand the need for dissociation and the protective function it affords. Also, the perils involved in the discontinuity of the mental life and the need to gradually integrate different states of mind, or "personas" into one more flexible and capable one, rather than to continue to split the states into fragments that are "super-specialized' for one function (fighting, facing the world, eliciting affection, etc.). Clinicians should be alert to the presence of these phenomena in order to institute early intervention as soon as possible to promote the improvement in the mental health of the mother and as a strategy to prevent in the baby the negative consequences of living with a constantly scared and possibly scary mother.

References

ALLEN, J., FONAGY, P. & BATEMAN, A.W. (2008). *Mentalizing in clinical practice.* Washington DC: American Psychiatric Publishing.

BATEMAN, A. & FONAGY, P. (2006). Mentalization-based treatment for borderline personality disorder. Oxford: Oxford University Press.

HAUGGARD, J.J. (2004). Recognizing and treating uncommon behavioral and emotional disorders in children and adolescents who have been severely maltreated: dissociative disorders. *Child Maltreat* 9:146-153.

GUTIÉRREZ-PELAEZ, M. (2009). Trauma theory in Sandor Ferenczi's writings of 1931 and 1932. *International Journal of Psycho-Analysis* 90(6):1217-1233.

HENNINGSEN, P. (2010). Disordered self: Any chance for therapeutic integration? In *The embodied self,* T. Fuchs, HC Sattel & P. Henningsen (editors), Stuttgart, Germany: Schattauer, pp.293-298.

JANET, P. (1904). L'amnésie et la dissociation des souvenirs par l'émotion. *Journal de Psychologie* 1:417–453

LIEBERMAN, A.F., PADRON, E., VAN HORN, P. & HARRIS, WM. (2005). Angels in the nursery: the intergenerational transmission of benevolent parental influences. *Inf Ment Health J* 26:504-520.

MAIN, M. (1996). Introduction to the special section on attachment and psychopathology. Overview of the field of attachment. *J Consult Clin Psychol* 44:237-243.

LYONS-RUTH, K., BRONFMAN, E. & ATWOOD, G. (1999). A relational diathesis model of hostile-helpless states of mind. Expressions in mother-infant interactions. In *Attachment Disorganization,* J. Solomon

& C. George (editors), New York, NY: Guilford Press, pp. 33-69.

LYONS-RUTH, K., YELLIN, C., MELNICK, S. & ATWOOD, G. (2005). Expanding the concept of unresolved mental states: hostile/helpless states of mind on the adult attachment interview are associated with disrupted mother-infant communication and infant disorganization. *Dev Psychopathol* 17:1-23.

LYONS.-RUTH, K., DUTRA, L., SCHUDER, M.R. & BIANCHI, I. (2006). From infant attachment disorganization to adult dissociation: relational adaptations or traumatic experiences? *Psychiatr Clin N Am* 29:63-86.

MALDONADO-DURÁN, J.M., LARTIGUE T., FEINTUCH, M. (2000). Perinatal Psychiatry: Infant mental health interventions during pregnancy. *Bull Menninger Clin* 64 (3): 317-343.

SWICA, Y., OTNOW-LEWIS, D. & LEWIS, M. (1996). Child abuse and dissociative identity disorder. Multiple personality disorder. The documentation of childhood maltreatment and the corroboration of symptoms. *Child Adol Psychiat Clin N Am* 5: 431-447.

SCHECHTER, D.S., ZYGMUNT, A., COATES, S.W., DAVIS, M., TRABKA, K.A., MCCAU, J., KOLODJT A. & ROBINSON, J.L. (2007). Caregiver traumatization adversely impacts young children's mental representations on the MacArthur Story stem battery. *Attach Hum Dev* 9:187-205.

VAN DER HART, O., NIJENHUIS, ERS & STEELE, K. (2006). *The haunted self. Structural dissociation and the treatment of chronic traumatization.* WW New York: Norton and Co.

www.ingramcontent.com/pod-product-compliance
Lightning Source LLC
Chambersburg PA
CBHW062215270326
41930CB00009B/1740

* 9 7 8 6 0 7 9 1 3 7 1 3 7 *